Rethinking the Civil War Era

RETHINKING THE CIVIL WAR ERA

DIRECTIONS FOR RESEARCH

PAUL D. ESCOTT

UNIVERSITY PRESS OF KENTUCKY

Scholarly publisher for the Commonwealth,
serving Bellarmine University, Berea College, Centre College of Kentucky, Eastern Kentucky University, The Filson Historical Society, Georgetown College, Kentucky Historical Society, Kentucky State University, Morehead State University, Murray State University, Northern Kentucky University, Transylvania University, University of Kentucky, University of Louisville, and Western Kentucky University.

Editorial and Sales Offices: The University Press of Kentucky
663 South Limestone Street, Lexington, Kentucky 40508-4008
www.kentuckypress.com

Library of Congress Cataloging-in-Publication Data

Names: Escott, Paul D., 1947– author.
Title: Rethinking the Civil War era : directions for research / Paul D. Escott.
Description: Lexington, Kentucky : The University Press of Kentucky, 2018. | Series: New Directions in Southern History | Includes bibliographical references and index.
Identifiers: LCCN 2017043860| ISBN 9780813175355 (hardcover : alk. paper) | ISBN 9780813175362 (pdf) | ISBN 9780813175379 (epub)
Subjects: LCSH: United States—History—Civil War, 1861–1865—Causes. | United States—History—Civil War, 1861–1865—History. | United States—History—Civil War, 1861–1865—Influence.
Classification: LCC E468.9 .E83 2018 | DDC 973.7/11—dc23
LC record available at https://lccn.loc.gov/2017043860

This book is printed on acid-free paper meeting the requirements of the American National Standard for Permanence in Paper for Printed Library Materials.

Manufactured in the United States of America.

Member of the Association
of University Presses

Para Candelas,
ahora y siempre

Contents

Preface

The Civil War was vast in its scope and impact. We tend to remember first the preservation of the Union and the end of legal enslavement, but the war also brought enormous changes to government and society, produced between 752,000 and 851,000 deaths by recent estimates, and drove roughly 250,000 civilians from their homes. Close to 3 million men left their families to serve in the two armies, and as many as 50,000 turned to some form of irregular warfare or guerrilla violence before the war was over. Hundreds of thousands of soldiers roamed the landscape at various times as deserters, stragglers, or skulkers. Approximately 60,000 fighting men suffered amputations, and 15,000 of them died. Alarmed slaveholders moved 150,000 slaves to new plantations more distant from the scenes of battle, while 500,000 African Americans seized their freedom by escaping into Union lines. Along with immense destruction of property, there was an enormous impact on the physical environment. Every year the rival armies destroyed or consumed 400,000 acres of timber, and they converted an additional 2 million trees into corduroy roads, bridges, houses, forts, or firewood. There were immense losses of livestock and new inroads by disease among the animal populations.[1]

Not surprisingly, an event of this magnitude and significance has inspired an enormous scholarly literature. Estimates run to 60,000 books about the Civil War and 15,000 titles about Abraham Lincoln alone. More important than the quantity of studies is their quality. Within the history profession, the war has attracted an abundance of talented researchers, analysts, and interpreters. The quality of the modern literature they have produced is high. Literary figures also have weighed in, on occasion, with sound insights.[2]

Through the decades, various themes have captured the most attention, but as Frank Towers argued a few years ago, Civil War studies seem to be at an inflection point. Broad themes that had organized much of the research in past generations successively gave way to an overarching interest in questions and aspects of modernization. But the centripetal force of that concept also seems to have dissipated in the current climate. New approaches—whether they center on "deep contingency" or "disunion rhetoric" or new interpretations of the Slave Power or the clash of modern nationalisms—indicate that various new directions for study of the Civil War are at hand. Towers also noted a shift of tone in recent works.[3]

We should welcome a change in the tone of interpretations. It is time to modify the long-held and determinedly positive perspective on the Civil War, for celebration of the war's results has been exaggerated. Although war preserved the Union and brought about the legal demise of slavery, its story also includes less cheering but fundamental elements. Not only did the nation's proud democracy run head on into an enormously destructive conflict, with immense human suffering, but key elements of what caused the war remained unresolved, as demonstrated by the grievous racial problems that have plagued subsequent generations. It is impossible for citizens or scholars to understand contemporary conflicts and injustices if a dominant popular narrative suggests that the Civil War resolved the nation's racial dilemma. One of our functions as historians is to write history that, as Carl Becker once put it, is "useful" for society and for our democracy. With respect to the popular understanding of the Civil War, part of our job, according to Becker, is "to correct and rationalize for common use Mr. Everyman's mythological adaptation of what actually happened."[4]

The celebratory gloss that used to characterize much writing about the Civil War is changing as times and experience change. Historians, like anyone else, react to events and are products of a certain time and place. In the twentieth century, they lived amid the influence of American victory in World War II, the nation's rise to superpower status, and thermonuclear confrontation during the Cold War. Ideas of an "American Century" or "the end of ideology" naturally encouraged positive, patriotic interpretations of an era that had encompassed both progress and failure. Today, we can hope, a different outlook has taken shape. Failures in foreign policy have shown the limits of American power and the fallibility that our citizens and leaders share with all other human beings. Certainly a powerful and influential nation needs to bring a realistic mentality to world affairs, and we must hope that our society can be informed and mature enough to recognize and learn from national failures as well as successes.

The new directions that Frank Towers mentioned are justified, and new tools are available for historians. Both invite innovation and fresh discovery. They give us new routes to explore events and relationships and offer the possibility of discovering connections that had previously been hidden. Exciting work is already under way, exploiting large databases to show and map changes over time or to explain actions in terms of their spatial and social context or to make routes of travel and intersections of people visible. An era of much wider digital research has begun, and it is sure to continue and to attract fresh talent into the field.

Given these developments, what is the justification for a book like this one? And why did I accept an invitation to try to write it?

It is easier to answer the first question than the second. Books such as this one traditionally attract the attention of many young scholars, and historians assume that discussion of research questions will stimulate some new ideas or new approaches among all those working in the field. For the historical enterprise, ideas that are mistaken sometimes provoke as much good work as sound insights. Whether scholars adopt suggestions or reject them, taking stock of where we are and where we are going can prove useful. In fact, it may never be a waste of time to stand back, assess the current situation, and think about the future.

Answering the second question requires something beyond humility. (Perhaps a better way to put the question would be, "What was I thinking?") Although I was and am grateful for the invitation, I make no claim to be specially qualified for the task and am offering comments and suggestions only in the hope that they may contribute to our collective research enterprise.

I also appeal for understanding and pardon, at the outset, from the many talented scholars who may not be mentioned here by name. It is impossible for me to give citations for all or even a small part of the impressive scholarship that I have surveyed. This project required an effort to read widely in the literature, far more widely than I had ever done before. That effort necessarily is incomplete because one's time is too limited and the task—the immense corpus of fine research—is too great. I am deeply impressed with the work of scores of talented researchers, most of whom I have never met, and I make no claims to greater insight than they. In fact, I have become convinced that we often are like the blind men touching and trying to describe the elephant. In some respects, we all are identifying part of the reality—but only part, while the larger truth eludes us.

My intention is not to make a comprehensive historiographical review of the existing literature or to offer ideas on every potentially important area of inquiry. I instead want to present chapters that focus on issues and questions to which I think I can contribute and that read more like essays than a historiographical summary. In places, I use a personal tone because I am offering my opinions or speculations, and they tend to reflect my interests or way of looking at the world. I hope this format proves interesting and provocative. The ideas expressed, the suggestions made, and the questions posed are, of course, my own and are fallible. Other perspectives and approaches may be equally valid, and nothing in the chapters that follow is ex cathedra. My comments may omit important possibilities or be wrongheaded, and surely I have not mentioned or foreseen important directions.

Given the large amount of ground to cover, my format does not allow many long, detailed, and nuanced descriptions of scholars' interpretations. I have tried to capture the essence of arguments without omitting essential points, and I apologize if I have short-changed any key elements. I offer my comments and ideas in a spirit of cooperation, humility, and occasional puzzlement. If my approach stimulates thought, I will be satisfied. Because I have benefited throughout my career from the generous community of scholars, I will be glad if this work returns something to the profession. I am grateful for the intellectual pleasure that I have derived from the work of so many.

1

Understanding the Roots of War

A fundamental part of Civil War studies has always been analysis of the causes of the war. Except for books about Lincoln and military history, which have included the work of many nonacademic historians, probably no other topic has attracted as much attention. And perhaps in no other area have change and progress been so great. The overall way that we try to understand the roots of the war is very different now from the way it was understood in the 1960s or 1970s.

When I began graduate school, many important studies focused their attention on the events of the sectional conflict, the friction points that eventually led to civil war. Through careful research, historians tried to understand the sequence of North–South conflicts, how each collision affected the Union, and how these successive clashes aggravated the tensions that brought about secession. Some interpretations had a pro-Southern slant, whereas others showed more appreciation for abolitionists or Northern antislavery sentiment. If many scholars were moving away from James G. Randall's earlier argument that a "blundering generation" of politicians caused a needless war, the focus of their attention had not changed. Their priority remained to elucidate the debates and crises that produced growing tension.

The efforts of this period produced some outstanding research and trenchant analysis. If Roy Nichols previously had identified the way battles over the right to petition broadened into fear of a Slave Power, others such as Joel Silbey and Michael Holt offered important new insights about party realignment. To understand the actions of political leaders, we continue today to turn to studies of the Compromise of 1850 as well as of Henry Clay or Stephen Douglas or John C. Calhoun or others, and valuable studies of such prominent leaders continue to appear. One of the most enduring of all the political histories is David M. Potter's book *The Impending Crisis, 1848–1861.*[1] Through extensive archival research, Potter was able to show what key leaders were thinking as their goals and measures collided, and his insightful analysis clarified the dynamics and dimensions of their disagreements.

We can note that much of this work was history written from the inside out rather than from the outside in. That is, such studies moved from the particular to the general; they scrutinized certain events and selected individuals in order to move toward an overall interpretation, an understanding of the larger dynamic. Their careful research placed us in the minds of sectional leaders and positioned us with them in the arena of their conflicts so that we could better grasp the decline of consensus and the march toward conflict. From individual events, historians would assemble a larger picture; from details and the analysis of them, they would construct a broader interpretation.

Additional evidence that this approach could be very fruitful came from the work of Bertram Wyatt-Brown. In his writings about the culture of honor, Wyatt-Brown demonstrated how the thinking and values of elite Southerners were different from those of our era. His description of their emotional patterns could be revelatory because those patterns have faded from modern society. Explaining and putting himself into the angry reactions of Southern leaders, Wyatt-Brown offered explanations for the coming of the war that were grounded in emotional states. He concluded, for example, that "the lower South separated from the Union out of a sense of almost uncontrollable outrage. . . . Southern whites increasingly felt deeply insulted to the point of disunion and war. . . . Anger and frustration were the root emotions that drove Southerners to secede, a visceral response to a collective sense of degradation and disgrace." It would be difficult to imagine a clearer example of analysis that moved from the inside, or personal dimension, to the outside and its larger picture.[2]

Essentially different was history written from the outside in—that is, history that offered an interpretation of the big picture in order to explain and illuminate the smaller elements that played their role in successive events. Noting the difference, Paul Quigley has recently argued (in praise of a book by Michael Wood) that emotions "ought to be seen not as the fundamental cause of the war, but rather as a means by which Americans converted underlying socioeconomic differences into highly charged northern and southern sectional identities."[3] Such socioeconomic differences have been a focus of important and expanding research. In a previous era, Charles and Mary Beard had presented an overarching argument about the dynamic and meaning of the Civil War that inspired various studies to test the validity of their argument about industrial versus agrarian forces. In the early phases of my career, the most influential example of this approach to understanding the war's causes was the interpretive work of Eugene G. Genovese.

For all that Genovese knew about Southern agriculture or about individual leaders, their writings, or particular crises—and he knew a great deal—his analysis was outside in. It began with and grew out of a Gramscian and Marxist conceptual framework that determined the big picture. The Slave South, insisted Genovese, was not a capitalist society like that of the North. Rather, it was at an earlier, precapitalist stage of Marxist development, and its social relations derived from the hegemony and societal prestige of the planters, whose values had a dominant influence. Those values were seigneurial and patriarchal rather than crassly profit oriented. Slavery was the foundation of their prestige and the central pillar of their social dominance. Because the world these slaveholders made had to expand, the territorial conflict with the North was unavoidable.

As a powerful thinker and prolific writer, Genovese stimulated many studies that sought to examine, test, or modify his interpretation. It is not necessary here to specify in detail what parts of his work have been most supported or rejected. What is striking, however, is that his effort to identify the largest, most systemic causes of the conflict has become a dominant direction in impressive new work. A great deal of the influential research in recent decades has focused on the big picture rather than on the particular events. That is, the approach taken by many fine historians has been from the outside in, and as a result we have a much fuller, more compelling sense of the *forces* behind the sectional conflict. Our attention rests now on large systems, economic movements, and trans-Atlantic and global patterns that reveal the roots of the Civil War.

For me, a striking illustration of the usefulness of a big-picture approach came in an article published by Chandra Miller [Manning] in 2000. She documented the close friendship and mutual respect that existed between John Quincy Adams and John C. Calhoun when both were members of James Monroe's cabinet. At that time, Adams regarded Calhoun as being "above all sectional and factious prejudices more than any other statesman of the Union, with whom I have ever acted"! When the Missouri crisis arose, however, they discovered the gulf that lay between them. To Adams, slavery threatened both republicanism and the Union, and he assumed that its end in some way was ultimately necessary. For Calhoun, in contrast, the protection of slaveholders' interests—or rights, as he saw them—was essential to liberty and the Union, and he made clear that he would choose disunion whenever necessary to protect slavery. The unexpected scope of disagreement between these two friends showed how ineffective compromises would be in removing a clash that was fundamental. Large forces that had not previously been visible to these close friends immediately overrode their personal relationship.[4]

In the early days of the Union, Adams and Calhoun had been able to overlook the deep differences that related to slavery. So had many of their contemporaries, who saw evidence of nationalism and then an "era of good feelings" following the War of 1812. But early clashes over slavery had been common, though contained, as John Craig Hammond, Brian Schoen, and others have documented. The fact that early disagreements did not create a sense of crisis before 1820 was due more to Congress's weakness than to any shared consensus between North and South. That crisis was coming, and it would reoccur.[5]

The message that powerful economic forces and financial interests were behind the growing crisis emerges unmistakably from recent important work that has sharpened and immensely broadened our frame of reference. James Huston argues that "property rights in slaves generated the sectional conflict, that the concentration of valuable [slave] property in one region thwarted any attempt at compromise and undermined the genius of the democratic process." Using congressional debates and other speeches, Huston has marshalled many quotations from Southern leaders who emphasized exactly that point, decrying that property worth $2 billion "was in peril" in 1850 or that Lincoln's election in 1860 rendered "insecure a property valued at $3,000,000,000." Moreover, he documents how vast the South's $3 billion worth of slave property was in the world of the nineteenth century. The value of slave property at that time was far greater than all US investment in railroads and manufacturing combined. Planters, who owned somewhat more than half of all slaves, by themselves had almost as much wealth as all northern railroads and manufacturing combined. Those large slaveholders made up only 3 percent of Southern society, yet they made up 70 percent of the richest persons in the nation. Because Northerners thought of wealth in terms of land and buildings rather than in terms of slaves, it was easy for them to think of the South as less wealthy, "even though . . . they were peons compared with southerners."[6]

Determined to protect their wealth, Southern leaders worried that governments defined what property rights were and were not, and so they demanded absolute security for their "property" in slaves. The struggles over the territories were not about state rights, argues Huston, but about property rights, and Southerners "used a property rights argument . . . unabatedly until the moment of secession." Protection of their rights had to be national in scope, even though the Constitution gave Congress power over the territories. Therefore, they insistently sought protection for slavery in the territories. Their demand for an absolute guarantee of their property rights in slaves collided, however, with Northern interests because "property rights in slaves created an unfair labor market that ruined the opportunities for free northern village labor." Northerners could not let the South define property rights "because it meant the possible extension of slavery into the North and the ruination of their society." One valuable aspect of Huston's work is that he attempts to identify changes in the political system that caused conflict to become especially sharp in the 1850s. More could be done, especially at the level of popular culture, to explain the timing of this clash. After all, many Americans had accepted Henry Clay's argument that the differing economies and labor systems of North and South were complementary and mutually supportive.[7]

Huston makes his economic case for slavery's massive importance by concentrating on the South and the United States, and Edward Baptist documents in impressive fashion how important slavery was to the entire American economy. Others have powerfully enlarged that argument by taking an Atlantic or global perspective. Their work has located slavery and the cotton economy firmly within the currents of Atlantic events and thought and even more within the global rise of the cotton-textile industry. Earlier studies of abolitionism, of course, had devoted much attention to the cross-fertilization of British antislavery and American abolitionism and to the influence of emancipation in the Caribbean. Edward Rugemer has more recently made those Atlantic connections even more tangible by showing how they affected many ordinary citizens. For example, in various cities near the Atlantic coast in the North, local groups celebrated the First of August—the day when emancipation arrived in the British West Indies. These celebrations grew in number through the years and became part of local traditions. By the 1850s, they had spread beyond the Atlantic coast into more western states.[8]

That phenomenon showed that events in the Atlantic were inspiring some Northerners to address questions relating to slavery at home. Events in Europe also affected attitudes in America, particularly the nature of nationalist feelings on this continent. The democratically inspired revolutions in Europe in 1848 had a strong impact on nationalist feelings in the United States. The preexisting pride in the Union, as an example to the world of rule by the people, gained additional strength. Many American politicians and editors praised European patriots' efforts to bring a more democratic government to their lands. They lauded and feted men such as Louis Kossuth in Hungary, who toured the United States and gave inspiring speeches about democratic ideals. The "Young America" movement gained strength and had Southern as well as Northern advocates. In the 1850s, it was even a subset of the Democratic Party. The failure or defeat of the revolutions of 1848 initially convinced nationalists here that America was exceptional. Within a few years, however, nationalist feelings in the United States diverged along sectional lines. The growing conflicts over slavery then convinced some Northerners that Southern politicians were introducing alien, undemocratic, and dangerous values. Southern efforts to plant slavery in Kansas and the violence that broke out there seemed a descent into European-style violence and despotism. Thus, the comparison with Europe began to suggest to some Northerners that pro-slavery forces must be resisted, even by violence if necessary.[9]

Edward Rugemer also has shown how Southerners reacted to and were affected by international developments, at least by those occurring in the Caribbean. A series of slave revolts or uprisings on various islands in the Caribbean received extensive newspaper coverage in the United States. That startling news, when added to slave uprisings in this country, convinced alarmed Southerners and many Northerners that all talk of liberty for slaves was dangerous and that a gag rule was necessary and justified. One topic for further investigation is how foreigners viewed this energized defense of slavery and the extent to which citizens of the United States worried about their nation's reputation abroad. Certainly, Abraham Lincoln decried the damage that slavery did to America's image as a republican government. It remains less clear how much Northern Democrats or Southerners thought about their standing in the Atlantic world. Little more than a decade before secession, Stephen Douglas was one of the Northern Democrats most involved in the Young America movement. After taking great pride in the example of self-government that the United States set before the world, did Douglas or other Democrats worry about the damage that sectionalism was causing to the country's international image? Did Southern radicals give much thought to international reactions as they pursued their interests? Did they have connections with British or European leaders comparable to those that abolitionists and Northern reformers enjoyed?[10]

Sven Beckert's impressive book *Empire of Cotton: A Global History* anchors Southern economic and social developments within not just an Atlantic context but a global frame of reference. European powers first employed war capitalism to conquer new lands and create global networks of trade in cotton. It was this war capitalism that "opened fresh lands and mobilized new labor, becoming the essential ingredient of the emerging empire of cotton" and the forging of industrial capitalism. But as British mills expanded, by 1800 they needed ever more cotton, and the fertile lands of the US Gulf of Mexico region could answer that need. After the invention of the gin, cotton production in the Gulf South soared because the US government seized Indian lands and legitimized the power of masters over their slaves. The "combination of expropriated lands, slave labor, and the domination of a state that gave enormous latitude to slave owners over their labor" proved to be "fabulously profitable." As a major supplier of this empire of cotton, Southern planters amassed the wealth described by Huston. Beckert goes on to highlight the extensive ties between slavery in the South and American industrial development in the North. "Capitalism rested on the *coexistence* of war capitalism . . . with industrial capitalism," in which "state power rather than masters" legislated property rights and encouraged "a powerful new system of wage labor." Industrial capitalism, based on wage labor, legal definitions of property rights, and repression of workers' movements, would become the giant of the postwar era.[11]

But if we now have a far clearer image of the slaveholding cotton South as a wealthy part of the developing, global system of capitalism, we face new questions about its economic nature. An additional body of new work has revived old complications about descriptive or conceptual categories and created a new challenge for historians. The former debate about whether the slave South was capitalist or not has taken on new dimensions, and historians need to develop new categories for understanding the South's character and the outlook or mindset of its leaders. What kind of economy did the South have? If not precapitalist and seigneurial, was it modernizing, partly capitalist, capitalist, or something else? How did its special features fit within the model of capitalist development? What is the correct way to describe the views of its leaders on political economy?[12]

On the one hand, the slave-based economy and wealth of the South were not an advantage for industrialization. "Slave states" worldwide, noted Beckert, "were notoriously late and feeble in supporting the political and economic interests of domestic industrializers" simply because their slavery interests were stronger and more prominent. As Gavin Wright has pointed out, all interest groups compete for support, but industrial interests did not achieve priority in the South until near the end of the nineteenth century. The South also ran into problems "symptomatic of early industrialization when a new region enters into competition with a more established industrial center." Aspiring industrialists faced capital constraints, a generally less-developed banking system, "difficulties with the quality of the regional labor," and problems due to "long-distance interactions with machinery suppliers." In addition, federal policies were not oriented toward industrialization of the South, with one telling exception: the federal government spent large sums on river improvements, which aided the successful development of Southern steamboat companies.[13]

Although wealthy, the slaveholding South remained so rural that even its mercantile sector was undeveloped. Merchants were a tiny part of the free population, only 1.8 percent according to a recent study drawing on twenty-two counties selected from nine states in the 1850 census. They lived and operated "within a cultural and economic no-man's-land." Although merchants tended to locate in the wealthier, settled portions of the region and were dedicated to slavery (with one-quarter of them owning slaves), their activities were distrusted: "the region's farmers, planters, and artisans often viewed the merchant's commercial world" with "suspicion or outright hostility." Their business required them to travel frequently to the North, and they were united by some distinct interests, but they did not develop an ideology or truly become a bourgeois class in the South.[14]

On the other hand, industrialization was not moribund in the antebellum South. The 1840s and 1850s saw a variety of investments, particularly in the upper South. Most important were the railroads. Except for a slowdown in the 1840s, railroad construction in the South started later but proceeded at a healthy pace similar to that in other parts of the country. In the 1850s, railroad construction in the South enjoyed a surge like that of the Old Northwest, when the amount of new mileage built put Virginia, Georgia, and Tennessee at sixth, seventh, and eighth place among all the states in the Union. Other Southern states doubled their length of track during that decade. The South, says Aaron Marrs, was "on a trajectory that embraced railroads" and was "striving for technological advancement while wholly committed to slavery." By 1860, the South's railroad network was one of the most extensive in the world, and nearly all of it had been constructed by less-expensive slave labor. In fact, with more than 10,000 slaves building lines each year during the 1850s, the railroads' demand for their labor was, according to William G. Thomas, "a primary reason for the rise in slave prices throughout the region." Railroad companies were among the largest slaveholders in the region, and southeastern slaveholders were most numerous in belts served by rail lines. Such combinations seemed to indicate that many Southern leaders saw no conflict between social conservatism and economic modernity. Southerners felt, concludes William Thomas, "that railroads and slavery together could transform the region." State funds had provided half of the railroad investment in the 1850s. Thomas also points out that the South had brought proportionally more of its citizens into contact with the railroad system than had the North, and although its lines used different gauges of track, the system there was no more disunified than that of the North.[15]

Agricultural reformers in the Southeast also had an economic vision that linked the improvement of agriculture to a modern development of the region's economy, including industrialization. The predominant pattern of shifting cultivation, which left much land fallow for as much as two decades, created unimproved land that functioned as "economic 'dead space'" by reducing population density, increasing transportation costs, and limiting "the size of markets for southern merchants and manufacturers." Agricultural reformers urged government support for more intensive cultivation and favored government aid to railroads and other transportation projects. "Many secessionists," concludes John Majewski, "envisioned industrial expansion, economic independence, and government activism as essential features" of the new Confederacy. Favoring a "modern economy" that would integrate "slavery, commerce, and manufacturing," they believed that "moderately protective tariffs" would exclude Northern goods while encouraging more commerce with Europe, more local production, and a more balanced economy. Many argued that their conservative slave society "could industrialize and urbanize without class conflict or fear of socialist revolution," a danger that Calhoun had attributed solely to the

North. Some even believed that in the future, when the Northwest would join the Confederacy due to the lure of river trade, the North would succumb to Southern manufacturing.[16]

With this scholarship, historians have a challenge to define more convincingly and comprehensively the South's economic system, its visions for the future, and its relation to modernity. Tied into the economic picture is the evidence that some influential advocates of secession, far from being on the defensive, were aggressively confident about the South's future power and influence. The decades of careful attention to events of the sectional conflict may have encouraged an overemphasis by historians on defensive Southern reactions or statements. Other Southerners looked at the region's prosperous place in the global empire of cotton and predicted a bright and powerful future. They contrasted the South's booming productivity with a decline in exports from the Caribbean, where freed slaves seized any opportunities to flee from plantation discipline and pursue family farming. Since the world economy needed cotton, and Southern production was increasing, these Southerners declared their system to be vindicated. The future prosperity of the Atlantic world would thus depend on slavery. It alone could supply the needs of a textile-based industrializing world, and in that future the South enjoyed the advantage over slaveholding Brazil or Cuba. An imperialistic mindset about the Caribbean characterized many Southern leaders' views.[17]

New research and analysis is needed to probe these questions and to determine how widely shared these confident, expansive, and imperialistic views were. In the same way, it would be important to see how widespread was the view that slavery and industrial development could go hand in hand. If some leaders were sanguine in these expectations, we also know that others were doubters. One key variable may be region, for it is clear that the older states of the Atlantic coast and upper South differed with the Gulf area on various issues. It also is possible that there was an emerging generational difference among influential Southerners in that different life experiences could produce different outlooks. In addition to traditional research in letters and speeches, it could be important to know who was investing in railroads or industries and how most wealthy planters invested their money. Because some states owned or invested in railroads, it makes sense to examine those governmental decisions and the debates about them. Immanuel Wallerstein's work has explained the weakness of economies that were suppliers on the periphery of world economic systems, and one wonders if any

Southern leaders had a suspicion of the potential weakness of their position. British manufacturers, says Beckert, certainly worried that slavery made their American supply of cotton potentially unreliable.[18]

The fact that regional differences are relevant to these questions should alert us to another large area that is fertile ground for new research. We are accustomed to talking about the South as a whole and about a binary conflict between the North and the South. But new work has shown us the value of treating the slaveholding states as well as the free states in a more differentiated manner. William Freehling probably deserves the credit for first bringing this theme strongly to our attention. In his important work, he not only divides the South or identifies its regions in a different way but also documents how important those regional differences proved to be during secession and in the Civil War. Others have now taken the insight even further.[19]

New work goes beyond a recognition that some leading politicians in the border region between the North and the South opposed aggressive pro-slavery measures, such as the Lecompton Constitution, and considered making a political alliance with conservative Republicans. This work calls for a new way of looking at the border region in the sectional clash. The dynamics of sectionalism played out differently along the border than they did in either the South or the North. We can conceive of this middle, border region as consisting of an upper or border South and a lower North. Its northern portions barred slavery but contained many residents with Southern ties or sympathies. The slaveholding elements of this border area were economically and culturally different from the Deep South and its black belts. Political and cultural values, for example, among slaveholders in Kentucky or Missouri were similar both to those of "Unionist Whigs in North Carolina, Tennessee, and Virginia" and to those of "conservative Democrats in Illinois, Indiana, and Ohio." Such similarities between this border South and lower North could even be seen as far west as Iowa.[20]

Despite these similarities of outlook, the fact that slave property had a will of its own and could move—escape—became an irritant that drove a wedge between border South and lower North states. The physical situation of border South states, adjacent to free soil, also tended to separate them from the Deep South. Thus, the realities stemming from location proved doubly important. Looking northward, slaveholders in the border South sought and later demanded help from the lower North in recapturing runaways and sealing the border. As time passed, however, their efforts to capture runaways became more irritating to citizens in the free states along the border. Even in conservative Indiana, resistance to slave catchers and violence between pro- and antislavery forces over escaped slaves grew. Thus, slavery interests in the border South came to feel that slavery was "under siege" and that they could not trust the North. But looking southward, the border slave states found that their slavery-related concerns had far more to do with flight than with expansion into new territories. In contrast to the Deep South, they sought security for slavery through federal protection, an outlook that shaped their stance when secession arrived. Territorial issues and the need to expand slavery were matters of far less concern to them.[21]

Yet racism was a force that channeled thinking and emotions into similar paths on both sides of the line between slave and free states. Many whites on either side of the border despised African Americans, were reluctant to surrender their love for the Union, and blamed conflict on extremists of both the North and the South. In the North, these sentiments characterized much of the Democratic Party. Do we know enough about the prewar strategy of the Northern Democrats? How strong were their ties to Southern Democrats? Why were they not more successful in linking the Republicans to the unpopular abolitionists? As for the Republicans, they may have benefited most from the overreaching by pro-slavery Southern leaders, but an active, visible segment of them promoted colonization as the solution to the nation's racial problem. It seems unclear whether those racial arguments strengthened the Republicans' appeal or merely shielded them to some extent from attacks by Democrats. In the slaveholding border states, those whites who favored secession were often the minority. But the activities of African Americans, who sought freedom during the war, immediately stimulated the white racism that was strong across the border region. Both slave-state Unionists and free-state Democrats would turn bitterly against the federal government when it meddled with slavery. This racism would challenge the North's war effort and would destroy Unionist sentiments in the border slave states.[22]

Considering these facts more broadly, we might ask if we have been describing the sectional conflict in a partial and incomplete way. Instead of North versus South, was the nation experiencing a crisis affecting three regions? Were the North and the South moving in different directions and pulling the nation apart, while a third region—the border—was uncomfortably strained in the middle? Was the sectional crisis a crisis in three parts, not two? Aaron Astor has argued that "the perspective of the middle third of the nation—home to a mass of small landholding whites and, in many localities, African Americans scattered on isolated farms—challenges the dominant sectional narrative."[23]

Another way to consider this "middle third" of the nation is to apply a generational perspective on the way the United States approached the problem of slavery. The Founding Fathers' generation accepted the reality of slavery but regretted its existence. Indulging vague hopes that the institution would eventually fade away, they were sometimes willing to talk about compensated emancipation, and a spectrum of leaders actively supported the idea of colonization. Then, as time passed, the North developed more critical feelings about slavery, while the Deep South became aggressive in defense or promotion of the institution. Yet along this border area attitudes changed less and more slowly. Henry Clay of Kentucky continued to voice attitudes like those of the Founders until his death, saying in 1850 that he would never vote to extend slavery into new territory. Abraham Lincoln enjoyed friendships with Kentuckians of similar character who were quite willing to discuss ideas of gradual emancipation. Their attitudes probably influenced—and misled—Lincoln in his understanding of Southern slaveholders.[24]

In any case, it is clear that greater scholarly concentration on the nation's "border third," as we might call it, could be productive. The intransigent, bitter resistance to the fact of emancipation that characterized the defeated Confederacy first appeared along the border, in Kentucky, which never left the Union. Postwar praise or vindication for rebels and guerrillas such as John Hunt Morgan, William C. Quantrill, and Jesse James also began in some of those border areas and foreshadowed the development of the Lost Cause ideology. The racism that plagued postwar society may have taken its most revealing form there because emancipation turned even staunch supporters of the Union into hostile opponents of an emancipating federal government. How much could further study of the "border third" of the country tell us about national developments later in the nineteenth century?[25]

It makes sense to ask if we have given all the attention that is needed to race and racism and their role in the sectional crisis. Our appreciation of slaves' initiative has been steadily growing. Despite the relative scarcity of written documents, on which historians are trained to rely, it is becoming increasingly clear that the slaves played a major role in the sectional crisis. The number of successful escapes during the 1850s was a significant issue for slaveholding interests, a source of encouragement for abolitionists, and an influence on nonabolitionist Northern whites.

Those who couldn't escape may also have shown an initiative that affected events. Comments by slaveholders both before and during the Civil War attest to their amazement at how well informed the slaves were. At times, complained masters, their slaves knew about significant events a day or two before the white family. The so-called slave grapevine was evidently an effective tool of communication. The skills and mobility within the slave population also contributed to the slaves' ability to gain information. Perhaps one point that should not be overlooked in Robert Fogel and Stanley L. Engerman's controversial book *Time on the Cross* concerns its data on the varied skills of slave workmen. The Civil War confirmed that slaves did much more than routine labor. The Confederate government put tens of thousands of slave artisans and craftsmen to work, and the range and number of skilled positions in which slaves were forced to work is truly impressive. For example, blacks in the Confederate Navy Department worked as machinists, carpenters, boilermakers, firemen, molders, shop hands, axmen, sawyers, cooks, caulkers, joiners, bricklayers, and boat hands. In the Tredegar Iron Works, more than a thousand slaves worked as iron puddlers, bricklayers, painters, packers, blacksmiths, and teamsters. Before the war, skilled artisans often earned money for their masters by being hired out on either a long-term or a short-term basis. With greater skills, these slaves typically had greater opportunities to observe, learn, and gather information.[26]

An important research goal would be to learn more about what slaves knew in regard to the developing sectional conflict and how they viewed it. We know they were gathering news from a variety of sources, but it will be a challenge to discover what their information was. We do know from the arguments put forth by Steven Hahn and others that within the slave community African Americans were developing networks and connections that facilitated political activity. Indeed, some of their prewar actions had political effect and should be regarded as politically motivated. Similarly, as soon as the war ended, black Southerners began to speak up for themselves in ways that indicated a sure grasp of the democratic process and the roles of government institutions. Studies of the nature and content of political ideas within the slave community are under way and will be of great interest.[27]

In these ways, it is time for historians to recognize Southern slaves, not just Northern free leaders, as full-fledged actors in the historical developments. It is lamentable but admonitory that a debate developed between James McPherson and Ira Berlin over who deserves the credit for freeing the slaves. Whereas Berlin and his collaborators in the Freedmen and Southern Society Project documented the ways in which slaves seized freedom and pressured the government to act, McPherson insisted on the importance of the traditional view that freedom came from the president. Certainly, the actions taken by Lincoln and other government leaders were a necessary part of legal emancipation. But it is equally clear that tens of thousands of slaves by their actions created situations that forced the government to respond and pushed the political agenda in the direction of freedom. Without their initiatives, taken at great risk, it is uncertain what might have developed and even which side would have won the war. We cannot let the difficulties of research stop us from trying to illuminate the slaves' thinking and actions.[28]

If we turn our attention from what the slaves did to how their actions affected whites, we encounter the contradictions and significance of white racism. It is a common observation that Southern whites discussed slavery in contradictory ways, with a mixture of self-delusion and anxiety. They knew on some level that slaves hated their bondage and racial subordination, but they could not afford to look steadily at the implications of that fact. They needed to deceive themselves in order to enjoy a comforting level of security. Their expressed feelings about slavery thus oscillated between declarations that the master–slave relationship was warm and affectionate—a blessing for happy and contented slaves—and frightened or sometimes panicked warnings about monstrous, hidden assassins who threatened every household.

The role that such fears played in the run-up to secession needs to be assessed more thoroughly. If decades ago Steven Channing described a crisis of fear in South Carolina, Donald Reynolds has more recently provided startling evidence of "mass panic" leading to violence and secession in Texas. Fearing Lincoln's election in the summer of 1860, Texas newspaper editors and politicians encouraged rumors and suspicions of a slave insurrection inspired by abolitionists and Republicans. With such encouragement, some citizens turned to violence against Northern immigrants and visitors as well as against African Americans. Reynolds was able to document no fewer than thirty killings but believes there were more. "A variety of sources," he concludes, "indicate that killings were commonplace occurrences that had become entirely acceptable to a majority of the population."

Violence on this scale invites further investigation, especially since Reynolds notes that there were similar events in other states beyond the scope of his detailed investigation. "Texas-like 'plots' were exposed in several other slave states of the Lower South," he points out, and there were reports of supposed abolitionist activity in at least eight other Southern states.[29]

Such fear undoubtedly affected elections in Texas, as Reynolds argues, but it is worth asking additional questions, starting with how deeply other states may have been affected. Where did such nervous reactions *not* occur, and why? In the absence of actual revolts, one wonders about causation, the factors that fed or created such panic, and here blacks' initiative must be considered. To what extent had the actions of African Americans in Texas put the white population on edge? The more informed the slave population was about the coming election, the more whites may have attributed insurrectionary motives to their slaves. It seems likely that whites were sensing some kind of optimism or expectation among the black population. If so, this possibility underlines the importance of learning more about the slaves' thoughts and actions. Extensive research in white people's letters and diaries may be the primary way to gain such information.

In places such as Texas, did external triggers—such as the nation's political crisis—send a long-established mechanism of social control into overdrive? For decades, threats to slavery or uprisings had unleashed violent repression, and rumors and suspicions spread rapidly whenever there was alarm among the white population. It would be valuable to understand this social pattern more thoroughly. Where in the social structure were the leaders of these movements? What role did sheriffs, editors, ministers, or judges play in justifying or inhibiting violent acts? An extensive analysis of violence, including mobs and riots, in the thirty-three years before the Civil War reveals striking differences between North and South. David Grimsted documents the frequent individual acts of violence in the South and finds that mobbing was "a sanctioned mode of social control" not opposed by the authorities. Mob violence sometimes occurred in the North as well, but whereas Northern mobs typically attacked property, Southern mobs attacked people. To explain the difference, Grimsted applies a psychological explanation to the white society. He argues that violence suppressed moral ambiguities and fears about slaveholding. Riots against nonexistent "abolitionists" could handle internal threats, silencing any questioning of the institution of slavery and identifying the problem as external rather than endemic. Nearly half of the 403 Southern riots that he identifies had to do with insurrection scares or mobs against supposed abolitionists, "although usually there was no evidence of abolition activity." As valuable as these data are, it would be good to have a more fine-grained understanding of the mechanisms of repression.[30]

With mob violence, the South was controlling white people as much as the slave population. Such control was a distinguishing feature of society throughout South. Parts of the South would qualify as a "slave society"—that is, a society so dependent on slavery that the institution shaped all other aspects of social life. Other parts of the South were merely "slaveholding." But everywhere individual rights and liberties counted for nothing when slavery needed support. Maintaining order was always the priority, despite an emphasis on liberty, small government, and the unrestrained individual.

Should we be giving more credit or blame to Southern ministers as the theorists and defenders of a hierarchical racial and patriarchal order in society? It is striking the way in which sermons on the eve of secession and during the war emphasized order and hierarchy as absolutely necessary to a good society—indeed, as God's plan for human life. Southern ministers—at least those in well-established congregations that arranged for the printing of favorite sermons—castigated the North as sinful and un-Christian because it was too democratic. A God-ordained hierarchical order supposedly had given way before a multiplicity of dangerous reform movements above the Mason–Dixon line. Feminism, Fourierism, utopianism, socialism, and other "isms" defied God's will and ignored the Bible's teachings. Therefore, order had the benefit of religious authority in the South. Did this religious endorsement of the slave system contribute to a sense of political security among Southerners? Christians were told they were virtuous to revere not only the hierarchy of masters over slaves and whites over blacks but also and significantly the hierarchy of husbands over wives and parents over children.[31]

Such teachings fit in well with the social patterns of a slaveholding society whose most characteristic unit was the plantation. For masters, the plantation was the realm of their racial authority and their patriarchal power, the center of their imagined world. Clothed with such authority on his plantation, the slaveholder went out into society to claim his influence and respect. Women, children, and slaves had to obey. Ministers justified gender subordination as strongly as racial subordination was justified, and their words likewise defended the political power of rich over poor, the privileged over the common folk. Larry Tise has shown that these ideas had their roots in antidemocratic thought in Federalist New England and in a few northeastern seminaries and universities. But as Northern society moved toward a stronger embrace of democracy, the South, aided by many ministers who came from or had studied in the North, developed its proslavery ideology.[32]

To what extent was the religious justification of hierarchy as a basic principle for society limited to elite or to urban congregations? One wonders whether rural, evangelical churches or ministers who preached to nonslaveholding small farmers advanced the same arguments. One of the inherent contradictions of the slave South was its championing of both inequalities in society and the equality of white men in government. The explanation put forward by leaders such as Calhoun or Jefferson Davis, that slavery made all white men equal and erased any division between rich and poor of the same race, could convince on a racial level. But when whites only were considered, it could be more difficult to square concentration of power and democracy. The importance of hierarchy and the dominance of the deserving rich over the undeserving poor contradicted democratic values. If ministers preached this doctrine to poor farming families, did the nonslaveholders accept it? Was there a difference in the churches' message from one denomination to another or from one region to another, given the considerable diversity among Southern whites? Did the message that God ordained the authority of the slaveholder contribute to overconfidence among politically active planters, or was that merely window dressing for their primary reliance on economic power?

Finally, we can ask what forces were shaping the way Northerners and Southerners thought about the meaning of the nation. There appears to be a difference in the literature between the view that nationalism for Northerners depended largely on the idea of the nation and the notion that nationalism arose from local circumstances. Older interpretations based nationalist feeling in the pride that citizens felt about America's self-government and the representative nature of their institutions. A more recent analysis stresses the success of antebellum Northern village society. Because the country was growing and individuals were improving their lot, it was natural for Northerners to feel pride in what they saw as a supportive society and successful country. Valuing the local experience they had had in the Union, people believed in keeping the national framework in place—a kind of "localism as nationalism." With growth, the nation appeared to be an enabler of progress for villages, towns, and individuals.[33]

The transportation revolution in the North not only stimulated the economy but also multiplied the means of communication. As it created a regional market that united almost all of the North, it tended to give citizens in their local communities a sense that they were participating together in a successful enterprise. With greater communication, Northerners progressively heard more about other towns and states and learned more about the nation of which they were a part. One wonders how much of this description could apply to the South. Population density was far lower in the South, and settlements were much more spread out. Nonslaveholding white Southerners had, in most cases, not yet been pulled into the commercial market economy. Though as individuals they might feel that they were progressing, they probably felt that their progress depended more on personal efforts than on any contribution government was making to society. Southern perspectives were certainly local, and the connection of the local to the national was much weaker. Given the prevailing small-government rhetoric of that region, it is less clear what national loyalty actually meant.

A new study of the content of national feeling in both sections—and the differences between them—would be valuable. For the South, one important challenge for such a study would be to examine possible differences in outlook between political leaders and ordinary nonslaveholding small farmers. Those in positions of leadership had much more reason to think about national issues, whereas subsistence farmers normally lived very locally centered lives. As tensions grew, political officeholders may have become more resentful of the United States, whereas subsistence farmers who lived in areas with few slaves may have retained more national loyalty. Another challenge would be to examine regional differences within the South because different attitudes toward secession were related to people's feelings about and concepts of the Union. Looking at both sections together, we might see if their ideas of what the nation should be were at all congruent as a destructive civil war approached.

Exploration of the war's causes certainly has not ended, and many challenges remain. The diversity within the South as well as the differences within the nation continue to challenge understanding. Slavery rightly has grown in our understanding of the forces leading to war, but we continue to explore its relationship to other forces and causes, whether political, social, or economic. The conjunction of all these elements formed the reality in which the nation split apart and went to war.

2

Understanding Societies in War

Challenges and Opportunities

Just as enormous effort has gone into understanding the roots of the war, historians have energetically investigated the social and political history of the Union and the Confederacy. With the rise of the "new social history" and with greater attention to gender and cultural developments, there has been little danger that wartime society would be neglected in Civil War research. Here again the quantity and quality of work in recent decades are impressive. Although some might wonder what directions are left to explore, a few scholars have called for research in some neglected documents—the Provost Marshal Records, medical corps reports, and military tribunals of the US Army—and as Mark Neely has demonstrated, some large documentary collections contain gems that have been overlooked. Even without the attraction of such documentary sources, the possibility of understanding better the Northern and Southern societies in war is an exciting area for research.[1]

Considering the war years from a general perspective, both the North and the South struggled onward through four bloody years while also experiencing significant internal difficulties. For both regions, persistence *and* internal division were realities that can give thematic unity to our narratives. Both sides seem to have expected a short conflict and easy victory, and both were mistaken. The North as well as the South had to adapt, innovate, and find the means to continue fighting. In the process, however, internal problems and divisions—social and political—appeared, and they were serious. Though we should never minimize the distress and human suffering of the war years, the difficulties that affected the wartime societies can offer an attractive intellectual challenge for historians. They also have relevance for today's world.

War is a crucible in which unusual conditions or intense pressures can put society to the test. War brings unexpected change, introduces new ideas, and almost always imposes strains on a social system that may have seemed to be in equilibrium. In the process, societies under stress reveal much about their structure, reigning values, and centers of power or protest. For the historian, the events of war present an opportunity to understand in greater depth the nature of society in both the North and the South. The scope of the Civil War meant that both regions were going to experience change, division, and conflict. Analysis of wartime developments thus is an exciting area for scholars, who have the chance to benefit from greater insight but also face significant challenges.

Let me admit that the emphasis on "challenges" reflects a personal feeling, yet it is one that potentially has wider validity. Much of my career has been devoted to the study of Confederate society and politics, and I had the advantage of being raised by southern parents whose age gave them some understanding of life in the nineteenth century. Yet I sometimes wonder if I will ever truly understand the personality or thought patterns of Confederate Southerners. As British writer Leslie P. Hartley famously wrote in his novel *The Go-Between,* "The past is a foreign country; they do things differently there." His words capture a fundamental challenge for historians. It is easier for us to understand people who lived in times and situations similar to our own. Yet even those whose experience is closest to ours may differ from us in important ways, and the farther away we are in time or social distance, the more difficult it can be to enter into the thoughts and feelings of those we study. This applies to our research on the Civil War North, and—for me at least—it has particular relevance for Confederate society in wartime.

Emory Thomas deserves great credit for directing our attention to the startling changes that occurred within the South during the Civil War. His work in the early 1970s opened new directions and went far beyond earlier studies that had attributed much division to conflict over state rights. Thomas made us aware of the extent of unexpected change not just in policies and practice but also—at least for some Confederates—in values. Although aware of opposition and division, Thomas tended to put his accent on the positive, calling the glass half full rather than half empty. His insights inspired much new work that often reversed his emphasis and argued instead for the importance of conflicts, divisions, or resistance that damaged the attempt to create and maintain a new nation.[2]

After years in which scholars explored and developed this latter theme, a reaction set in that insisted on the strength of a Confederate war effort that was potent enough not just to last four years but even to convince Abraham Lincoln in August 1864 that his reelection was doomed. Some studies have documented continuing dedication to the Confederate cause in particular areas or high morale among troops or renewed hostility to the North. In fact, there was both persistence and division, and the Confederacy did carry on the fight for four bloody years. The debate over the strength or weakness of Southern will and national determination probably has reached a dead end, for it cannot illuminate simultaneously the two opposed facets of Confederate morale. Documentary evidence abounds for both determination and disaffection.[3]

To understand that double reality better, we should admit that human beings are sometimes inconsistent and that a given individual can be both ardently patriotic and despairing. We also may need to be more conscious of differences affecting particular regions, varying circumstances, and military situations. We should be asking how morale differed in areas that were safe from Federal invasion compared to areas where the war's destruction hit home. How, also, did time or the duration of suffering affect attitudes toward the Yankees? It would not be surprising that invasion could produce an immediate reaction of angry defiance, but months later would that reaction endure amid depressing circumstances? Would the continued presence of Federal troops matter? We also know that attitudes toward the Yankees in occupied areas were not always the same; in some areas occupation generated hatred, whereas in other areas economic cooperation with the enemy developed. What were the factors that accounted for such differences? When and at what points did the war's events most affect emotions on the home front, and where were civilian attitudes most unrealistic or well informed? How much did social pressure and governmental policies of coercion and control shore up support for the cause? In short, a more fine-grained, particular, and localized approach is needed to understand the positive and negative aspects of Confederate morale.[4]

But life in the wartime Confederacy had dimensions even more intriguing than the coexistence of commitment and disaffection. A wave of new studies has made us appreciate the fact that violence was at the center of many Southerners' experience. This internal violence—that is, violence not inflicted by Federal armies—arose quickly, took multiple forms, and plagued many regions. Moreover, the startling amount of violence seemed to have its roots not only in the unusual events of war but also in features inherent in Southern society or in individuals' mentality.

From the war's outset, neighbors often turned against neighbors. In many areas, differences of opinion on the wisdom of secession quickly degenerated into violence. Pro-Confederates resorted to punishment or repression of Unionists, who usually were in the minority. Hostility often took personal forms but sometimes was clothed in law. Local or state officials arrested outspoken Unionists, even if the writ of habeas corpus remained in place. The Confederacy's legal code favored seizures of property in a way that the Union's confiscation laws did not, and this code soon led to a great deal of rapacious sequestration, which Confederate loyalists used to punish those they viewed as disloyal, to take advantage of absent neighbors, and to enrich themselves. In the face of neighbors' hostility, many stubborn and determined Unionists fought back, and the conflict became more intense. Some Unionists showed great inventiveness, using their knowledge of kin and friends to remain in resistance and work stubbornly to undermine the Confederacy. When their outspokenness or their actions to aid Union prisoners and deserters provoked a violent reaction from pro-Confederates, many then turned to guerrilla warfare.[5]

Daniel Sutherland has shown that for a great many Confederates guerrilla or irregular warfare was the Civil War. Its source was often local conflicts among residents. "The heart of the contest," says Sutherland, "had always been a struggle between unionist and secessionist neighbors for political and economic control of their communities. Many of those battles were intensified by family or personal feuds rooted deep in the past." Overall, however, there were three types of irregular warfare: partisan warfare, in which the Confederate government authorized certain cavalry units to raid independently and take plunder as spoils of war; raiding warfare, in which regular cavalry units such as John Hunt Morgan's conducted punitive expeditions; and guerrilla war or "people's war," in which small, irregular bands often descended into uncontrolled brigandage, robbery, and disorder. Sutherland writes that there were 50,000 guerrillas operating all over the South as well as in Missouri, Kentucky, and the Ohio River valley. Robert Mackey emphasizes the importance of guerrilla warfare in Arkansas, Tennessee, and Virginia. Almost from the start, some guerrillas ran amok, with heavy violence occurring already in the summer of

1861. Sutherland's detailed research concludes that guerrillas altered grand strategy and brought disorder, insecurity, destruction, and chaos to broad regions throughout the South. Such warfare made life horrible for all who experienced it, brutalized all who practiced it, and eventually sapped the Confederate will to resist.[6]

At the beginning of the conflict, the Confederate government allowed and sometimes encouraged guerrilla or partisan warfare. For example, in Arkansas early in the war General Thomas Hindman called on the citizenry to organize into bands of ten to help him defend the state. Many individuals enthusiastically complied, eager to pursue an irregular type of warfare. Their bands were supposed to be under the control of provost marshals in the various towns, but that control never became a reality. Before long, as the guerrillas seized food and supplies from residents in order to maintain themselves, their actions degenerated into frequent robbery and the settling of old scores among individuals. The guerrillas became the scourge of Arkansas, whose alienated residents longed to move into any secure area, Union controlled or not, in order to escape the violence. The Confederacy's "failure to control and support the guerrillas created a vicious cycle in which the only winner was the Union army."[7]

Before the end of 1861, the Confederate government was having serious second thoughts about the use of guerrillas because of the "mania" to form or join guerrilla bands. Many Virginians "seemed possessed by a ruthless, almost murderous, instinct to destroy the invader." Leaders saw how this type of warfare spiraled out of control, with damage to both internal morale and the Confederacy's international image. The Partisan Ranger Act, passed in early 1862, was an effort to get a grip on independent operations by bringing them under regular army control. But within a few months the Confederacy needed a disciplined irregular war in several states, whether to oppose Unionists or to aid the small, inadequate regular forces. Thus, it committed itself to "at least a limited partisan war," with the indiscriminate violence it entailed. By the beginning of 1864, it was clear that guerrillas afflicted the civilian population as much as the Union army, and the government all but repealed the Partisan Ranger Act, hoping to retain only a few elite, more disciplined units, such as John Singleton Mosby's.[8]

Where guerrilla violence spiraled furthest out of control, the results were appalling. Men such as Champ Ferguson and William Quantrill, who personified violence along the Kentucky–Tennessee border and in Kansas, became ruthless murderers. Ferguson, who may have had "the bloodiest single career of the Civil War," killed almost without compunction. He often murdered preemptively and later justified himself by claiming that he killed men in order to prevent them from posing a threat to him. Ferguson personally killed at least fifty-three Unionists, and his actions and those of his followers spread fear and devastation throughout the area where they operated.[9]

But the government could not limit or control "people's war," which also fed on the growing disorder within Southern society. A vast amount of "people's war" was locally focused, aiming at the defense of one's family, property, and home. If the government could not protect its people, citizens armed themselves to do the job. Men fought against threats or impositions by either side. Moreover, as hunger and suffering spread on the home front, many soldiers deserted out of concern for their families and resisted when local authorities tried to arrest them and send them back to the army. An increasing number of citizens were fighting their government.

If men did most of the actual fighting in guerrilla conflicts, they never could have sustained themselves without the help of women. Guerrillas often were on the run or needed to find shelter or a hiding place, and women were the people who made these things possible. Aside from some information about Unionist families or kin networks that resisted the Confederacy, we know little about the women who supported or encouraged guerrilla activities. Some women went even further, with great effect. Rebellious women took to the streets of cities, towns, and villages in numerous bread riots. Moving beyond the limits of their traditional gender roles, they threatened merchants and workers at government depots in order to seize food for their children. Can we learn more about how women felt about these efforts and how they combined rebellion with the traditional concern for feeding their families? Their actions demanded a response from the Confederate and local governments.

All of these factors help to explain the widespread disorder and absence of real government in North Carolina. Barton Myers has shown that "less than 60 percent of North Carolina was under firm control of the Confederate government by 1864." More than thirty counties suffered an "anti-Confederate people's war of self-defense and resistance that emerged among disaffected citizens, deserters, conscript evaders, and unconditional Unionists." Efforts by the government to capture deserters or round up conscripts were often seen as "tyranny and military occupation in their home communities. This experience included approximately seventy-five counties (nearly

90 percent) out of the eighty-six counties of North Carolina." With roughly 5,000 men fighting Confederate authorities in irregular warfare, a force the size of General Robert E. Lee's army, Myers calculates, would have been necessary to suppress resistance. The result was "destabilization and loss of control" by the government and not only in North Carolina.[10]

Home-front suffering, guerrilla war, and disorder exposed the weakness of Confederate authorities and caused people to lose faith that their governments at any level could protect or serve them.[11] "By 1863," notes Laura Edwards, "it was no longer clear who held legal authority in the Confederacy."

> At the point when people needed services the most, local governments literally crumbled. Federal and state policies left local governments with too many needy people and too few resources. Not only were there no resources to distribute, [but] there were not even enough men to fill the necessary positions, keep local courts running, and maintain a semblance of order. . . . [T]he Confederacy descended into a chaos of competing governing bodies, in which everyone claimed to be in charge and no one could actually do much to resolve the problems that people faced in their daily lives. . . . When their entreaties met with silence, white southerners took the law into their own hands.[12]

Nor was this collapse of governmental services and law the only type of disorder. Moving through the landscape were thousands of fugitive slaves, Confederate deserters, stragglers, and skulkers, few of whom met the description of peaceful, law-abiding citizens. Deserters needed food and shelter as they traveled, and therefore many preyed on local families. Their depredations grew in scope as the Confederacy's military fortunes declined. One-third of the Confederate army was listed as absent in November 1863, two-thirds by the end of the war, and in the four months after October 1864 the War Department estimated that 72,000 had deserted. In addition, thousands of imprisoned US soldiers escaped from their confinement. Between September 1864 and February 1865, for example, almost 3,000 Union prisoners in South Carolina escaped and traveled across the state with little hindrance from Confederate or state officials. All these developments forced Southerners to take up arms to protect themselves and their families, a fact that increased the violence.[13]

Some aspects of this widespread violence have causes that are easy to understand, but other features challenge our analysis. For example, it is clear that much violence was not wholly defensive. Confederate authorities had far more eager partisan rangers than they wanted. Many white Southerners did not hesitate and were quick to attack Unionists, political enemies, and neighbors against whom they had a grudge. Local authorities wanted to punish deserters, but deserters armed and organized themselves to steal from the wealthy and to impede courts and governmental meetings. Some men made it plain that they would not permit the government to enforce conscription, collect taxes, or otherwise interfere with their lives. Such resistance to government policies became so widespread that some Confederate officials complained in official communications that their work had become impossible or that to carry out their duties meant risking their lives.

As historians, we need to understand how this tendency to resort to violence or take the law into one's own hands was related to the culture of the prewar South. How did it fit into the extremely local and personal orientation that Southerners brought to their idea of community? What was its connection to the ordinary person's concept of liberty? David Grimsted has shown that violence in the prewar South was common and not dependent on frontier conditions or the code of honor. "Violence," he argues, "served less any communal code than a system of individual winning by intimidation." It often "served such practical ends as gaining political clout, avoiding paying bills, winning property, eliminating rivals, settling court cases one was losing, silencing opinions one couldn't refute." Was the purpose of society, as understood by many white Southerners, to allow to each man the maximum freedom and opportunity to exercise his will, free from restraint? The desire for mastery that has been identified in wealthy slaveholders and public figures seems to have had its counterpart among the ordinary small farmers. In the culture of honor, ambitious or prominent men understood that brash assertiveness was a means to demand respect and status, and if that recognition was denied, violence was the next step. Did this way of thinking apply in a broad manner to ordinary folk as well?[14]

Unlike the North, where most agriculturalists lived in villages or towns and where cities were growing rapidly, settlement in the South was widely dispersed. If Northerners were accustomed to pursuing their goals within a well-established, ordered social structure, Southerners were more isolated and seem to have seen themselves more as unhindered free agents. Joined to a very rural style of life in the South was a long-established political ideology that went beyond celebrating small, limited government. Not only was governance "highly localized" and state-rights rhetoric pervasive, but there also was "a fundamental disdain for centralized government" or authority. Individual white Confederates "thought that legal authority rested—at least in part—with them." When the war began, patriotic Confederates were ready to fight, but many offered their support to the government on "their own terms," assuming they could dictate the type or length of service.[15]

In such a setting, what did freedom or liberty mean to the ordinary Southerner? What was to be expected of his relationship to those who wanted to limit his freedom of action, and what did manliness or self-respect require of a person? Many individuals' fierce determination to have their way is striking, whether they were foes or champions of the government. George Rable notes this characteristic in his analysis of the theoretical weakness and contradictions in Confederate nationalism. The Confederates' "impressive staying power" derived from a national feeling that "proved far more visceral than intellectual, more emotional than ideological, more stubborn than consistent." In all parts of the Confederacy, as conflicts and disorder grew, people exhibited personalities that often were belligerent, viscerally emotional, and stubborn.[16]

Yet there were unspoken, unspecified, but real assumptions among the Confederate population about what different classes and groups owed to each other. To use a biological metaphor, Southerners were part of an interpersonal ecological system whose rules the war disrupted. When that disruption occurred, individuals and groups acted on their own to defend their rights or regain what they felt was owed them. Along with the rhetoric of "decentralized government and the importance of individual white men's interests," there was a conviction that resistance, food riots, and other efforts "to reclaim the social order" were justified. Along with a fierce or barely limited individualism, there were "expectations that government—at all levels—would respond directly to their needs." Hungry, suffering nonslaveholders blamed their wealthy neighbors and charged that they had failed to fulfill their social obligations. Army privates, whose families could not subsist deprived of their labor and were supported only by their small military wages, angrily asserted that the government had breached a duty to them.[17]

To understand more fully how this social system operated remains an intellectual challenge. How did individual Southerners see themselves and their communities? How were individual violence and the social order related? At least to me, it seems clear that the violent character of Southern society still poses challenges to students of the Confederacy. Those challenges represent opportunities as well to historians who will take up the task. Perhaps deeper analysis of social patterns (what groups actually did in different situations) and closer reading of individuals' letters and papers (to deepen knowledge of their motives) can yield greater understanding.

This discussion of the South is not meant to suggest any lack of opportunities for studying Northern society in the war. If there has been much debate about Southern nationalism and the strength of Southern will, there may be less debate but more theories about nationalism in the North. The Civil War was the greatest crisis of the nation, so it seems obvious that it affected American nationalism, and there is an unspoken but general assumption in our society that the war's outcome strengthened nationalism. Such thinking, however, runs the risk of being simplistic or unchronological, and it short-circuits a meaningful, scholarly approach. Much recent attention to the Union's nationalism has focused on the idea of citizenship—what duties were a part of citizenship and what the nation meant to its citizens are closely related—and these studies are valuable. But more direct investigations are also justified.

The concept of nationalism is protean, hard to pin down, even slippery. Scholars differ as to whether nationalism has an ancient history and always existed or is exclusively a product of modern eras characterized by superior communications and strong central governments. In human beings' emotional makeup, there seems to be some kind of tribal impulse or predilection. Many people want to belong to some larger group that is impressive or favored and that gives them a sense of belonging to something greater than themselves. They choose to affiliate with a team, a party, a belief system, a region, or even an entertainer. Thus, people who live close to each other and have similar personal characteristics can be fanatically dedicated either to the Tar Heels or Duke, to the Crimson Tide or Auburn, to Chicago or New York, to France or Great Britain. Scholars have analyzed these affiliations from the point of view of communications theory, structural theories, politics, psychology, ethnicity, linguistic groups, gender, shared history, and other approaches. A recent volume that seeks to review and advance this field has more than a dozen chapters devoted to different theories of nationalism.[18] Not all of these theories have been applied at this point to the study of nationalism in the Civil War North, and comparative investigations that utilize the history of other nations have barely begun.

Conceptually, one problem is that the visible reality of nationalism—

the nationalism that we see expressed in the political affairs of a country or in its international relations—appears to be unitary, yet the roots of national feeling may be highly diverse. People may feel devotion to their nation based on religious beliefs, military power, economic progress, ethnic identification, shared history, or social mythology. In fact, it is often true that national identity and the myths associated with it are based on exaggerations, misrepresentations, inventions, or propaganda. Thus, national feeling is a many-headed creature, a kind of emotion shared among many people that may arise from many different sources. Logically, too, that national feeling can be affected by many different kinds of events.

Works by George Rable and Harry Stout have drawn our attention to religion as a motivating force in the Union's war effort. As the death toll mounted and the carnage and destruction of the war exceeded anyone's expectations, the Northern clergy did not lose faith. With minor exceptions, they instead preached with greater conviction that victory and the destruction of slavery were necessary. Their congregations heard that God's hand was in the war. For pious Northerners, such preaching undoubtedly affected their sense of nationalism. Not all citizens were pious, however, and not all favored emancipation. Chandra Miller Manning is among those who have revitalized the idea that emancipation became an inspiring goal, sustaining the long war effort and increasing devotion to the Union. Taking careful notice of racism, she argues that white Northern soldiers wanted to separate the national cause from slavery, but the war forced them to confront questions of race, equality, and civil rights. Because they wanted to win the war and uphold the Union, most soldiers accepted emancipation as a necessary or inspiring goal. Susan-Mary Grant has argued that in a prolonged war democracies often need a new stimulus, and the emancipation of slaves provided the idea of a "new birth of freedom" for Northerners. Undoubtedly for many Northerners, though not for all, the destruction of slavery strengthened nationalism by fulfilling America's founding ideals.[19]

Melinda Lawson has produced the most ambitious study on the nature of Northern nationalism and how it changed during the war. In agreement with earlier scholars, she argues that devotion to the nation had been based principally on the *idea* of America, the idea that the United States was an example for the world as its first representative democracy. She also mentions the earlier influence of "notions of Christian charity, sacrifice, and redemption; ideas of liberal self-interest and republican virtue; local and partisan identities; free labor tenets; the longing for 'self and freedom';

a profound faith in the founding fathers; and a providential view of history." The experience of the war, however, changed American nationalism. It moved citizens toward the kind of nationalism that characterized other countries—a nationalism "rooted in existing religious, political, and cultural values and identities." A second important change was that the state came to be seen as a benefactor and not a threat to the individual. In addition, Lawson sees Lincoln's leadership and his martyrdom as adding "a missing 'organic' element" that was both emotional and unifying. Because Lincoln "infused his synthesis with a profound ideological significance" drawn from the Declaration of Independence, his leadership and death helped to envelop the nation "in a mystical aura."[20]

Heather Cox Richardson's study of economic policies gives some support to Lawson's idea of the state as a benefactor. She argues that Republican legislators were passing new laws under the conviction that these laws would benefit individuals and add to prosperity. All these points about what shaped and contributed to nationalism have value, and David Potter argues that nationalism can gather up various loyalties in a supportive relationship.[21] But this multiplicity raises some analytical questions. Did nationalism in the North come to have a meaning that most patriots understood? Did these different elements cohere in some way, or did nationalism mean different things to different Northerners? Or was it just as likely that nationalism remained a fragmented or diverse kind of belief, however strong it may have been? Did its meaning vary by region or according to native or foreign birth? To what extent did the changes in the nature of nationalist feeling affect Democrats, who remained unhappy with the war, as well as Republicans? Did belief in and loyalty to the nation continue to mean quite different things to different people or different political parties?

In fact, it makes sense to ask whether the Civil War damaged or lessened the feeling of nationalism among certain groups in the North. The Peace Democrats were steadfastly opposed to the war, and many other Democrats seemed convinced that prosecution of the conflict was unjust to Southerners and certain to cause serious damage to previous unity. The numerous supporters of Clement Vallandigham, the leader of the antiwar Copperhead Democrats, deeply deplored restrictions on civil liberties. Certain immigrant groups, such as recently arrived Irish immigrants, expressed hostility to the war and the government's policies, and the fact that the Union won most likely did not erase their resentment. Wartime events adversely affected the assimilation of German Americans.[22] Racists, of which there were many in the North, were not reconciled to emancipation or convinced that such a change in society was part of God's plan. Here I am echoing an argument that for certain topics a more localized, particular, situational analysis—distinguished from an overall interpretation—is justified. This is one such topic, and investigation of it might lead to a different overall understanding. Isn't it possible that much of the new, stronger nationalism coming out of the war had its impact in the future? Was it the substance of an inspiring set of beliefs for later generations rather than a shared reality in 1865 or 1866?

Political differences are among several other fascinating challenges relating to Northern society. The Union experienced sharp political divisions during the war, yet Northerners, too, found ways to persist under pressure, eventually reaching victory. Moreover, scholars in recent years have opened up new areas of investigation relating to the North, its political competition and conflict, and its social values. The important area of race presents an exception to the fact that there was less violence in the North (at least between whites) than in the South. Violence against African Americans was very common and widespread as strong divisions over race spread beyond the political arena. Along a series of dimensions, wartime political and social clashes in the North left society with significant challenges to reintegration after the war.

Internal division over the war could become deeply personal, but it usually had its roots in Northern politics. Any description of these political roots in broad, summary terms reveals that from the start Democrats and Republicans had very different ideas about what caused the war and what should be done. Republicans saw slavery as a threat to Northern society, a blight on the nation's future, and a moral issue. Democrats defended slaveholders' rights and felt few concerns over the treatment of a race they regarded as inferior, unwelcome, and undeserving. To Republicans, the South and the Slave Power were aggressors; to Democrats, the dangerous fanatics of the North and the irresponsible extremists of the South had brought on a needless war. Republicans were open to or desirous of change, whereas Democrats repeated their mantra of continuity: "The Union as it was, and the Constitution as it is."

Such political differences could arouse potent emotions on either side, and surely there were many arguments among friends and within families. Some political issues, whether they involved emancipation or constitutional principles, were deeply felt and became more significant as the war went on. Conflict may have been most acute and painful within some evangelical Protestant churches. A recent investigation suggests that such conflict took its strongest form in the states along the Ohio River or farther west. In this region, migration had influenced politics because many Democrats there had origins in the slaveholding South, whereas many who became Republicans had family roots in New England or the Northeast. But religious belief intensified the normal political differences. In their churches, many Democrats and Republicans took the scriptures as God's teachings and therefore as their guide, but they reached opposite conclusions. Controversy grew during the fall of 1862 as these evangelical Protestants divided over Lincoln's emancipation plans. The notion that God commanded their obedience raised the political questions to a transcendent level. The sincere and conscientious believer, many thought, had to take a particular stand or offend God. Slavery was the North's worst sin to some, whereas antislavery sermons were unbiblical, wrong, and offensive to others.[23]

Physical violence occurred in some congregations as congregants differed. Mutual hostility over emancipation grew until in 1863 Clement Vallandigham's candidacy for governor of Ohio proved especially divisive. Many Northern ministers by then had adopted the view that God's hand was in the antislavery events of the time. In angry rejection of that view, some Methodists broke from their denomination to form the Independent Methodist Church. Others worked to create a new denomination called the Christian Union. Before the end of the war, the Democrats' negative reaction to the clergy's pro-Union, antislavery stance "precipitated an ecclesiastical crisis of immense proportions" as many Democrats abandoned churches in Indiana and elsewhere. Because both sides felt they knew God's purpose, religious beliefs made differences unbridgeable.[24]

These conflicts became most acute in the middle years of the war, but historian Sean Scott has argued that religious beliefs continued to encourage social divisions. Among many church-goers there was a drift toward favoring retribution against traitors or rebels. The carnage on the Virginia battlefields in 1864 encouraged unforgiving attitudes, and anger grew against the Copperheads, whom Republicans denounced. Religiously inspired zeal, Scott argues, had left many Northerners unprepared for the compassionate, forgiveness-oriented message of Abraham Lincoln's Second Inaugural Address. The assassination of the wartime president dismayed and confused many who usually believed they could see God's purpose. In response, they "clamored for vengeance," adding another complication to the many that would make national reintegration difficult. Such emotions must be considered along with the many others that made Reconstruction problematic.[25]

The clash between Republicans and Democrats has posed many questions for historians—including questions about the parties' strategies and the dynamics of their competition. A panel at a recent meeting of the Society of Civil War Historians concluded that our understanding of the Democrats remains weak. Others have argued that the Democrats themselves struggled to define what being the "loyal opposition" meant. Mark Neely Jr. has declared that "the loyal opposition in the North during the Civil War remains to this day in crying need of analysis." Despite what he says was a principal lesson of the first party system—that the minority party cannot fundamentally oppose the nation's war effort—the Democrats "indulged in poisonous criticism of the country and lapsed into suicidal factionalism, to this day not satisfactorily explained by historians."[26]

Given that the Democrats laid substantial blame for causing the war at the door of the Republicans, how far were they willing to go in trusting Lincoln's pledge that he would respect the Constitution and Southerners' legitimate rights? To what extent did partisanship prevent them from crediting the steps Lincoln actually took to attract and assure Southerners? In the early months of the conflict, there *were* many Democratic editors who saw Lincoln as a reasonable man pressured and harassed by the dangerous radicals within his party. But before January 1863 harsh condemnation of the president was virtually unanimous. How much of that change was attributable to the Emancipation Proclamation and how much to the adoption of harsher military measures? How energetically could Democrats support a war when they believed that Southerners were being wronged and that every day of warfare simply made reunion psychologically and socially more difficult? Was defeating the South completely mistaken in the eyes of many Democrats? One has to wonder if their basic perspective on the conflict allowed them much room to support any strong measure that would lead to victory. Surely in the papers of Democratic leaders and editors there is commentary relative to these subjects.

The split that developed in the Democratic Party also challenges analysis, with Neely declaring that "the power of the peace wing of the Democratic Party was especially anomalous." A two-party system was supposed to moderate extremes, and both parties knew they would suffer when their ranks were sharply divided in an election campaign. Yet the Democrats came out of their convention in 1864 as virtually two parties—one accepting that the war had to continue until victory restored the Union and the other demanding peace now.[27] What were the ideological reasons for this split? What role did Lincoln's supposedly tyrannical policies or violations of the Constitution or curtailment of individual rights play compared to emancipation and racial change? We should ask whether the Peace Democrats' motives differed from one part of the North to another, and we should try to determine when or where their opposition to the war effort became irreversible.

Modern historians, following the argument among the Democrats' contemporaries, debate whether the Democrats' opposition was disloyal or not and whether it damaged the national cause. Jennifer Weber sees the Democrats' opposition, especially that of the Peace wing, as a real danger to the Union, and she notes a number of sources for their ideology. Other studies conclude that Peace Democrats and Copperheads in Connecticut interfered with the war effort, whereas in Pennsylvania they were a local, nonconspiratorial movement that did little or no harm. How unified were the Peace Democrats? To what extent was there coordination of their efforts across the North? Did Federal government economic policies that aided some Democratic areas tend to modify their hostility to the administration? Whether two-party competition helped or hurt the Union has also come under debate. The notion that the North benefited from such competition but the Confederacy suffered from its absence rests on an assumption that the verdict of the polls resolves conflict and settles things. But the sharpness of wartime division certainly alarmed contemporaries, and studies should identify how much rapprochement there was between the parties once the voters had spoken and before Reconstruction introduced new conflicts.[28]

If wartime Democrats castigated the administration, Republicans in equal measure flayed the Democrats for failing to support the Union. This Republican tactic frequently blurred the line between loyal but critical Democrats and dangerous Copperheads who engaged in traitorous activities and advocacy. To overcome the Democrats, argues Adam I. P. Smith, Republicans tried to depict all opposition as illegitimate during the emergency while wrapping themselves in a virtuous cause, the cause of the Union. Advancing a "partisan antipartisanship," the Republican message was that all must rise above party and become antipartisan in the national interest. The Union Leagues and allied organizations generated propaganda designed to create "a new conception of loyalty and patriotism" that would submerge the opposition and armor-plate the administration. The title of Francis Lieber's pamphlet *No Party Now but All for Our Country* (1863) captured the Republican strategy.[29]

Smith's argument ties into older speculation that Lincoln and others expected a reorganization of parties after the war. In such a reorganization, Republicans would gain strength by moving to and claiming the center of the political spectrum, both regionally and nationally. Lincoln presumably had the former Southern Whigs in his sights as one pillar of strength for a reorganized, bisectional party. No less an authority than Michael Holt has argued that President Lincoln in 1864 "set out to destroy the Republican party as it existed in 1860 . . . an exclusively northern party whose sole basis of cohesion was hostility toward the South and the Democratic party." Other studies focused on the North show that the Union Party label was not simply a ploy to aid the Republicans in the election of 1864. It emerged before 1864 in some states, and in Pennsylvania, for example, the effort to forge a broader party by bringing in the "Bell and Everett" men from 1860 had the backing of Governor Andrew Curtin and others. There is sufficient evidence for this idea to explain why it remains one of the most intriguing, significant, and still unsettled questions about Northern politics of this period.[30]

Although Republicans maintained their unity as a party better than the Democrats did, that does not mean that all were agreed on the path to follow or the speed at which to move. Much evidence supports the long-established view that policy differences and tension characterized Lincoln's relationship with the Radical Republicans. James Oakes's recent, celebratory work tends to erase this difference and to portray all the Republicans as eager, from the start, to destroy slavery. Whatever Lincoln's private feelings may have been, the record shows that he did not set out to destroy slavery, that he moved slowly toward emancipation, and that his interest in colonization continued after January 1, 1863. His gradualism and the fact that he repeatedly argued for colonization surely seemed positive to some of his conservative colleagues as well as to many voters.[31]

The new Republican Party was a diverse mix of former Whigs and former Democrats, idealistic abolitionists and dedicated racists. More attention is needed to the differences in their perspectives. Someone should produce a successor volume to Eric Foner's book *Free Soil, Free Labor, Free Men* by analyzing the party's wartime ideology on race. How did abolitionists in the party plan to counter the colonizationists, whose active ranks included some western governors and various officeholders? Were the abolitionists merely hopeful that colonization would prove impractical? How close did they come at the end of 1864 to convincing a majority of congressional Republicans that freedmen in the South should vote? Also, before many years had passed, some former Democrats, such as the Blairs, left the party. That raises a question about how real the differences may have been during the war, on economic issues as well as on slavery. If the differences were slight, what was it about the wartime environment that suppressed division in what was, after all, a new political organization composed of diverse elements?[32]

Writing that "the major mysteries of Civil War politics remain unsolved," Neely adds that "it is the extremism of the Civil War political parties that to this day cries out for explanation."[33] For the Republicans, that extremism was the adoption of emancipation as part of a harsher conduct of the war. But that decision in itself is not too difficult to explain. The war was an emergency, one in which the existence of the nation was at stake, and military victory was proving far more difficult than expected. Lincoln clearly felt driven to what he viewed as a risky decision by military necessity and the plummeting morale of disappointed Northerners. His decision cheered elements of his party but offended a substantial part of the electorate. What made emancipation extreme was the status that slavery had enjoyed in the Union and in public attitudes. Not only was there constitutional sanction for the institution where it existed, something Republicans freely admitted, but also and more importantly emancipation involved the issue of race and the maintenance of white supremacy. The importance of widespread racism in the North demands continuing emphasis in new investigations.

I am not aware of a strictly wartime counterpart to Forrest Wood's book *Black Scare: The Racist Response to Emancipation and Reconstruction,* and many accounts focus on progress rather than on the persistence of racial hate. We should describe more fully the extent to which racism dominated developments in Northern society, impeding or diverting progress and setting the limits for political change. Many historical accounts have celebrated the gradual change in Northern attitudes toward emancipation as a combination of moral inspiration and practical realities pushed the Union in that direction. Soldiers backed emancipation in order to win the war and give meaning to their hardships and sacrifices. Most recent works, to their credit, acknowledge Northerners' continuing racism. For many in or out of the army, the need to prevail in the war or to preserve the Union triumphed over resistance to emancipation. But racism always imposed significant limits on change, and voices repeatedly calling for fair treatment or wiser policies went unheard. Whether coming from military officers in direct contact with the freed people, members of the American Freedmen's Inquiry Commission, or abolitionists black and white, voices calling for equal rights, the right to vote, or a chance to obtain confiscated land were ignored. And the limitations of Lincoln's policies and Congress's laws are well known.[34]

Racism's impact may be even more determinative in relation to the Democratic Party. We should ask how strongly racism dictated Democrats' opposition to the administration and the war. Racism was not just one among many issues exploited by the Democrats. Rather, it seems to have been the taproot from which many additional complaints sprang—such as the charge that huge sums were wasted to feed contrabands or that white soldiers were neglected or depreciated in favor of black recruits. Was race also the most intensely emotional issue in the Democrats' arsenal? How much emphasis did politicians and, more particularly, Democratic newspaper editors put on racial fears as compared to complaints about military arrests or violations of the Constitution? What aroused their most fervent rejection of Lincoln's administration? Analysis of the content of Democratic propaganda during election campaigns should shed light on the relative importance of various issues. One wonders if emancipation—given Democrats' basic views on race and the rights of the South—made any cooperation with the Republicans impossible. And was whites' fear of racial competition the strongest motivator for Democratic Party voters?

The Democrats presented themselves as the champions and defenders of the Northern white laborer. They sought his support through messages of fear. Just as the prewar Lincoln had used fear that slavery would become national, wartime Democrats encouraged fears that freed slaves would flood the North, drive down wages, take whites' jobs, and overthrow white supremacy. Their appeal to the common man in the North was a racist appeal. Where was it most effective, and why was it less effective in other places? How much racial hate and violence did the Democrats create, and how much of their rhetoric was a response to emotions that were already actively in play? Did the battle between Republicans and Democrats boil down to the Union versus white supremacy?

Violence attests to the importance of the race issue. Leslie Schwalm and others have presented evidence that racist violence was widespread in the North, despite the small black population in most areas there. The famous New York City riot of 1863 was only one of many. In 1861, when African Americans tried to volunteer for military service, the police in several cities ordered them to desist due to the danger of mob violence as well as to racist rejection of their service. Race riots occurred as early as the summer of 1862, when violence flared in Toledo, Cincinnati, Chicago, and Peoria. Attacks on black workers took place in Chicago, Cincinnati, and Boston, and black communities were targets in Massachusetts, Connecticut, New York, and New Jersey. "Numerous" attacks on African Americans occurred when blacks arrived by river in Minnesota and Indiana, and the largest or best-known riots were in Detroit and New York.[35] This list probably is not complete, and a more comprehensive study of race riots, including their causes and effects, is in order. Interestingly, economic motives sometimes were in conflict with racism, for some whites reacted to a shortage of labor by seeking freed slaves as workers. Tens of thousands of former slaves moved as workers into the upper Midwest during the war. Was the reaction against their presence always violent? Were there some areas where they became accepted as part of the community? How did Republican or Democratic officials react?

The study of antiblack riots opens a window on the place that racism held in white identity. It also can shed light on whites' attitudes toward other vulnerable minorities, such as the Irish and the Indians. Symbols of social status were in play, proving as potent as events that actually affected a person's employment or opportunities. Midwesterners who felt that the government had failed to protect them against Indians resented the administration's concern for the slaves. How did attitudes and prejudice toward Indians then influence the treatment of African Americans? Why did the Irish sometimes encounter greater prejudice than blacks? What action, if any, did churches take against racist activity? In all of these events, the ugly character and structure of white supremacy—the Northern version—is waiting to be fully described and identified. A foundation of high-quality work can aid investigation now in a way that was not possible even twenty years ago.

Amid the conflicts of Northern society, there also was significant social change, in particular change affecting women. Some who struggled when their husbands or sons went into the army used their dependency to claim government aid. Others who took up paid work sewing uniforms with material furnished by subcontractors petitioned Congress or used publicity and political action to demand better wages. As nurses, missionaries to the freedmen, and the hardest-working and most reliable workers in wartime sanitary or fund-raising fairs, Northern women stretched the definitions of their gender role to take on wider responsibilities. These activities certainly had some kind of lasting impact. "The lessons of the war were not lost on the women of this nation," declared Elizabeth Cady Stanton. If new roles taught lessons, so did the criticism directed at Northern women by 1863. Nina Silber argues that complaints that women were not being patriotic enough had the effect of encouraging women's sense that they should have their own principles and political beliefs. Stanton took a similar view: "Through varied forms of suffering and humiliation, [women] learned that they had an equal interest with man in the administration of Government, enjoying or suffering alike its blessings or its miseries."[36]

A question for historians to explore is how changed thinking translated into changed societal and institutional arrangements or the extent to which it did. It would seem that some of the most explicit ideas for modeling the process of change in gender roles have come from Morton Keller and J. Matthew Gallman. Endorsing Keller's view that change occurs slowly with considerable continuity in social relations, Gallman describes an incremental or gradual change in actual behavior coexisting with "ideological conservatism organized around gender roles." As women did the actual work in large-scale sanitary fairs, men continued to occupy the leadership positions, women remained subservient, and local rather than centralized action continued to be the pattern. Lyde Cullen Sizer agrees that middle-class women came to feel "a personal stake in national politics," but "public rhetoric and social reality" remained far apart.[37]

Conditions of war seemed to have opened some doors through which women could enlarge their influence, but change on the ground did not mean that new roles were promptly accepted as a legitimate social reality. A degree of actual, wartime change preceded acceptance of change. That women sensed this dynamic also appears to have occurred in the Confederacy, where protesting women became "a salient constituency in Confederate politics." Nevertheless, they did not make their claims "based on perceived rights as citizens of the nation." Like Northern women, Southern women expanded their influence within the accepted definitions of wives and mothers. Male civilians and especially army officers who dealt with slaves likewise insisted on defining women as wives rather than as citizens.

The power of patriarchal patterns and the barriers to ideological change were firmly established in society, and the processes by which they slowly began to change are sure to claim additional attention.[38]

Defining women as wives meant that they did not have full rights as citizens, and they were not alone. The status of others and the meaning of citizenship came into question during the war. What citizenship meant, as I mentioned earlier, is one of the new areas of study that are already proving valuable. The number of conferences, articles, and new books dealing with duty and people's understanding of what citizenship entailed indicate that new insights will come from this subfield. One product of some of this work is that it takes us directly into the feelings, thought patterns, and social assumptions of Northerners during the Civil War. But an additional benefit is the light that it sheds on the nature and operational values of Northern society.

When Lincoln spoke about citizenship in time of war, his comments concerned voluntary choices that individuals could make rather than requirements that should be met or obligations that must be discharged. He invited public appreciation for the value of the Union rather than describing duties that individuals owed. J. Matthew Gallman has used enlistment data as well as public and private comments to demonstrate that in the matter of military service Northern men had choices. As long as a person was supportive of the cause and not guilty of cowardice or hypocrisy, he did not have to go to war to be patriotic. The public perception of citizenship's duties—like Lincoln's comments—reflected a free market for decision making rather than rigid responsibilities. Did the choices open to citizens contribute to their feelings of loyalty to the nation? Phillip Paludan has argued that localism served nationalism in the sense that Northerners' positive local experiences led them to affirm the nation. Building from that idea, Melinda Lawson describes how sanitary fairs became vehicles for national loyalty as towns and local organizations competed to give support to the nation. She then traces the development of a redefined relationship "between the individual and the national state"—one in which the state was a "benefactor, not [a] threat, to individual Americans." How much of that relationship was a product of a free market for decision making?[39]

The idea of a free market for decision making by citizens prompts intriguing speculation about the relations among capitalism, freedom, and what Northerners perceived as the social contract. I suspect that there is important work to be done to clarify the penetration of free-market, capitalist notions of freedom into Northern society. Although this book does not address the Reconstruction period or the Gilded Age with any thoroughness, it is a commonplace that the era of big business followed swiftly upon the Union's victory in the Civil War. Moreover, the rapid dominance of large capitalist firms was not a shocking revolution that smashed through strong barriers but a kind of flowering that took place almost naturally. Heather Cox Richardson's fine study of Republican economic policies during the Civil War illuminates many of the events that followed the war. Her book is by design, however, a thorough study of men in Congress, their thought patterns, and the expectations they had about new laws and the future. Isn't there more that might be said, through some new approach, about the power of free-market, capitalist assumptions in the general society and how they had become embedded by the time of the Civil War? The transportation improvements that created an extended regional market before 1860 had furthered prosperity but had also caused many people to lose their jobs or forced them to find different ways to make a living. We probably need to understand better the overall reaction of society and of Northern farmers and workers to the market revolution that tied the Northern states together economically. Was the "connection between economic progress and human progress" that Daniel Walker Howe describes enough to create acceptance of the market economy? What do Northern workers' protests in wartime reveal concerning their assumptions about rights and contracts? Answering these questions is a large but important challenge.[40]

In regard to foreign affairs, there is one area in which Robert May's fine and pioneering work deserves more support. Although the North had to concentrate its efforts on winning the war, that did not mean that imperialistic dreams and assumptions disappeared or were rejected. The idea that the United States should dominate or control the Caribbean was very widespread among Northern leaders (as well as among leaders in the prewar South). Within the Republican Party, the influential Blair family worked closely with Lincoln early in the war to try to establish a kind of protectorate in Central America where African Americans could be colonized. The Blairs and members of the administration continued to pursue these ideas, and we now know that various European governments contacted the administration all through the war in hopes of gaining laborers for Caribbean colonies where slave labor had ended. The American interest in projecting national power throughout the Caribbean basin would become an enduring leitmotif of foreign policy. Closer scrutiny of the war years should be a part of that larger story.[41]

A final comment on Northern society during the war. The experience of war produced divisions and tensions in Northern society, just as it had within the Confederacy, and these divisions and tensions would be an often unmentioned part of the challenge of Reconstruction. After years of war and controversy, how would the political parties, the divided churches, the races and ethnic groups find their place in a reintegrated Union? Our focus in regard to such issues has largely been on the South. The fact that the North won has too often diverted attention from the rents sustained in its social fabric. What happened in the North as it faced problems of reintegration after the war is worthy of attention and constitutes another dimension of the divisions caused by war.

3

African Americans in the Civil War Years

African Americans were central to every aspect of the Civil War—its origins, its course, its politics, and its results. The decades since the civil rights movement have seen a great and greatly intensified investment of energy in the field of black history. Prior to that time, some scholars may have complained about the difficulty of finding abundant and eloquent sources such as were readily available for other fields. But rich sources increasingly have become available, and creative use may be made of documents that were created for other purposes. Nevertheless, much remains to be explored, and identifying sources is only one of the challenges awaiting historians.

African Americans were a very diverse population at the time of the Civil War, and their history is accordingly many sided. Free black people in the North, though surrounded by prejudice and beset by discrimination, lived in very different circumstances from those affecting the South's many slaves. In the North, their communities embraced different levels of wealth, education, and culture, and such differences were even greater when compared to the communities of the Southern black population. Free black men and women in the South constituted another group with its own special circumstances and interests. Then, once the war had begun, the situations of runaways, black Union soldiers, men and women in contraband camps, and slaves still trapped on plantations and farms all varied greatly. It is a large challenge to tell a unified history of a group so varied and affected by such different circumstances. Most recent work has not attempted to do so.

A great deal of research has instead focused on separate pieces of the larger story. One necessary step in dealing with such diversity is to pay a great deal of attention to the particular locales, situations, and conditions that affected African Americans. We know much more now than at the beginning of my career about black abolitionists, Northern organizations and leaders, Southern slaves, Union soldiers or army laborers, and those living in contraband camps or cultivating abandoned plantations. But important questions remain to be investigated for each of these groups, taken separately. Relatively little has been done to study elite or working-class black women in the North, and only now are a larger number of studies of Southern black women emerging. Equally important is the fact that much more should be done to examine the connections or contacts between these different groups, to learn more about how they interacted, and to address the questions of how and to what extent they constituted a single social entity that we label with the words *African American.*

The author of a recent, important study of illness and suffering among Southern blacks during the war, Jim Downs, has raised a question about our profession's general approach to these topics. He argues that the political correctness that is the norm for current discussion and writing is impoverishing the historical record. From sensitivity over past injustices and prejudice that marred the historical record, our conclusions tend to be romantically positive—we always emphasize, he feels, success against the odds rather than defeat and failure. He even suggests that because of similar political goals the records of the Freedmen's Bureau and the Freedmen and Southern Society Project may have been slanted at the time of their creation.[1] Whether his concerns are valid or not, it surely is necessary to tell the full story of African American history. Inevitably, that story contains abundant evidence of injustice, suffering, death, and disappointment, even in the period when a profoundly important advance—the end of slavery—occurred. Inevitably, too, it contains instances of human error or failure among blacks as well as among whites.

Beyond the importance of telling all parts of the history, both good and bad, triumphant and tragic, let me offer one additional overall comment at the outset. A priority for future studies must be to continue to identify the various ways, whether subtle or dramatic, that African Americans exercised initiative during the war years. For many years, much history emphasized what white Americans did to or about black Americans, but the recognition of the inadequacy of this approach is not a case of misguided political correctness. White Northerners, white Southerners, *and* African Americans in both sections were the major actors in the Civil War drama. African Americans as well as whites changed the dynamics of events by the decisions they made and the actions they took. Some actions by African Americans caused decisive change, and that reality must alter our approach to historical analysis. To accept its importance is not to insist that all African Americans were heroes or that they always made wise decisions, only to give them their rightful place in the narrative. Once we identify black initiatives, we then need to note their types, motives, and effects in order to write good history.

We can begin to discuss black initiative in the place where Confederates least expected to see it—among the enslaved population and even among those blacks who were under Confederate military supervision. A substantial part of the wartime experience of Southern black people took place in Confederate army camps. Because Confederate officials hoped that slaves could perform most heavy military labor, the government first requested and then requisitioned slave laborers through impressment. Tens of thousands of enslaved men had to labor under military supervision to build forts, mount canons, move supplies, and otherwise advance the proslavery cause of the Confederacy, and a smaller number of slaves accompanied the Confederate army as body servants for slaveholders.[2]

Our knowledge of these experiences remains somewhat thin. Decades have elapsed between the publication of James Brewer's book *The Confederate Negro* in 1969 and Jaime Martinez's recent study of impressment in the upper South.[3] Thanks to those investigations, we know a great deal about the system and duties of impressment, but detailed information is still restricted to Virginia and North Carolina. We actually know little about that experience, except that it occurred and except for the types of work required. The path lies open to study impressment of slaves in other parts of the South, where its circumstances, conditions, or effects might have differed.

One striking fact emerges from these studies, however. It concerns the breadth and level of skill among the slave population. It is undeniable that the Confederacy put thousands of slaves to work at simple manual labor—digging trenches and throwing up fortifications, often under miserable conditions of rain or mud or water up to a man's waist. Others did heavy labor repairing railroads or bridges or moving cannon. But thousands of others worked for Confederate bureaus in dozens of skilled jobs, as blacksmiths, carpenters, wagon makers, wheelwrights, bricklayers, caulkers, joiners, harness makers, machinists, iron puddlers, painters, teamsters, boat hands, and so on. This list of skilled categories could run on at some length. Another area in which many thousands labored with or without previous skills was nursing. Confederate leaders assumed that through such labor the slave population would prove a great advantage to the war effort, and slaveholders' initial patriotism seemed to support this belief.

This kind of detailed information is important not only for what it tells us about white Confederates' plans but also for what it indicates about the slave community. The skills of these thousands of impressed laborers imply both a higher-than-normal level of knowledge and a wider access to information and means of communication. Skilled slave artisans were often hired out before the war on a long-term or short-term basis, and their work frequently involved or required some degree of travel. Such movement gave them a greater knowledge of the society that they could use for their own benefit or pass on to others. Moreover, once they were impressed, slaves went to new cities, forts, or army camps, where they could gain additional information.

Partly for such reasons, a key result of the army's impressment of slaves was not what Confederates had expected. Proximity to Union lines was usually a by-product of service in forts and camps, and that fact gave slaves important opportunities to escape—opportunities they would not ignore. The chief engineer with one Confederate army unit lamented that out of almost 1,000 slave laborers, little more than a third were working. Why? "Most of them have run away." One slave whose presence in a Confederate army camp had involved him in some fighting against Federal troops used what he learned to slip into Union territory. Like other impressed slaves, he just wanted a chance to escape.[4]

A zeal to help the Union army went along with the desire for personal freedom. In 1861, when Allan Pinkerton, chief of the US Secret Service, surreptitiously visited Memphis, he found that impressed slave laborers were "ever ready to answer questions and to furnish me with every fact which I desired to possess." Such attitudes led many slaves to spy for the Union, and throughout the war black Southerners gave information and aid to US forces whenever possible. When Union soldiers managed to escape from Southern prisoner-of-war camps, they found that the slaves were their ready allies.[5]

It is now well known how three impressed slave laborers—Frank Baker, Shepard Mallory, and James Townsend—escaped across Chesapeake Bay in May 1861 to offer information and help to General Benjamin Butler at Fort Monroe. Their arrival was the start of a mass exodus of slaves that could not be stopped, and Butler's decision to retain them as "contraband" of war was the beginning of a Northern debate that within a year would change US policy. With any proximity to Federal troops, slaves became "insubordinate" and would run away to the Yankees. Thousands started arriving everywhere there was a fair chance to reach safety, despite the fact that for several months many Union lines did not represent safety because commanders frequently turned runaways back to their owners. At that point, the war was not a war against slavery. But the slaves kept coming and in effect demanded to be heard. This was an example of the way slaves, who were not supposed to have a political voice, compelled attention from the government and essentially forced a broadening of the political community. The tidal wave of "contrabands" forced the North to address slavery directly and discard the belief that the conflict was "a white man's war." By risking danger to seek freedom, these escaped slaves changed the law and the agenda of the Lincoln government. Congress passed legislation forbidding the return of runaways, and Lincoln began to move toward emancipation.

It is regrettable that there has been an unnecessary debate about who deserves the credit for bringing about emancipation, Lincoln or the slaves. There is no question about the overall facts. In the first fifteen months of the war, the action of tens of thousands of slaves forced the North to deal with runaways and consider the benefits they could bring to the war effort. President Lincoln's policy originally supported slavery anywhere that it already existed, and for some time army officers were under orders to return runaway slaves to their owners. It is likewise true, however, that Lincoln responded to events as they happened and that other Republicans urged emancipation with greater enthusiasm. Without the response and the actions taken by lawmakers, the president, and the army, the legal end of slavery would not have occurred. But the actions of thousands of slaves precipitated that response. Both elements were necessary to achieve the result, and both should be noted. To insist that only Lincoln deserves credit is to deny the slaves' vital contribution to achieving their own freedom.

Just as slaves' initiative shaped these developments in the North, their actions had an equally far-reaching impact in the South, with ramifications that damaged the Confederacy in multiple ways. Confederates found that their measures of control over slaves were weakening everywhere, whether on the plantation or in the army. Slaveholders whose "property" disappeared into Union lines soon lost their initial enthusiasm for helping the government. Instead of volunteering their slaves to the military as laborers, slaveholders held back, forcing the government to resort to the compulsion of law. Then they resisted the measures of legal impressment. Their reaction to the slaves' initiative caused one Confederate official to denounce "the folly and wickedness of our own people," whose behavior showed that slaveholders, in Stephanie McCurry's words, "were more concerned with property than nation."[6]

Planters whose slaves had not yet escaped also faced a loss of control. Slaves took advantage of the absence of owners or overseers to extract better conditions from the whites left behind. Others who were reasonably close to Union lines exploited the substantial leverage that the possibility of escape gave them. By using the threat of flight, they could extort better conditions of daily life. By 1864, for example, slaves in Tennessee were demanding better conditions and pay for their labor, and owners had to agree in order to keep their slaves at all. Many worried planters decided to relocate their slaves to areas that would be more secure from Federal operations, but others found that they could not do it. "The slaves resist it," explained one Mississippi slaveholder—"every negro on this place will go to the Yankees before they would [submit to relocation]."[7]

Thousands continued to "abscond," and once slaves made their way to freedom, in the process setting an encouraging example, they did more—they returned to help others escape. Acting as "missionaries," men who had made it to the Federal lines in Mississippi in 1863 went back into Confederate territory to free their wives, children, and others. The same thing was occurring in Virginia and elsewhere as black troops found opportunities to go "recruiting." Federal officers asked, "Are you not afraid to risk it?" "No" was a typical answer—"I know the way." These brave runaways also knew, as a white officer put it, that "colored men will help colored men and they will work along the by paths and get through." These actions continued despite stern reprisals by Southern officers, who convened "drum head court martials" and lynched on the spot any men they managed to capture. Every slave "recruited" made the institution more unstable.[8]

General Patrick Cleburne was one Confederate commander who deplored the effect that the slaves' flight had on white Confederates' attitudes. He complained that slaveholders' support for the war effort evaporated whenever their human "property" was threatened or gained the chance to flee. Charles Roland has concluded that "even the temporary appearance of northern troops in any part of the South so disrupted the labor force and the economy that they could never be returned to normal." Slaves' flight, adds Yael Sternhell, "gnawed away at the social order of the Confederacy until it finally came tumbling down."[9] Thus, scholars have noted the influence of slaves' actions, but only in general terms. Can we do more to assess, measure, and quantify their impact and effects—on Confederate attitudes, voting, and military strength? How and when did planters pressure Congress? Was there a direct relationship between the approach of Federal armies and the reactions of whites? Can the slaveholders' complaints and their timing be correlated, for example, with voting in the legislature or the sending of Confederate units into the interior? We need to make more tangible the connections between the observed phenomena and their importance.

Slaves in the Union's border states played an especially transformative role because slavery remained legally sanctioned there and was not supposed to be challenged. Nevertheless, thousands of slaves who struck for freedom virtually determined the character of the war in such states—for instance, Kentucky. A majority of whites in these states were pro-Union, although they also backed slavery and abhorred abolition. When pro-Confederates opposed them, the ensuing violence disrupted normal mechanisms of order. Slaves then exploited the confusion and a weakened patrol system to liberate themselves. To gain freedom and aid the coming of emancipation for all, slaves ran to recruiting centers, even in other states, so that they could join the Union army. Despite resorting to violence in response, Kentucky's slaveholders, whether pro-Union or pro-Confederate, could not control the slaves' restiveness and desire for freedom. Pro-Confederate whites engaged in guerrilla warfare against blacks, and pro-Union slaveholders, enraged by the loss of their slaves, became sharply critical of Lincoln's government. The initiative of Kentucky's slaves helped turn the war there into an "abolition war."

So many Kentucky slaves wanted to join the US Army that the War Department eventually established eight recruiting centers there, despite the anger of supposedly loyal slaveholders. Almost 60 percent of Kentucky's male slaves of military age joined the army, the highest percentage in any border state. In three other border states where slavery remained legal—Delaware, Maryland, and Missouri—large numbers of slaves also seized their freedom and undermined the institution. With slavery falling apart and many pro-slavery men off in the war, the latter two states passed emancipation ordinances before the fighting came to an end. Resentful racist whites in Kentucky and Delaware eventually forced their states to hold out longest against ratification of the Thirteenth Amendment.[10]

We need to understand much more about how the slaves were able to translate their desire for freedom into such effective actions. How much coordination of their efforts took place? What were the sources of their knowledge, and what lay behind their impressive initiatives?

As Steven Hahn has argued, there was a communal foundation for the actions that slaves took once the war began. That foundation encompassed shared values, spiritual inspiration, means of communication among the slaves, access to sources of information about national politics, discussions and debates that were unknown to the whites, and "meetings, discussions, and organizing" that preceded the war. Once the war was under way, slaves promptly reacted in an intelligent manner. Even in the border regions where slaves often lived on scattered, "isolated" farms, "these widely dispersed slaves knew exactly what to do and what the war meant." The process of politicization and information gathering then continued. "Communications between contrabands and home plantations" provided new sources of up-to-date information about local conditions and the evolution of national policy. We remain unsure about how the slaves managed to be so well informed, but whites at the time had no doubt of the slave grapevine's effectiveness. A Northern observer heard a captured rebel soldier admit "that one of his negroes had told him of the [Emancipation] [P]roclamation five days before he heard it in any other way." Others, this Northerner reported, "agreed that their negroes provided the first news of the proclamation."[11]

Some insight into the so-called slave grapevine can be gleaned from comments made by whites, and scattered hints about it can be found in the Federal Writers' Project Slave Narratives. But Elizabeth Regosin and Donald Shaffer have pointed us toward another possible source. African American army veterans filed approximately 100,000 claims for a federal pension. The records of their claims contain much testimony they gave in response to examiners' questions. Although information about the communities in which slaves lived and communicated surfaces indirectly, a detailed picture can sometimes be ferreted out of these US Pension Bureau files as applicants and their neighbors described the interpersonal ties that existed in slavery. Interviews revealed how long people had known each other, how "intimate" their relationship had been, how close to each other they had lived, and what activities they shared. It would be valuable to learn more about the ways slaves consulted with each other and shared information between different plantations, sometimes over distances of several miles.[12]

Even more fundamentally, historians face a major challenge in trying to understand better the slaves' mentality or political and social perspective. Slaves paid attention to politics among the whites because it would affect them; they developed their own analysis of events; and they had their own political ideas. We know that they had a thorough understanding of the norms and processes of representative government because even before the Civil War ended, slaves and free blacks in the South began writing petitions to federal or military authorities. They were, in fact, the first to call for a new legal system with different definitions of rights. These documents show that they had a clear understanding of what their rights should be and how those rights were denied or impeded by white people's laws. They knew how democratic discussion and debate were supposed to take place and how citizens could call on legislatures to make changes. Some conclusions can be inferred from what African Americans wrote or said. But learning more about their political ideas should be a high priority for Civil War scholars, and some efforts in this important area are fortunately already under way.[13]

Our lack of sure knowledge of the slaves' political ideas and their view of themselves, their status, and their future is at the root of one of the most debated issues in Civil War studies: How should we understand and interpret the slaves' initiatives for freedom? How did they see their future? What did their actions signify for Southern society, for the nation, and for themselves?

Well into the twentieth century, the prejudiced view of African Americans determined the interpretation of their actions during the Civil War. According to this canard, the slaves did nothing to gain their freedom; they were merely the docile, passive recipients of an undeserved gift from whites. Supposedly loyal to their owners or inert, they did nothing to dismantle the institution that bound them. W. E. B. Du Bois was, of course, the most prominent dissenter of this view with his insistence that the slave population engaged in a "general strike" that had enormous importance. More recently, Steven Hahn has asked, "Did we miss the greatest slave rebellion in modern history?" Blaming this omission on the habits of thought that dominate the profession, he argues for the affirmative by comparing the events of the Civil War to Caribbean slave revolts. "In its course and outcome," he concludes, "the slaves' rebellion . . . may well be . . . most similar" to the revolution that shattered the colony of Saint-Domingue in the 1790s. Other scholars have put forward a number of other descriptive phrases, such as "rebellion," "revolt," "the enemy within," or "an array of insurrectionary activities calculated to destroy the institution of slavery."

The Confederate army's General Cleburne viewed the slaves' actions with deep alarm and described them as "insurrection in the rear."[14]

The sharpest and most well-developed difference of interpretation on this point is that between Hahn and William W. Freehling. In *The South vs. the South,* Freehling paints a picture of a determined but shrewd, careful, and politically well-informed slave population. Rather than being rebels animated by the spirit of revolt, Freehling's slaves were always aware of the power of racism among Northern whites. Instead of moving too precipitously or too boldly, they struck for freedom with a nearly sophisticated awareness of how best to influence Northern opinion and gain Northern support. At numerous points, an overreach could have backfired against them because Federal officials and army generals were resolved to crush any sign of a bloody uprising and because the Northern public was only slowly reconciling itself to freedom. But the slaves avoided such possible setbacks. They handled the developing situation and advanced their interests, Freehling almost suggests, with the kind of sensitivity to and insight about Northern feelings that marked the first phase of the civil rights movement.[15]

The gap between Hahn's "massive slave rebellion" and Freehling's shrewd planning is great. It would be difficult to close it without addressing the slaves' worldview, for that gap calls to mind and stems from other interpretations focused on the mentality of the slaves and the nature of their community. Hahn's work speaks of "a nation under our feet" in a way that reminds us of Eugene Genovese's concept of a protonationalism that characterized the slave community.[16] Were the slaves merely suspicious of whites, or did they reject the society that oppressed them? Did they seek their rights in the American system, or did they want to escape from that system and create a society of their own? Were they seeking inclusion and justice, or did they ultimately want separation and black nationhood? Were they a class, a race, or a nation?

Historians can find evidence to bolster either interpretive direction. To cite just a few examples, many runaway slaves enthusiastically volunteered their services to the Union, and in contraband camps they seized the opportunity to be considered citizens, despite the partial and limited nature of what citizenship for them meant in that context. As the war came to an end, they petitioned for the ballot, an end to discriminatory laws, and recognition of their rights. Blacks' political participation in Reconstruction was strong, persistent, and widespread. But it also is true that a group of leaders in Savannah, Georgia, with virtual unanimity, told Secretary of War Edwin

M. Stanton that they would prefer to live off by themselves. In the North, a significant portion of Northern black leaders in the 1850s had favored emigration to establish a black nation elsewhere. Even Frederick Douglass, usually the exemplar of black protest within traditional American ideals, for a while endorsed such separation. In both the nineteenth and twentieth centuries, some black nationalists in both the North and the South favored emigration. The Exodusters hoped to establish all-black communities west of the Mississippi River after the failure of Reconstruction, and a little later thousands of farm laborers pinned their hopes on what turned out to be failed or fraudulent efforts to leave the country by ship. Marcus Garvey subsequently made such possibility a reality with his Black Star Line, and Malcolm X made it crystal clear that the Black Muslims wanted no part of a rancid and doomed white society.

How should historians interpret these nationalist efforts? Were they evidence of a commonly held, dominant, and nationalist outlook that usually was not expressed, or were they instead an understandable, frustrated reaction when hopes of inclusion once again ran up against the solid wall of racial prejudice? Did they represent one among several differing political outlooks found within the black population? I will not try here to offer a solution or develop a complete argument to respond to the challenge, but I do want to suggest the importance of the interplay of two analytical factors: black people's aspirations and their fundamental understanding of white racism.

The injustices of slavery naturally produced in African Americans a fervent desire for opportunity, fair treatment, and equal rights. African Americans thus were attuned to any chance to better themselves and their loved ones, regardless of what the overall ideological implications of an opportunity might be. As Chandra Manning has put it, for example, contrabands seized the degree of citizenship that army officers offered them "not because such rights comprised the sum total of all they hoped freedom would achieve, but because they recognized such rights as vehicles for achieving their aspiration for themselves, their families, and their communities." The remarkable enthusiasm of slaves and freed people for education is another example of this desire. Their hunger for education was overwhelming. One Northern missionary marveled at the eagerness of the freed people: "Go out in any direction and you meet negroes on horses, negroes on mules, negroes on foot, men, women and children . . . all hopeful, almost all cheerful, every one pleading to be taught, willing to do anything for learning." During Reconstruction, roughly half of all the schools for freed people were supported by tuition payments from the impoverished black population. Why? Because education mattered greatly for the future of the race. The eloquent demands or carefully phrased appeals for equal rights and the ballot similarly had an obvious importance to black people's future. After generations of repression, black people were going to pursue any possibility for advancement that came their way.[17]

At the same time, African Americans, whether enslaved or free, had an awareness of themselves as a despised race that was so deep and fundamental that it may be impossible for whites to understand it completely. Everything in their life experience had taught them that white racism was ubiquitous and enduring. Joined to the injustice and suffering of enslavement was a merciless racism that denied the slaves' humanity and envenomed every interaction with whites. This racism infected the entire society, while on the plantation the enforced intimacies that arose from living and working with whites rarely caused slaves to respect their owners. They instead sharpened the sense of racial identity as blacks learned that they should expect hostility and unjust treatment at every turn. The situation was the same in the North, where Charles Lenox Remond concluded from his experiences in the abolitionist movement that "it is impossible, for any of our white friends, however much they may have tried, fully to understand the black man's case in this nation." Such experience put African Americans in a separate reality from whites. The two races lived in two different worlds, and blacks knew that they could never wholly trust the white world even though they desired to gain as many advantages from it as possible.[18]

These facts could contribute to a view of the world that equipped African Americans to move in multiple directions. Without being bound to one exclusive ideology, perhaps they entertained a range of alternatives. Perhaps their experience equipped them to adopt a variety of strategies as different circumstances presented themselves. Are our interpretive categories too narrow and restrictive? Do we need to move beyond the either/or choices of black nationalism or American inclusion, protonationalism or protest, separatism or civil rights? If African Americans fundamentally doubted the capacity of whites for fair play yet were determined to gain for themselves all the benefits that American society might offer, their worldview might have been more flexible or adaptable than our conceptual categories. Nor should we forget that African Americans—as historical actors who could not have perfect knowledge of the overall political environment or its future—would have tried different strategies and changed their viewpoints. At the level of theory or conceptualization, the challenge to create a better and thoroughly developed theory of the fundamental outlook of slaves and free black people in white American society awaits historians.

Turning to the North's black leadership, we see that the question of emigration was an important source of division, and debates over it certainly relate to questions of separate nationalism or integration. On the eve of the Civil War, the idea of abandoning the United States had substantial appeal. Martin Delany devoted a book-length effort to make the case for emigration, and others such as Henry Highland Garnet and Henry McNeil Turner supported the idea. In addition, the appeal of emigration and the logic behind it were not limited to the leadership class but extended into at least part of the general black population in the North. A few days before the war began, a correspondent for the *Weekly Anglo-African* argued, "We must have a strong nationality somewhere—respected, feared," a black nation that could be "a power" and give "hope of progress" to black people everywhere. More striking is the fact that in the spring of 1862, "just days after slavery was abolished in the District of Columbia, at least sixty free blacks petitioned Congress" for a homeland in Central America where they could "'secure, by their own industry[,] . . . an honorable position'" in the world."[19]

Too little is known about the characteristics of those who favored emigration (whether leaders or ordinary black Northerners) compared to those who opposed it. Among leading men who had made a name for themselves, there were some on either side of the issue, and although we have studies of a few individuals, there seems to be no analysis of this issue for the larger leadership group. How strongly might economic interests have affected viewpoints among the elite? Did wealth imply a deeper commitment to trying to change things in the United States? What role did occupation, region, or past travel play? Even less is known about the reasons why ordinary black Northerners favored or rejected emigration. Although documentation might prove hard to find, there are important questions to investigate in regard to emigration.

Those who opposed emigration or colonization had emotional reactions that are easy to understand. Many felt like Robert Purvis, who denounced Lincoln's pro-colonization advice of August 1862 by saying, "We were born here and here we choose to remain. . . . [T]his is our country as much as yours." Beyond that, the fact that the nation was now at war, with slavery potentially in the balance, made a tremendous difference to the leadership class. Most agreed with Frederick Douglass that it would prove impossible "to separate the freedom of the slave from the victory of the Government." Once the Emancipation Proclamation was issued, almost all doubts were erased, with Henry Highland Garnet, for example, convinced that "we must fight! fight! fight!" Martin Delany set to work recruiting black soldiers and joined the army. Robert Hamilton, the editor of the *Weekly Anglo-African,* sagely pointed out that "a century may elapse before another opportunity shall be afforded for reclaiming and holding our withheld rights." As a result, the vocal leadership of the North led determined efforts against colonization, rejecting and denouncing it at every turn. Nor did the idea, once the war had become a war for freedom, generate much interest among the common people.[20]

One wonders how much influence ministers and abolitionist leaders had in encouraging the rejection of emigration. They spoke out strongly, and they had the best platforms from which to spread their message of rejection. On this point, the North's black leadership was determined and adamant. Even after former emigrationists had changed their tune, concerns surfaced at the National Convention of Colored Men held in Syracuse in October 1864, where the stance toward the American Civilization Society became an issue. Although that organization was focusing its wartime efforts on helping the freed people and promoting emancipation, it had favored emigration in the past. Therefore, many delegates wanted to distance themselves from it as much as possible and wished not to mention the society in a passage praising the work of various organizations. The tensions over the American Civilization Society were as significant as any other axes of division, such as class or generational differences or the clash of personal ambitions.[21]

The commitment of most Northern leaders to inclusion and to the United States, despite its history of enslavement and discrimination, merits further exploration. One of the basic elements underlying this commitment seems to have been pride in the role that an earlier generation of African Americans had played in winning independence from England. Pride in that revolutionary heritage mirrored the kind of historical awareness found among many whites. Moreover, there was a devotion to the ideals of the nation, ideals of liberty and equal rights, that had not been realized yet were inspiring. Such nationalism was in large part a nationalism based on the idea of America. For some—and one wonders for how many leaders and in which communities—the commitment to true American ideals went even deeper. Boston's John Rock believed that an important reason for staying in the country was to work at "civilizing the whites." He was committed to remaining in the United States and "try[ing] to make it worth living in." Stephen Kantrowitz has found among Boston's black abolitionists a desire to achieve not just equal rights but a true democratic community based on acceptance, inclusion, and mutual respect. There is some evidence that in other localities biracial cooperation and understanding pointed the way toward real community. Black leaders with such goals could claim to be virtually the only true Americans—the people most dedicated to the ideal of equality expressed in the Declaration of Independence.[22]

As politicians, Northern black leaders—though they were excluded from office and in some states the vote—showed an impressive ability to strategize. The arguments they made on political questions kept them ahead of events, where they could continue to put pressure on the government and take advantage of events. Almost as soon as the war began, black leaders began to insist that the war must be a war against slavery. The nation was in crisis, they argued, and it needed the assistance of the slaves. "Any attempt now to separate the freedom of the slave from the victory of the Government," said Frederick Douglass, "will be labor lost." Even before emancipation became a war aim, they raised a chorus of demands that black men be allowed to fight. Then, as the government began to accept black soldiers, abolitionists and other black leaders insisted repeatedly that military service entailed citizenship and the right to vote. As J. W. C. Pennington put it in 1863, "We are now fighting . . . with the distinct understanding, that WE ARE TO HAVE ALL OUR RIGHTS AS MEN AND AS CITIZENS, and, that there are to be no side issues, no RESERVATIONS, either political, civil, or religious." The way these leaders sustained a unified, coherent message invites us to look further at their mechanisms of coordination.[23]

On racially charged social questions that threatened to derail political progress, the Northern black leaders likewise were united in putting forward a logical and potentially disarming message. "I do not ask you to invite me into your parlors," declared H. Ford Douglas even before the war began. "I ask not to be recognized, socially, by any man in the world. We are not demanding social equality. All we ask is the same rights, legally, as yourselves." The address of the Syracuse convention of 1864 similarly declared, "Whatever prejudice and taste may be innocently allowed to do or to dictate in social and domestic relations, it is plain, that in the matter of government . . . prejudice should be allowed no voice whatever." And to further bolster their claim to equal rights, men such as Frederick Douglass argued that if there were to be any "condition of voting, you shall apply it equally to the black man." Yet these arguments raise a question about how much African Americans wanted "social equality" or invitations to white parlors. Was the argument a sound tactic or an expression of separate identity? What did the behavior of black leaders in their personal lives indicate about the relationships they wanted to have with whites?[24]

Pride in one's race and rejection of unequal treatment were strong in the North's black population. The prompt reactions against discrimination that surfaced at the very beginning of the war help to explain the insistence on equal rights that characterized leaders' rhetoric. In many places in the North, free black men offered their services to the military, only to be turned away and told that the war was a "*white man's fight, with which niggers had nothing to do.*" Would-be volunteers angrily denounced the government. Editors published letters that pointedly asked why any African American should "invite injustice at the hands of those we prefer to serve" or risk his life to support a government that had not rejected "the perpetuity of human bondage" and favored "the African colonization scheme." Even the newspaper of the African Methodist Episcopal Church sharply declared that to enlist would be "to abandon self-respect and invite insult."[25]

Equally impressive was the criticism that black leaders launched against the Lincoln administration's failures and hesitations. In the first two years of the war, they kept up a stream of sharp and accurate criticism. They pilloried Lincoln when he reversed the emancipation proclamations of General John C. Frémont and General David Hunter, chastised him for failing to move against slavery, and angrily accused him of encouraging racist attitudes when he urged colonization on a group of black ministers. What historians call the gradualism of Lincoln's administration excited their ire. Once Lincoln signed the Emancipation Proclamation, they enjoyed a brief respite for celebration.

But even after emancipation became the administration's policy, a keen awareness of deficiencies remained. The *Christian Recorder* noted that slavery continued to be legal in several states or areas, and an assembly of blacks in Harrisburg, Pennsylvania, observed that welcome though the Emancipation Proclamation was, it was "simply a war measure." Because Lincoln had said nothing about equality, black leaders demanded more. The short-lived candidacy of John C. Frémont in 1864 caused a split in their ranks.

His nominating convention came out in favor of not only a constitutional amendment to end slavery but also complete equality before the law, so Frederick Douglass and others rallied to his support, but men such as J. W. C. Pennington and John Rock defended Lincoln for the progress that had come under his leadership. When Frémont withdrew from the race, the leadership elite quickly closed ranks, pragmatically giving all its support to Lincoln, the remaining candidate most favorable to their cause.[26]

The Syracuse convention gave close and alarmed attention to a Lincoln administration maneuver that historians have insufficiently noted. The reactions of black leaders and radical Republicans and any contacts between them need closer attention. That summer, as Lincoln and Republican leaders worked for his reelection in the fall, war weariness overtook the Northern public. General Ulysses S. Grant's campaign against Robert E. Lee in Virginia had produced no breakthrough, only an appalling and ever-growing list of dead and wounded. General William T. Sherman's army was somewhere in Georgia, but again no definite news had arrived to lift the public's spirits. Then Horace Greeley of the *New York Tribune* pressured Lincoln to talk with Confederate commissioners who were in Canada, just across from Niagara Falls, and were proclaiming their interest in peace. In response, Lincoln issued a "To Whom It May Concern" letter that he made public on July 18, 1864.[27]

In this letter, the president declared that he would be willing to discuss peace with "any person anywhere" who had a proposal from Jefferson Davis "embracing the restoration of the Union and the abandonment of slavery." This letter ignited a firestorm of hostile reaction precisely because it included abolition as a condition of peace. Democrats pointed out that Lincoln and his party had always justified emancipation as a tool to win the war, not as a sine qua non. "Why has he now taken this extreme ground?" asked the *New York Herald*. Democrat editors charged that Lincoln's letter revealed that abolition was the Republicans' "main object" and that "tens of thousands of white men must yet bite the dust to allay the negro mania of the President." The white electorate of the North recoiled in large numbers. On all sides, Republican leaders and editors saw defeat ahead, deplored Lincoln's "blunder," and reported to the president that "the tide is setting strongly against us."

To deal with this crisis, Republicans tried to backtrack. Lincoln himself drafted a letter in which he argued that just because he had said he would discuss peace *with* the abolition of slavery, that statement did not mean that he would refuse to discuss *something less.* Although he decided not to send that letter, his supporters made the argument for him. The *New York Times,* for example, declared that Lincoln had "*never 'refused* to receive or consider any proposition looking to peace or Union unless accompanied with the abandonment of slavery.' . . . Mr. Lincoln did say that he *would* receive and consider propositions for peace, coming with proper authority, *if* they embraced the integrity of the Union *and* the abandonment of slavery. But he did not say that he would *not* receive them even if they embraced neither."

Even more disturbing were the words used in a public address by Secretary of State William Seward. After admitting that the "chief complaint" against Lincoln was "the abandonment of slavery," Seward first argued that the events of war were destroying slavery anyway. But then he declared that as soon as the rebels laid down their arms, "the war will instantly cease; . . . and all the moral, economical, and political questions, as well questions affecting slavery as others, which shall then be existing, . . . will, by force of the Constitution, pass over to the arbitrament of courts of law and to the councils of legislation." What exactly did that mean? Would the South be able to claim its rights under the Constitution? Would it have a role in the "councils of legislation" that would settle the issue of slavery? Lincoln echoed Seward's disturbing and vague formula in his end-of-the-year address to Congress.

General Sherman's capture of Atlanta resolved Lincoln's fears over the election and brought victory to the Republican Party, but for African Americans deep and legitimate disquiet remained. It would be good to know if there was any cooperation between Northern blacks and white abolitionists in or out of Congress to bring pressure against the positions taken by Lincoln and Seward. At the Syracuse convention, black leaders publically sounded the alarm over these developments, saying that it was "very evident that the Republican party . . . is not prepared to make the abolition of slavery, in all the Rebel States, a consideration precedent to the re-establishment of the Union." With all the force they could muster, they condemned this possibility and the administration's action. The Republican Party was still "under the influence of the prevailing contempt for the character and rights of the colored race." The American Anti-Slavery Society also earned condemnation as a weak friend for its denial that it supported voting rights for African Americans.[28]

The black-convention movement, which had been under way for much of the early nineteenth century, was a very important expression and tool of black leadership. Questions connected with its leaders, declarations, and supporters deserve more attention. We know, for example, that in 1864 the convention delegates and many of the 2,000 spectators traveled to Syracuse through various cities that gave them a hostile reception on route. We also know that many delegates benefited from the generosity of local residents who opened their homes to them on the way to or in Syracuse. These facts raise the question of how the convention and its delegates were financed and whether, besides the efforts made in black churches, other organizations or individuals contributed. The matter of financing becomes even more important in 1865 when the National Equal Rights League, outlined at Syracuse, began its operations. The fight for equal rights would be both local, in various communities, and national through the league. Knowing more about its organizational structure and financing is important.

The national meetings of black leaders in 1864 and 1865 suggest topics relating to the issue of black ideology. The Syracuse meeting urged "frugality" among the freedmen, along with property ownership, education, and "vigorous moral and religious growth." In drawing up the constitution of the National Equal Rights League that met in 1865, these same delegates identified its purpose as to encourage "morality, education, temperance, frugality, industry" and a "well-ordered and dignified life." Education, religion, and morality seemed to be hallmarks of the leaders' thoughts, along with other solid Victorian values. Among some of the leading families, an elevated moral and intellectual culture was of great importance. How different, then, was the culture of black leaders from that of religious members of the white elite? Were these values simply shared with whites, or were they a prescription for economic progress and the acquisition of respectability? One resolution from the convention in 1865 had a more separatist tone, when the delegates pledged to support Southern schools but emphasized that it was critical that black men and women staff them. Accordingly, they urged well-educated Northern blacks to go south as teachers. It also was notable at this convention that James H. Harris of North Carolina spoke out in agreement with the assertions by John Mercer Langston that "white men are white men the world over." Accordingly, "the elevation of the Negro depends upon his own right arm."[29]

Despite the establishment of the National Equal Rights League, it seems that most of the fight against discrimination during and immediately after the war took place in local areas through local organizations. We know too little about these important efforts. Some states, such as Pennsylvania and New York, evidently had a more robust level of organization, probably due in part to the larger black population in those states. For example, in 1860 New York blacks formed sixty-six local suffrage committees and distributed thousands of tracts and sample ballots. Though they failed in that year to gain the right to vote, they increased the number of pro-suffrage votes.[30]

Blacks throughout the North used protests, petition campaigns, lobbying of legislators, and legal challenges to fight racially discriminatory "black laws," mistreatment on streetcars, denial of voting rights, and segregated schools or other discrimination in education. Notable campaigns took place in New York, Cincinnati, Philadelphia, Chicago, and other major cities. But efforts also occurred in Connecticut, Kansas, Minnesota, and others. Successful black businessmen, as opposed to ministers or traditional abolitionist spokesmen, led some of these efforts.[31] From examination of these organizing efforts, we could learn more about the black community, about what factors aided success, and about where and why different types of leaders had the most influence. We can also study hostile white reactions, and from comparison of blacks' successful and unsuccessful efforts we might learn more about the character of white resistance and the effectiveness of black strategies. The research might prove difficult, but the findings valuable.

We know very little about the situation of Northern blacks who lived in rural areas amid overwhelmingly white populations. Their situation may have been far more tenuous than those who lived in cities and enjoyed stronger institutional support. They may have been subject to greater restrictions, or they may have gained a measure of acceptance over time in certain areas. The fact that blacks of long-term residence in the upper Midwest were sometimes hostile to newly arrived freed people from the South suggests that their experience may have had parallels to that of some long-established European immigrants: having gained some acceptance, they feared that new arrivals would alter the situation for them.[32]

Research has shown the importance of gender as a variable, for black female educators and writers and black women in eastern cities or the Midwest were often outspoken. Although black men dominated the abolitionist effort, Edmonia Highgate and Frances Ellen Watkins were delegates to the Syracuse convention in 1864. Watkins's wartime poems and writings urged black women to be active before the suspension of publications such as *The Liberator* limited her outlets after the war. In urban areas, African American women who depended on street railway systems to get to work or attend church played a major role in protests against discrimination on the streetcars. Protests and legal challenges brought success in New York, San Francisco, Cincinnati, and Boston. After 1864, "Philadelphia was the only major northern city . . . that had not desegregated some or all of its railroad lines." In the Midwest, black women who had arrived from the South may have observed local conventions that would help establish their respectable, civilized character, but within the black community they asserted themselves and did not allow men to have a patriarchal authority over all areas.[33]

Black women who gained their freedom in the South also spoke up and were not satisfied with a docile, subservient gender role. Once arrived in contraband camps, they immediately found ways to be useful and earn some money or support. They urged and often pressured their men to join the army and help the Union cause. Those who suffered sexual assault by US soldiers protested so strongly that military courts began to take their testimony and respect their rights. The Republican Party also was influenced by their stands and began to pay more attention to the status of slave women. Nevertheless, the white society's patriarchal assumptions were starkly evident as the army and the government thought of black women only as wives, not as citizens.[34]

One of the most important contributions of former slave women in the South was economic and therefore, in the context of the time, social and political as well. The army had not planned to feed and care for tens of thousands of contrabands, and from an early date it began to put them to work. In the Sea Islands, Virginia, occupied areas of the Atlantic coast, the Mississippi Valley, and elsewhere, contrabands worked the land in what were the first large-scale experiments in free labor by the former slaves. Much of this labor was done by women, for the healthy men had usually gone into the army. The fact that these women, working under difficult and sometimes dangerous conditions, were able to produce large quantities of foodstuffs and cotton was a triumph that tended to vindicate the Republican Party and to bolster African Americans' claims to rights and equality.

The experience of many thousands of contrabands in occupied areas of the South was tragic, however, and often fatal. As Jim Downs and others have shown, the Union was unprepared to receive the contrabands, gave their treatment low priority, and sometimes abused and mistreated them. Without sufficient clothing, adequate shelter, sanitation, and medical care, many contraband camps became death traps. The flight of Southern slaves into Union lines was "one of modern history's most significant episodes of human migration," and the army was neither ready for it nor at times properly concerned. "Caring for emancipated slaves was not a primary goal or concern of the military," and poor conditions and "explosive epidemic outbreaks" caused thousands of deaths. Racist mistreatment and neglect helped to make "life behind Union lines . . . toxic." It is an interesting fact that Democratic newspapers in the North often publicized these tragedies as an argument against the Republican administration and its policies. Black leaders and white abolitionists were occasionally able to gain the public's sympathy over such events, but only occasionally, and we should ask in what circumstances they managed to be successful.[35]

The treatment of black US troops was equally neglectful, unjust, and depressing, but it has been studied much more extensively. The record of black troops was a solid one. They died at a higher rate than white soldiers, partly from disease but partly, too, from their valor in battle. When given a chance to fight, even minimally trained troops fought fiercely, notes Joseph Glatthaar, and they acquitted themselves well in the Mississippi Valley. Their bravery won some attention in the North, and the battle for equal pay eventually established a precedent that would benefit black veterans.[36]

But every report of gallantry and sacrifice on the battlefield seemed to provoke a backlash from prejudiced whites, and it is particularly sad that the Lincoln administration failed to take any sustained action in response to Confederate mistreatment of black troops. After the Fort Pillow massacre in April 1864, in which Confederate troops killed most of the black Union soldiers garrisoned at the fort instead of taking them prisoner, President Lincoln threatened retaliation against captured Confederates if the Southern government failed to recognized black US soldiers as legitimate prisoners of war. But he did not follow through. Thus, soldiers fighting to maintain the existence of their government found that their government did little or nothing to protect them in case of capture. Acts of murderous violence against captured African American soldiers continued to occur. There is an opportunity here, in this lamentable historical episode, to probe the Northern government's failure and learn more about the nature and operation of white racism.[37]

Prejudiced treatment by Southerners *and* by the black soldiers' own army plagued these soldiers in many ways. Poor medical care, inferior weapons, lack of training, unequal pay, and frequent failure to provide the pay on which men's families depended were common problems. In addition, black troops were often mistrusted and given secondary assignments or heavy fatigue duty. "We are not Soldiers but Labourers," complained one man, and another protested "the hell" caused by "nearly eighteen months of service—of labor—of humiliation—of danger, and not one dollar." Insufficient attention has been given to the impact of black labor in the US military. William Thomas has pointed out that "by the end of the war the U.S. Military Railroads was running the longest, and possibly the largest, most comprehensive experiment in black free labor employment in the occupied South."[38]

The suffering of so many freed slaves in the South and in the army galvanized the Northern black community. We know well how black leaders fought for better treatment of black soldiers. It also was the case that from the start of the war that Northern black leaders showed their awareness of the needs and priorities of members of their race in the South. Before the end of 1861, the *Weekly Anglo-African* argued that the slaves would need land once they were freed. Arguing that slaves had "bought and paid for" land in the South "by their sweat and blood," the newspaper asked, "What course will be so just, so humane, so thoroughly conducive to the public weal and the national advancement, as that the government should immediately bestow these lands upon these freed people who know best how to cultivate them?" By 1862, prominent ministers were sounding a moral appeal for aid to the contrabands. Henry McNeal Turner, citing the contrabands' "condition of extremest suffering," described them as members of "the race that we are inseparably identified with" and urged free blacks "to extend a hand of mercy to *bone of our bone and flesh of our flesh.*" Robert Hamilton, editor of the *Weekly Anglo-African,* expanded on that argument, declaring that "it is for this trial that God had given us the partial freedom, and such education, and the irrepressible desire for equality which consumes our souls." The challenge of "transforming three millions of slaves into citizens requires the aid of intelligent colored men and women."[39]

The black community of the North mobilized to help the freed people, both through material aid and the work of individuals who went South to teach, preach, or serve. Although we know that many shipments of clothing and other aid came from Northern blacks, mainly through their churches, there has been little study of this effort. We need to learn more about how the relief effort was organized, how it interacted with white charities or the government, and how it affected the Northern black community. We also know that black ministers from the North went south to spread the gospel and to extend their denominations' influence and that some of these men later became active in politics, yet the detailed story of how these things occurred remains to be told. Similarly, there have been studies of the missionary efforts of teachers, and in their experience lies another subject to consider.[40]

It was natural, indeed inevitable, that the cultural gap between freed slaves and the educated, moralistic, and upwardly striving leadership of the Northern black community would become apparent. Charlotte Forten Grimké's journals exhibit the issue. As a highly educated, highly respectable woman from an elite family, she could not help but find the contrabands whom she went to teach at Hilton Head, South Carolina, "the most dismal specimens I ever saw." Their enthusiastic worship was a surprise to her, and some of their headdresses were "ridiculous." To her credit, she developed some empathy for "the poor creatures" plus an appreciation of aspects of their culture, and she undoubtedly helped them. But the social and cultural distance between her and them was undeniable.[41]

This illustrates an important issue that I believe has received almost no attention. What kind of relationship did Northern blacks develop with the freedmen? How did the educated and culturally ambitious leaders of the North treat the freed people in practice and over time? There is no question about their good intentions or about the zeal that former slaves demonstrated for education and self-improvement. Even in the army, black soldiers seized every spare moment to study and try to learn to read, and most of them made progress toward literacy. But there was a cultural gap that was not easily erased, and Northern blacks would face many challenges and problems of their own after the war years came to an end. It makes sense to ask how much aid they continued to provide once the war was over and how much actual contact developed between the two geographical branches of the race. In practice, was there much social or cultural unity within the ranks of African Americans before the Great Migrations of the twentieth century, when many Southern African Americans moved to the North? Just as black migrants from the Caribbean would influence the intellectual history and ideology of black leaders, freed people in contact with the Northern elite could have influenced that community. Therefore, to comprehend the full history of African Americans, it would be valuable to investigate the interaction of Northern black leaders and Southern freed people. That is just one of the challenges in illuminating the history of a people who lived in very diverse and challenging circumstances.

4

Military History

I came late to an interest in the Civil War's military history. My preference was for the study of political controversies and social changes, and I admit that I tended to think of military history as the province of detailed, even obsessive, accounts of the movements of particular units at certain hours of a battle. But teaching a Civil War course requires attention to the military events, and I began to develop an interest in the decisions and personalities of leading generals and then in larger strategic questions. I am surely less qualified to offer sage advice on this subfield than many who specialize in military history, but I now approach it with genuine interest and a few personal convictions.

Fortunately, others who are superbly qualified have identified gaps and opportunities for study that add much to the perspectives I have to offer. As Gary Gallagher, Richard McMurray, and others have pointed out, a striking omission is the absence of any thorough study of the camps of instruction for either North or South. The Civil War was fought by civilian soldiers because neither side had a large professional army, and it was in those camps of instruction that farmers, clerks, laborers, and businessmen learned what it meant to be a soldier. From a purely military point of view, it is important to know what those civilians learned and what important lessons may have been omitted. (We know that black troops often were thrown into battle with almost no training at all. It would make sense to compare the actions of well-trained soldiers and untrained soldiers in several engagements.) But in a wider sense, the experiences of a camp of instruction were significant in forming men's impressions of their cause, their leaders, and their country. Such camps should be studied from the perspective of social history, values, and national feeling as well as military training.[1]

Professor Gallagher also has pointed out avenues to gain a better understanding of the soldiers' motives. Instead of writing about their attitudes overall or in general, historians should compare them by different regions and by different generations. With different ages came different life experiences: older men had familiarity with periods of political compromise in the United States, whereas younger soldiers may have known only the years of ever-intensifying sectional conflict. Thanks to the outstanding achievement of Joseph Glatthaar in *General Lee's Army,* we have a model for the study of other major armies in both the Confederacy and the Union. Glatthaar has shown what kind of factors, such as social class, marital status, date of enlistment, or number of dependents, affected troops' longevity or decisions to desert.[2]

Gallagher, Barton Myers, and others agree on the importance of historians erasing any mental barrier that separates military events from the political and social developments in society. Myers believes that "the traditional line between battlefield and home front" has "impeded creativity in Civil War military history." The two realms need to be considered together because they were interactive. As the war unfolded, the battlefield and the home front influenced each other in direct and important ways. In this vein, Gallagher has called for greater attention to the impact within the South of US military forces and their operations and for analysis of the relationship between levels of slaveholding in Confederate regions and the extent of societal disruption caused by invasion. He is keenly aware of the fact that there were many local differences in military experiences, civilian attitudes, and reactions. Attention to these local differences is needed.[3]

In the essay "The Future of Civil War Era Studies: Military History," Myers offers many valuable suggestions after considering both gaps in the literature and new areas of interest. The experience of units composed of African American as well as Native American soldiers "remains largely deficient." Soldiers of various ethnic and racial backgrounds deserve more careful study, along with examination of their experiences as veterans. Some believe it is an open question whether military service increased or impeded the socialization of immigrant groups. The policy of the Union and Confederate governments on treatment of civilians was controversial during the war and has attracted a great deal of modern attention. Yet a "systematic study" of it is still lacking, and new studies are more likely to be on "atrocity, torture, and execution." Guerrilla warfare has rightly become a dominant focus, but Myers points out that there are no comparative studies of the American phenomenon and guerrilla warfare in other countries or periods. Similarly, the recent US experience in Iraq should remind us of the importance of undertaking comparative studies of military occupations and the civilian response. These and other recommendations, states Myers, will place "the soldier experience in fuller context before, during, and after armed hostilities by large field armies."[4]

In the same essay, Myers recommends attention to the unglorious side of battle, noting that "soldiers in many battles were jaded, lost, disaffected, and nihilistic." His words are not a criticism of the imperiled foot soldier but a call for greater realism. In a similar vein, I feel that a more realistic and critical approach toward Civil War generals is also in order. Granted, some harsh verdicts have been delivered by well-known scholars on the most controversial commanders, such as Joseph E. Johnston, Braxton Bragg, and George B. McClellan. Few can say more or make the point more effectively than has William C. Davis, whose analysis of the Atlanta campaign concludes that Johnston was a general who would not fight "even for a woman." Nevertheless, anyone who has read Rick Atkinson's trilogy on World War II will remember the damning, distressing evidence of thousands of lives thrown away due to the repeated errors of incompetent generals. Studies of poor leadership in the Civil War have somehow not produced the same emotional impact, despite the fact that many command decisions were so erroneous that in terms of human lives they seem unpardonable. Here greater recognition of the human costs of our most costly war is warranted, and Myers agrees that we need "more military histories that address pointlessness, imbecility, futility, and frustration."[5]

One place to start in the evaluation of both sections' high commands is the question of what constituted victory in battle. Perhaps surprisingly, on such a basic question there has been a lack of consensus and some confusion. The fact that the huge but slow-moving and clumsy Civil War armies usually pummeled each other without a decisive outcome created room for debate about what constituted victory. Was it dependent on which side lost more men? Or was the victorious side the army that lost a smaller *proportion* of its men? Was the crucial variable the damage inflicted or which side ended up in control of the battlefield? General McClellan was always prolific in arguments to defend his record, and some of his reasoning had the sound of an excuse. Nevertheless, there was some uncertainty about which army prevailed in a number of battles. Civil War historians might benefit from discussion with scholars who have analyzed this issue for other eras and other wars.

At a more fundamental level, there also was uncertainty—on both sides—about what constituted the proper strategy, and strategic questions constitute one of the most interesting areas of the war's history. Although Abraham Lincoln was unschooled in military matters, he read and studied military texts and deserves the credit historians have given him for grasping one crucially important point: that the North, with its superior numbers and military resources, should apply pressure at all points and in all regions simultaneously in order to deprive the South of any chance to concentrate its men against any single threat. If the opposed armies were similarly competent, simultaneous pressure by the numerically superior side would wear down and defeat the Confederacy. By exhausting the South's armies and diminishing its resources through occupation of territory, the North eventually prevailed—an example of the "persisting or logistic" strategy known to Julius Caesar.[6]

Nevertheless, Lincoln's strategic thinking had to go through a process of trial and error before he identified the key element for victory. Early in the war he went along with the thinking that the capture of Richmond or some other vital point was extremely important. He later realized that the Confederacy's true center of gravity was not a specific place. Yet he always had great difficulty in convincing his generals that destroying the enemy's army, rather than just stopping it, was essential. What explains that gap between Lincoln's thinking and his generals' behavior time and time again? Donald Stoker has argued that Lincoln also sometimes allowed himself to be distracted from the basic goal. In the spring and summer of 1862, says Stoker, the Union missed a good chance to seize Chattanooga. Early in 1863, Lincoln and his generals focused on controlling the Mississippi River even though the Union's "'real' war was in Tennessee." When the French intervened in Mexico, Lincoln wanted to mount a Texas expedition for foreign-policy and domestic reasons, but this idea indicated that he was "los[ing] sight of the main goal." It also was true that he was skeptical about the large-scale raids that General William Tecumseh Sherman proposed. The March to the Sea might not have occurred but for the fact that in 1864 Sherman and General Ulysses S. Grant had accumulated enough prestige to override the president's doubts.[7]

The challenges to strategic thinking on the Confederate side were even greater. Traditional interpretations, which James McPherson has recently supported, have held that Jefferson Davis adopted the strategy of an "offensive defense." The Confederacy would aim primarily at defending its territory, a goal in keeping with its claim that it only wanted to be left alone to enjoy the right of independence. Yet Southern leaders agreed with Carl von Clausewitz and other military thinkers that a defense should not be passive. The Confederacy would instead look for advantageous opportunities to strike at its foe. At the beginning of the war, Davis's approach emphasized defending territory. Under great pressure from governors, he hoped to hold the perimeter and defend all territory claimed by the Confederacy. But that kind of dispersal of forces was impractical, and by the time he gave his inaugural address as president of the "permanent" government in 1862, he acknowledged a change in emphasis. Thereafter, as Davis explained to various unhappy constituencies, the Southern government would take forces from some areas to concentrate them where the greatest benefit could be obtained. Instead of defending its borders, the Confederacy would focus its power against the most threatening or most vulnerable Federal armies.[8]

Yet basic questions have been raised about this description. Donald Stoker argues that the Confederacy never reconciled its announced strategy of an offensive defense with preexisting aims for territorial expansion. Rather than fighting defensively, if opportunistically, on its own territory, the South launched two invasions of the North. The first, in the fall of 1862, was a two-pronged offensive reaching into both Maryland and Kentucky. The second, of course, was Lee's invasion of Pennsylvania in 1863. Clearly, too, there was interest at high levels in the possibility of luring the Northwest to enter an alliance with the Confederacy and enjoy the future benefits of trade through the Mississippi River.[9]

I have argued that this ambiguity probably had most to do with Davis's respect for his most successful and cooperative general, Robert E. Lee. Lee's correspondence with Davis before the invasion in 1863 documents both Lee's tact and the divergence between his thinking and Davis's. The Confederate president always thought it was possible for the Confederacy to gain its independence by outlasting the North, and he had to cling to that idea after the two invasions failed. But the limited nature of Southern resources was evident, even after the early adoption of conscription. Therefore, Lee was keenly aware of the South's material disadvantages, and I believe he felt that victory, if it were to come, had to arrive sooner rather than later.

In 1862, Lee hoped to win a victory and inspire Marylanders to join the cause, which would allow the Confederacy to offer peace to the North as the latter was approaching its midterm elections. Then in the summer of 1863 Lee was impressed with the rise of a peace wing in the Democratic Party of the North. In conjunction with the planned invasion of Pennsylvania, he urged that nothing should be done to discourage peace-minded Northerners. Their stated insistence on reunion, he argued, was something that could be handled once the fighting stopped. Davis did not abandon his fiery rhetoric demanding independence, but because he had faith in Lee, the president authorized the offensive. In both instances, Lee may have seen possible secondary advantages, such as attracting recruits in Maryland and Kentucky or taking provisions from the fertile fields of Pennsylvania rather than from war-ravaged Virginia. But his greatest hope and central goal were to strike a blow that would cause the North to consider peace. En route to Gettysburg, Lee said, "If successful, [we] will secure our independence and win the war." Davis had reason to trust in Lee, but approving his ideas was a departure from the offensive defense. This ambiguity in the Confederacy's strategic practice is a key point of debate.[10]

Lee's decision to invade Pennsylvania in 1863 proved to be crucially important, and Robert May recently has focused new critical attention on it. Arguing that it was one of the key determinative moments in the war, May suggests that Lee made a fundamental strategic error. "Had Lee remained in Virginia and adopted a more Fabian strategy in 1863," May argues, "he could perhaps have avoided disastrous defeats, strung out the war, and induced enough war weariness in the North as to undermine Lincoln's campaign for reelection in 1864." Thus, instead of suffering a "catastrophic blow" to "manpower and morale" at Gettysburg, the Confederacy might have helped candidate McClellan win, an outcome that could have allowed the South to "eke out a fragile independence." The defensive or offensive elements of Confederate strategy remain controversial because they raise truly important issues for analysis.[11]

Another related question of broad scope concerns the possibility that Southern society put restrictions on the Confederacy's war effort and strategy that were not found in the North. At the beginning of the war, Davis's mistaken effort to defend his frontiers was not due solely to a desire to prove that the Confederacy was a nation. Even more it was the product of intense pressure from governors and the public. State leaders withheld thousands of men from the army, in large part to control the slave population, yet they insisted that the central government was never doing enough to defend their states. They constantly demanded reinforcements or the return of their state's troops. Charles Roland has identified this "localism" as a major problem for the military. He argues that although Davis resisted and fought against such pressures, too many troops were kept in garrison duty in the departments of the Carolinas, Georgia, and Florida. There they actually outnumbered their foes 45,000 to 27,000 in 1863, while the main armies elsewhere were in great need of more men. Confederate leaders always had to balance military goals against internal political necessities, and renewed attention to this dilemma can produce a military narrative that is tightly integrated with events on the home front.[12]

The Confederacy's "localism" also meant that the Davis government was not free to give up large chunks of territory, even temporarily, in order to use the resources it had more effectively. Early in 1862, when Davis admitted that he could not defend all of his nation's perimeter, General Braxton Bragg submitted a strategic analysis that Donald Stoker praises. Bragg urged a defense only of the Confederacy's core—the states north of Florida and east of the Mississippi. J. F. C. Fuller has also analyzed the problem of defending the long "western" frontier and concluded that the Confederacy should have abandoned the upper South and concentrated its forces near Chattanooga. Such ideas, however, were extremely risky in terms of internal politics and morale. The Confederacy was a government that needed to prove its ability to defend its citizens. Many soldiers believed that protecting their families was their first priority, and "keeping an army in the field," writes Mark Weitz, "meant keeping the Union out of the South." Wherever the Confederacy ceded territory, it lost the support of Southerners there and considerable morale among Confederates elsewhere. Charles Roland dismisses Fuller's idea by saying that abandoning the upper South would have "undone the Confederacy without a battle."[13]

These realities had a great deal to do with the adoption of a departmental system for the Southern armies. That system grew out of the "exigencies of politics, society, and logistics" and illustrated the severe constraints that society and politics put on military operations. By dividing the Confederacy into separate departments, each with troops and a commander responsible for its defense, Davis tried to meet the local demand for safety while distributing troops in a manner more consistent with the nation's overall needs. He changed the boundaries and definitions of these departments as the war went on, and it seems that the system worked better at the beginning of the war than later, but no one has systematically examined the departmental system. The reasons for the decline in its effectiveness ought to be investigated.

A fundamental principle of this departmental system was that its commanders had to be flexible enough to cooperate as exigencies arose. It was inevitable that one department would be threatened while others were not, and therefore troops should move between departments as necessary. In reality, this kind of cooperation proved almost impossible, leading Donald Stoker to criticize an "unnecessary and inefficient compartmentalization of forces." But the fault may have been less in the system than in realities of the society. Local politicians and increasingly the troops themselves resisted any transfer of forces. By 1864, for example, commanders in the Trans-Mississippi declared that their men would adamantly refuse to cross the river and go to the aid of states farther east. Such defiant or insubordinate attitudes masked a deeper problem and showed that the deficiencies of the departmental system perhaps should not be laid solely at the feet of unimaginative or uncooperative commanders.[14]

We should ask whether there was any similar problem facing Northern strategists. At first glance, it seems that Northern society did not hamstring the military strategists, for the North enjoyed some important advantages. Its population was so large that increasing demands for troops could be met and were met without widespread or lasting social disruption. The North did not have to deal with the loss of significant territory. Fierce resistance to measures such as conscription occurred in only a few places. To identify societal restrictions that might have affected the North's strategy in a manner similar to those that Jefferson Davis faced, we may have to consider politics. For example, had the government attempted to free the slaves in the summer of 1861, it seems likely that public outrage would have been severe enough to stymie the war effort. But emancipation did not come about until its usefulness had become clear and until the sacrifices already made had strengthened the public's determination to see the war through.

Other debated issues center on questions of strategy. One persistent controversy concerns which theater of war was most important—the "West" or the "East." Contemporaries considered the "West" to be that enormous area stretching from the Appalachian Mountains to the Mississippi River, whereas the "East" was Virginia and the Atlantic coast. For the North, the geographical features of the West presented severe military challenges. Federal armies would have to conquer a huge territory characterized by a large and hostile population and by "many difficult topographical features [that would] bog down Union offensives." If invasion succeeded, the Union armies then would face the problem of supplying their soldiers through vulnerable and extended supply lines. At the beginning of the war, General Winfield Scott proposed taking control of the Mississippi River as a way to hem in the Confederacy and choke off its access to material and human resources. But the North probably gave almost equal attention to the West for political reasons than from respect for Scott's "Anaconda" plan. Citizens in the Northwest had long viewed the rivers that made up the Mississippi Valley system as vital to their commerce and their future. Fear that a Confederate government would restrict or tax their trade through New Orleans surfaced as soon as the war started. To the Northwest, the Mississippi River as well as the Ohio seemed essential. Although railroads were beginning to carry a larger percentage of the region's products, that fact was not obvious to people at the time, for in the 1850s steamboat traffic was heavy and was increasing. Hundreds of steamers departed each year for New Orleans from Cincinnati, Louisville, Memphis, Pittsburgh, and St. Louis. Lincoln understood the region's concerns because he was a westerner.[15]

But Federal forces had to struggle to achieve success in the West. The size and topographical features of the region posed a severe challenge, and Grant and Sherman overcame them only through a process of learning and innovation. Grant sometimes used traditional methods to secure his supply lines, as in the case of Chattanooga. But he also learned during his operations against Vicksburg that the agricultural richness of the area made it possible to live off the land. Sherman was equally determined and daring, and after Atlanta he did not hesitate to cut his army from a long umbilical cord. The Union's western armies often supplied cheering news to a citizenry that too often learned of defeat in the East. Given that fact and the importance of the West, one wonders why the number of soldiers in the western armies was always smaller than the number in the major eastern armies.

One reason that Federal forces did not have an easy time in the West was the amount of guerrilla warfare that Northern soldiers encountered there. The disastrous results of Napoleon's invasion of Russia had shown military theorists that invasion of any large enemy region posed great dangers. The deeper an army marched into the enemy's country, the greater was its vulnerability to harassing guerrilla attacks. The Confederate secretary of war in 1862, George Wythe Randolph, confidently believed that no army would be able to conquer a territory as large as the Confederacy as long as its people resisted. And, in fact, the Union army ran into a great deal of guerrilla resistance in the first part of the war. This is obviously an important issue for any analysis of the western theater. Yet two scholars who can claim the greatest expertise in these areas differ in their assessments.

Earl Hess, who has analyzed the war in the West, does not give Union forces high marks for dealing with guerrilla warfare. Yet Robert Mackey has concluded that the Confederacy lost the "uncivil war" because "the Union army was able to adapt to irregular warfare faster than the Confederacy expected." Throughout the upper South, he claims, Northern forces learned how to defeat the various types of Confederate irregular warfare. A more searching analysis of this important issue would be valuable.[16]

The question of how much importance should be attached to the West stirred a great deal of debate in the South, where there came into being a wartime lobby of generals and politicians that Thomas Connelly and Archer Jones have dubbed the "western concentration bloc." These advocates of the heartland region stretching to the Mississippi River argued that too much attention and too many resources were going to Virginia. The Confederacy quickly lost territory in the West, a fact that undoubtedly fed the concerns behind the western concentration bloc. But was that all that was involved? Did the generals' and politicians' agreement stem from conceptual analysis, or were there political, personal, as well as geographical motives in play? It would be worthwhile to study the connections among the civilian and military members of this lobby in favor of greater attention to the West.[17]

Debate has not completely settled the question of whether advocates of the West were right. Karl Marx, earning money as a newspaper contributor in Europe, shared their view that the war would be won in the West, and the balance of modern opinion seems to have shifted in their favor. But Charles Roland has stressed that Richmond and Washington, DC, had great symbolic value and that Virginia gave the Confederacy a dagger's point with which to attack the North. General P. G. T. Beauregard took the lead in proposing bold schemes for western operations, and his ideas pleased various congressmen. But most historians agree that Beauregard's ideas were always exaggerated and unrealistic. His plans for bold movements by whole armies, leading to rapid concentrations of force, scarcely resembled the kind of armies that actually fought the Civil War. What more realistic plans might have accomplished has not received much discussion.[18]

For the North's point of view, Sherman's western army was key to bringing the war to an end. Its destructive march through Georgia to the sea had as its purpose to demonstrate Federal superiority and inflict psychological damage as well as to destroy a huge amount of valuable material of war. Sherman himself said that he wanted to "make Georgia howl" and that his aim "was to whip the rebels, to humble their pride, to follow them to their inmost recesses, and make them fear and dread us." He believed the war would not be won until Southerners were "not only ruined, exhausted, but humbled in pride and spirit." How great was Sherman's success? There can be no doubt that many Confederates in Georgia, the Carolinas, and elsewhere were profoundly discouraged by the success of Sherman's march. But a gendered approach to the actions of his army and the reactions of those directly in its path reveals a different, localized reaction. Both Lisa Tendrich Frank and Jacqueline Campbell have found that the experience of invasion enraged the affected elite women and hardened their hostility to the Union. This psychological reaction was visible in World War II as well, where bombing raids did not destroy civilians' spirit. One can also ask whether these women's reaction had a direct connection with anti-North hostility during Reconstruction or later in the formation of the United Daughters of the Confederacy.[19]

The gendered aspect of these events offers additional insight. Lisa Frank has developed evidence that Sherman's army followed a gendered strategy of psychological war. Although his army's formal marching orders stated that men were not to enter Southern homes, his soldiers wanted to punish the rich families that they blamed for the war, and frightening and humiliating the women who were left behind became their goal. Troops burst into houses, destroyed luxurious furnishings, and invaded women's bedrooms to search for goods. Southerners claimed there were many rapes. Sherman never gave official approval for this assault on women's bodies, homes, possessions, and clothing, but he was notably lax in restraining his men. Thus, issues of gender guided the army and fed the Southerners' reaction. In whatever ways this assault may have affected Confederates watching from afar and Southern men in general, who saw that they were failing in their duty to protect the home, it created elite women who were more patriotic toward the Confederacy than they had been before. What is most interesting about Frank's work is that it invites us to scrutinize other military events, where we may not have looked before, in order to identify gendered motives and reactions.[20]

The question of how important it was to control the Mississippi River remains controversial, as do a few other questions. Should the Confederacy have tried to hold onto Vicksburg, or should its troops have abandoned the citadel in order to fight another day? Vicksburg had great symbolic importance, but the eventual surrender of 30,000 troops was a blow to the Southern forces. Was Jefferson Davis justified in removing General Joseph

Johnston from command in front of Atlanta, and was General John Bell Hood the wrong replacement with the wrong plan? Did Lee give too much attention to Virginia and overlook the need to support other areas? Because such questions are important, they continue to be discussed. But they also continue to be live issues because any answers that diverge from what actually occurred have to be counterfactual and rest on many assumptions or suppositions. Is there a more fruitful way to contest these points? My suggestion is that future arguments should be supported as specifically as possible with data and detailed analysis of the alternatives. Too often now we accept boldly stated, conclusive-sounding declarations instead of scrutinizing a fully developed argument.

William G. Thomas, the author of a large, data-driven study of railroads, has raised a new argument. After 1862, he asserts, the war "became structured around the railroad network." As that era's new mode of transportation, railroads assumed an importance greater than rivers, and, in fact, from the first battle of Manassas their potential importance for putting troops into action was clear. Efforts to control or to destroy rail lines assumed increasing importance, and there was much vicious partisan warfare around the railroads. Thomas estimates that as many as 30,000 Confederate guerrillas operated along the railroad lines. On the Northern side, the Union hired or impressed many black workers at junctions and depots, a fact that encouraged many slaves' flights to freedom. But Thomas credits Robert E. Lee with recognizing the importance of the railroads. By moving the fighting away from railroad corridors, he says, Lee attempted to block any Union railroad strategy.[21]

Donald Stoker also has directed attention to an area deserving investigation by specialists. In modern military theory, "operations" constitute the important realm between strategy and tactics. Whereas strategy relates to the war in general and tactics to the choices made in a specific battle, operations constitute all the actions that must be effective to implement the strategy in particular campaigns. At the time of the Civil War, military leaders did not give the attention to the concept of operations that is typical today, but Stoker suggests that today's interest in operations can open up some new understandings of the Civil War's history. Brian Holden-Reid is one historian who has been working in this area, and others are sure to follow Stoker's suggestion.[22]

Another large and fruitful area for study concerns the variety of problems within the high command—problems that plagued both governments.

There was a great deal of conflict and misunderstanding in the personal relations between presidents and their generals. Another difficulty related to the process of decision making and the variety of actors who wanted to be involved. Political influence on decisions and appointments was a phenomenon that complicated matters and affected both the North and the South. Sometimes its origin lay solely with politicians, but at other times commanders themselves took part in lobbying to affect decisions.

It is noteworthy how often and how deeply poor personal relations between the president and his generals damaged each side's efforts. At important junctures, mistrust, lack of cooperation, and hostility played an outsize role. Jefferson Davis's working relationships with P. G. T. Beauregard and Joseph Johnston degenerated quickly, and Lincoln had a famously bad rapport with John C. Frémont and George B. McClellan. Other Northern generals, even friends or acquaintances, such as David Hunter, went behind Lincoln's back to affect policy or undermine his wishes. Both Johnston and McClellan were secretive and uncooperative, claiming that they could not trust their president to keep important military plans from the prying eyes of journalists. But Johnston had already bitterly accused Davis (incorrectly) of failing to give him the rank he deserved—namely, the highest position among all Confederate generals. McClellan's accusation against Lincoln is difficult to credit because early in 1862 the general gave details of his plans to a major newspaper, the *New York Herald,* "in a warped effort to gain Democratic political support and counter Republican criticism."[23]

Only with Robert E. Lee for Davis and with Ulysses S. Grant for Lincoln can we say that consultation and decision making within a framework of accepted authority worked well. It is obvious that many of the problems with others derived from egotism, but to make that observation is not to exhaust understanding. Modern sociological and psychological literature has much to say about small-group dynamics and interpersonal challenges of leadership. It would be worthwhile to apply that knowledge to analysis of wartime problems, just as it would be useful to compare systematically the troubled president–general relationships with the successful ones. What was the secret of Davis's smooth and trustful relationship with Lee? What should the Civil War's leaders have done to avoid problems in the first place? What were the indications that a partnership had gone off the tracks and needed to be terminated sooner rather than later? It also is relevant to ask to what extent institutional factors—such as support from the

Democratic Party in the North or the fact that the government of the South was new and insecure—played a role.

Political interference and complications had a great impact on command assignments during the Civil War. It is true, of course, that other periods have seen very public and high-level debates involving generals. Harry Truman had to fire General Douglas MacArthur, and President Barack Obama removed General Stanley McChrystal from command in Afghanistan, but the level of public controversy over commanders during the Civil War was elevated and persistent. In the South, there were frequent and loud demands that Johnston be put back in a high command, something that Jefferson Davis eventually did in 1864 against his better judgment. Southern officials who believed in Beauregard's genius also were numerous, and at one point Beauregard used that belief to encourage fifty-four members of Congress to petition for his reinstatement. In the last, desperate months of the Confederacy, there was a great deal of discussion about the idea of removing Davis in some way and putting Lee in charge of the entire war effort.

Nor was the North free from considerable intrusions of politics into military affairs and decision making. In 1861 and 1862, George McClellan actively entertained and sought the favor of Democratic leaders in Washington while he supposedly was preparing for a major campaign against Richmond. Advocating a gentler treatment of rebels and the least possible interference with slavery, McClellan allowed and encouraged such dismissive criticism of Lincoln that the president eventually cashiered one member of McClellan's personal staff for indulging in it. But it can be argued that Lincoln acted too slowly, for by that time the negative views at the top of the Army of the Potomac had infected the ranks and influenced the army's effectiveness. After the administration sidelined McClellan, controversies revolved around other generals. Even General Grant fell out of favor before he later was hailed as the commander who would surely bring victory.

These facts raise questions that I would like to see investigated. What do they say about the status of the constitutional principle of civilian control of the military? Had that principle failed to become firmly established before the war, or did special wartime conditions undermine it in new ways? I wonder if the principle had less strength in the South than in the North because, in the context of a new nation desperately fighting for its life, the culture of honor and masculine assertion lowered barriers and removed some restraints. Although civilian control was a constitutionally enshrined tradition, perhaps it was less important than other Southern values. I was struck by the words of a French visitor who dismissed talk of the "'great conservative cause of the South.' . . . The South is conservative of nothing except slavery."[24] Finding an extraconstitutional way to defend slavery—by deposing Jefferson Davis—was attractive to a substantial number of Southern leaders in the winter of 1864–1865. For the North, did Lincoln's early tendency to defer to the military experts encourage too much waywardness, or did the issue of slavery simply put serious distance between him and McClellan? Were congressmen of that era possessed of so much power relative to the president that they readily tried to expand their influence in a manner not seen today?

There are no "political generals" today, when the professional army supplies the upper ranks, but giving major responsibility to political figures was a feature of the Civil War. My impression is that it was more common in the Union than in the Confederacy, but hard data appear to be lacking. It also seems that the results of the practice were usually unfavorable, at least in military terms. On the military side, this outcome raises the question, How quickly were political appointments curtailed? On the political side, we need to assess what benefits of morale or recruitment or cross-party cooperation might have resulted from the appointment of popular politicians. One wonders if the greater size of the Northern armies created more posts than professional officers could fill or whether the North's partisan competition imposed politicians on the army. One article-length study has maintained that intensely partisan attitudes damaged promotions on merit within the Union army. Using the records of state adjutant generals responsible for recommending promotions to state governors (records that probably have seen little use), Timothy Orr has shown that Democrats blocked the promotions of deserving Republicans both in the field and in the halls of the state capitals, with negative effects on the war effort.[25]

The politicization of McClellan's army may have been only the most dramatic example of the way partisan politics affected soldiers' attitudes. It is a little-appreciated fact that many generals had served in Congress either before or at some point during the war. Their experience in Washington surely had an effect on their attitudes and political orientation, but I am not aware of any serious attempt to investigate the possible impact of these political careers on their military service. We also know that Lincoln benefited heavily from soldiers' backing in the election of 1864, and various scholars have argued that the troops backed him because they eventually adopted the view that emancipation would help them win the war. But Lincoln's dominance in the soldiers' vote did not necessarily mean that many soldiers had become Republicans or had decided to vote Republican. Another possibility, as one scholar has argued, is that many Democrat soldiers failed to support their party because they disliked its candidates, in particular vice presidential nominee George Pendleton, or its peace-oriented platform. Those men might have resumed their support for Democratic candidates right after the war. Because many army units came from particular towns and counties, it should be possible to scrutinize voting patterns before, during, and immediately after the war to see if army service turned some Democrats into Republicans.[26]

In both the South and the North, constitutional provisions made the president the commander in chief, and that fact has encouraged assessment of the two presidents' military leadership. It seems clear that Lincoln was too reluctant to trust his own judgment and assume control over McClellan in the early months of the war. Jefferson Davis has been accused of the opposite fault—interfering too much in the generals' command decisions. Donald Stoker has charged that Davis's desire to make the important decisions prevented a "clear chain of command and decisive leadership at the top." I think it is clear that Davis involved himself in too many low-level administrative decisions, including which officers should be promoted above the lower ranks. Also, in the very first days of the war the Confederate president did seem eager to be as much involved in battles as possible. But Davis himself later declared that he had to entrust decisions in the field to his commanders, and it is debatable whether Lincoln injected himself less significantly than did Davis. Stoker concludes that both presidents "sometimes interfered [with their commanders] more than they should have." There is consensus that at certain points both should have interfered *more* rather than tolerate incompetence, so these questions deserve more analysis.[27]

The question of resources was important for both armies and in two directions: the resources they needed and the effect of their resource-oriented operations on the rest of society. In the Confederacy, no important official was the target of more criticism than commissary general Lucius Northrop. The system that he established to supply the Southern armies never functioned adequately, and from the beginning of the war the Confederate army depended heavily upon impressments. The burden of supplying the army through impressments fell unequally on the population and caused much anger and resentment. Southern officials from Jefferson Davis on down deplored the situation but could not solve the problem, and the laws that tardily tried to regulate impressment were not very successful in removing public discontent. Northrop has been accused of creating a system that was too centralized, but it has been a long time since a study of his system and methods has been made. How much was possible given the South's less-developed railroad network, wartime crop failures, and dependence on midwestern supplies of meat?

The effect of resource issues on Southern society may initially have been positive in some respects because they spurred development. The government established strong incentives for industrial production of needed supplies, but we know that at least a substantial portion of new or previously existing factories was destroyed by the end of the war. Also on the negative side, areas that saw frequent battles suffered from the armies' demands. Large portions of Virginia were practically denuded of crops, livestock, and even timber. The impact on agriculture in Virginia was so great that it influenced Robert E. Lee's decisions to take the war onto Northern soil because he saw the advantage in collecting resources there and sparing certain areas of Virginia from continued, heavy demands. This problem of resources had important effects on the armies and on the morale of the civilian population (as is discussed further in chapter 6). Assessing those effects has often not moved beyond a general, descriptive stage. The same can be said for estimates that although the Confederacy actually had adequate supplies of food or uniforms, many crops never reached the armies, and certain governors hoarded uniforms, holding them for exclusive use of men from their states.

In the North, tremendous resources went toward supplying the armies. The Northern economy was able to meet that challenge, and the huge size of government purchases served to keep the economy humming. Cotton textile mills lost the raw material they needed, but some of them converted to production of wool fabric, and the government ordered huge quantities of cloth for uniforms. The list of war-related commodities that the government purchased was long, and those purchases stimulated the economy. At one point in the war, a Massachusetts business journal pointed out that strong business activity was due to government orders in almost every department. Thus, the Northern armies did not suffer from serious shortages of resources, and economic activity continued at a high rate. Economists have devoted a great deal of attention to the question of how the war affected the pace of industrialization, but it would be useful to ask how war-related demands changed the character of certain regions. Mechanized agriculture in the Midwest, for example, received a boost when many men went into the army.

Some additional topics in military history relate to the soldiers themselves and to society's treatment of them. Some good work has been published about the experience of African American soldiers, but there are important areas in which much more can be done. We are just beginning to know more about how military service changed the black men who fought. Attention has focused on certain units that protested unequal pay, but there is no thorough study of the racial dimensions of army prosecutions of its soldiers for crimes or supposed infractions. Various works have highlighted the black units that fought bravely in bloody battles, but less is known about the average black enlistee, who often ended up spending months in garrison duty. Likewise, thousands of black soldiers were kept on duty—usually in the South—after the war came to an end due to the government's desire to muster out white veterans and the fact that many African American soldiers had enlisted in 1863 or later. Surely much more can be learned about the conditions of these soldiers' service in the immediate postwar South and the conflicts that they had with hostile whites. Army duty changed these men in many ways—allowing them, for example, to gain at least the rudiments of an education. We have very few studies of the role these veterans played once the war was over and they had returned to their home communities. What effect did the war have on their relationships with their wives, and how did crippling wounds affect gender roles within the black community?

In-depth, long-range studies of such questions are only now beginning to be asked even about white troops. Not long ago, Maris Vinovskis lamented that almost "nothing has been written about the postwar experiences of Civil War veterans." We need to know more about them and about the long-term and community-related effects of military service in that bloody war. Many units consisted of men from a given town or village who signed up together. These men went to war together, thus emptying out a part of their home community at the same time, and they fought and died together. A smaller number came home, and some of these veterans returned with disabling wounds that affected their lives and their families and communities thereafter. For 45,000 amputees, life changed in a multitude of ways—practical, economic, social, and personal. "War unmade men," states Brian Craig Miller, affecting "their bodies, their souls, and their very identity." Most amputees, especially those from farming regions, would struggle to make a living and support their families. As a result, even a Southern gentleman such as General Richard Ewell, who lost a leg, found that strangers assumed he was a poor man.[28]

The psychological damage suffered by soldiers has been little studied, though it may have been serious. Diane Miller Sommerville has called for attention to "the psychological suffering of Civil War veterans and its impact on postwar households and families." North and South, surviving soldiers suffered, but the disabled Southern veteran faced particular difficulty in fulfilling the patriarchal role that was emphasized in his society. David Silkenat shows the way with a creatively conceived analysis of the levels of suicide, divorce, and debt among North Carolina veterans. His study wisely assumes that the ill effects of war could be wide ranging, appearing not just in physical problems but in many areas of personal life. Judkin Browning is at work on a comparative study of two units—one Northern and one Southern—that savaged each other at Gettysburg. By taking a long-range approach, he plans to study not just the men who survived but also their families and the impact of their absences and deaths on the communities from which they came. This kind of focus on both soldiers and their communities during and after the war could be a model for other studies. Such an approach would broaden and deepen our understanding of the impact of the war.[29]

Studies in women's history have rightly assumed that Southern wives faced a challenge in supporting the postwar adjustment of their defeated and wounded husbands. Brian Craig Miller has found a variety of attitudes among Southern women whose husbands or suitors suffered amputations or disabling injuries. Some married women expressed a kind of satisfaction that their men, who now depended on them, would need and appreciate their help and would never stray. The chance to play a more responsible role in the marriage also was appealing to some of these wives. Others, however, worried about how their families would be able to pay for food and shelter through future years. In a patriotic spirit and with an absence of self-centeredness, some young women remained true in their love for a maimed suitor and declared, "I love you better than ever." Probably an equal number of women, however, feared the economic and social consequences of their lovers' wounds or simply were repelled by the damage to the men's bodies. Some felt they deserved a whole man and would not marry a "wreck" or a "cripple." Young unmarried Southern belles would face a future in which there were fewer potential mates of their own age and social class. Some never married, and those who found a mate often entered matrimony with an older man and at an older-than-normal age. For these women as well as for their men, the Civil War had long-lasting, painful effects.[30]

If we change our perspective from the soldiers to the society and its values, we also encounter important questions to explore. The Civil War was such a powerful event that we should ask how it changed the character of society. In a sense, all Americans, North and South, spent four years in a highly militarized world. People's attention focused from day to day on battles and troop movements. Recruiting offices and provost marshals appeared in many communities. Confederates found that they had to get passports to travel and had to satisfy armed sentries on railroad cars and well-traveled roads. Though there were fewer of these phenomena in the North, there nevertheless were arrests of suspected spies or men interfering with military operations. Prison camps became a part of some social environments, with the threats of escapees and the spread of diseases. Did people's attitudes and thinking become militarized in some way?

As Emory Thomas pointed out long ago, the war changed values and altered the status of occupations.[31] Military careers were among those that became more highly valued. The society's attitude toward generals and military leadership seems especially intriguing. A man of fairly low status, such as Nathan Bedford Forrest, could become an admired figure in Southern society. Similarly, a man such as Ulysses S. Grant, who previously had left an undistinguished army career and failed in business, could become the fabulously praised and rewarded hero of the Union cause. Citizens showered gifts on Grant, from cigars to valuable properties, and presumably this behavior also involved a new estimate of the status of military men. Did military men become revered in a way they had not been in the decades before the war? Did veterans' organizations, as they pursued their interests in the postwar period, try to enshrine military service as the highest form of patriotism and service to the nation?

The fascination with military heroes and celebration of their deeds continued for some time after the war. Mark Twain saw the great commercial potential that could be realized in Grant's *Memoirs* and insisted on offering superior terms to Grant in order to be his publisher. Oliver Wendell Holmes became one example of a prominent man who in commencement addresses and other speeches praised the feelings of high purpose and intense experience he had known in wartime. The Century Company found great success in the 1880s with its series of publications titled *Battles and Leaders of the Civil War.* It is clear that the military experience exerted a fascination that persisted after Appomattox. Perhaps this fascination led to a new cult of the soldier or battlefield hero.

Yet it also was true that Northern society harbored enough suspicion of "the man on horseback" that President Grant worried about the public's reaction when he authorized military force against white Southerners. The sources of that suspicion and the roots of people's understanding of the civil–military relationship deserve more investigation and understanding. Whether the South had the same reservations about military influence is a question. The Confederacy in its final months seemed to have little reluctance about giving power to a potential military savior. Major newspapers and many leaders in the Confederate Congress had called for the replacement of Jefferson Davis with Robert E. Lee by some means. To the present day, the South is often thought of as a region with special respect for the military. Were the North and the South as fundamentally different in this respect as they had been in others? How war and those who made war were viewed in both sections would be a fascinating study in social values. Thus, the opportunities to reexamine how the war was fought and how it affected the nation, both North and South, are many and inviting.

5

New Techniques, New Opportunities

A century and a half after the fighting stopped, computers and digitization are breathing a new kind of life into the Civil War. We can almost say that they are giving us entirely new ways to revive the war and understand the contest. On nearly every campus, digital humanities projects are under way or under discussion, and presentations based on digital research are claiming a larger share of the sessions at scholarly conferences. Not only is it possible to do traditional research more easily and inexpensively, without traveling to distant archives, but in addition the advent of digitization has made historians more ambitious or ambitious in new and exciting ways. The possibility that ten years from now we will know many things that have been hidden from us or that we may see important aspects of the Civil War era from a new perspective is very real.

The attraction of digital history promises to be stronger, more energizing, and more widespread than cliometrics, or computer-assisted quantitative analysis, ever was. The reasons for this, to be honest, are not entirely complimentary to us as historians. Cliometrics typically demanded facility with computers and the use of analytical software programs in an era when both were far less accessible and user-friendly. More fundamentally, it required a level of mathematical understanding that many of us as humanists lacked and did not want to acquire. Although many of us were willing to spend long hours in an archive, working through hard-to-read manuscripts while sitting on hard wooden chairs, learning about multiple regression, ecological regression, binomial expansion, and other mathematical techniques seemed too difficult or too time-consuming a detour from regular research and publication.

Thus, although some quantitative cliometric research won respect and acceptance—historians of the South will think, for example, of J. Morgan Kousser's landmark book *The Shaping of Southern Politics*—most of us shied away from this type of research. Perhaps we felt better able to excuse that choice when we saw that cliometricians could have a very difficult time identifying data that would accurately *measure* what they wanted to analyze. The publication of *Time on the Cross* by Robert Fogel and Stanley Engerman took place amid unprecedented publicity and helped Professor Fogel win a Nobel Prize. Historians and other scholars rushed to read and discuss its controversial conclusions. But reviews by traditional historians soon pointed out questions or deficiencies relating to the kinds of data that went into the mathematical analysis. Critical reviews echoed the cliometricians' refrain "garbage in, garbage out." With relief, many of us, I'm sure, turned away not only from many of the book's conclusions but also from ambitious quantitative research.[1]

What we now can call the digital revolution is not likely to reanimate the cliometric revolution because the two approaches to research are quite different. But all of us who are basically traditional in our approach to research should remember some important lessons that quantitative, mathematical scholarship can teach us. The cliometricians are often more humble and more precise in their explanations than the rest of us. Multiple-regression analysis quickly reveals to them an important fact that we tend to de-emphasize—namely, that human behavior is very complex and is affected by a large number of forces or variables. Expertly conducted regression analysis often finds, for example, that the most powerful variable explaining some group's action accounts for no more than 20 or 25 percent of the observed variation in behavior. In our traditional, more literary habits of analysis, we tend to focus on one or two out of a large number of factors and build an argument for the important role of that small part of what is, in fact, a larger, multifactored explanation. Our arguments can be insightful or brilliant, but they often are narrowly focused on a part of what is in reality a much more complex picture.

Nothing about this point diminishes the excitement that we can feel about the possibilities of digital humanities research. The avenues that are now opening up to historians may well produce more new knowledge than the cliometric initiatives produced. Certainly, digitization can enable new research that addresses innovative questions and introduces fresh perspectives to our field. This chapter examines some of the methods in digital research that seem most promising and gives examples of some of the exciting work that is already under way.

Much of the potential of digitization lies in bringing together data that previously were scattered, inchoate, or unavailable or in making possible a coordinated approach to the analysis of separate sources of data. In both instances, we are talking about large collections of primary-source information that would be difficult to manage, much less analyze, without the aid of computers and digital means of organization and classification. Now, however, it will be much easier to study, say, a group composed of many individuals whose important characteristics might be described in very different records and whose lives unfolded through a number of decades.

For years, historians have used many different types of information that the United States government collected and published—census records are probably the best-known example. But poring through such information on microfilm or even in published form was laborious and time consuming. Governments and libraries are steadily digitizing their collections, however, and as records become available, it is possible to use software to simplify the search process and find what one needs much more quickly and easily. With more types of documents—both governmental and nongovernmental—being digitized every year, a wealth of data is much more accessible to historians. Tasks that used to seem impossible now are reasonable to undertake.

The many valuable and different types of databases that state and federal governments have created over the years include census records, military-service records, pension records, electoral results, and tax lists. Civil War historians will benefit immensely from a project at the University of Georgia that is fully digitizing the Official Records of the War of the Rebellion. Having that basic source available in digital form will facilitate many new studies. Land records are now available "in an unprecedented way," and for crop production we have "agricultural censuses, manuscript censuses, county and township data sets, family diaries and farm journals, US Department of Agriculture publications and Environmental Protection Administration reports, and Soil Conservation Service aerial photographs, as well as an abundance of state level surveys."[2] Corporations and other nongovernmental organizations also have produced valuable and accessible records. Sometimes private organizations digitize historical data and share them, but there also are corporation records as well as private manuscripts in the archives of major university libraries. Either cooperatively or singly, universities are supporting research through digitization and online repositories. For example, the Making of America collection was a collaboration between the University of Michigan and Cornell University, and its website (http://quod.lib.umich.edu/m/moagrp/) invites additional contributors. The Documenting the American South project (http://docsouth.unc.edu/) is a good example of a single university's effort, in this case by the Southern Historical Collection of the University of North Carolina at Chapel Hill.

Digitization also gives scholars the opportunity to create new databases. Through crowd-sourcing, historians can work together to find and assemble in one place information that has never been collected or unified by any previously existing agency or project—and do it inexpensively. Historians who share an interest in some question can combine information, each scholar collecting data relevant to the project and forwarding that information to a common, larger database. Collaborative effort such as this does not need to be limited to professors; students can be brought into the project, tackling small parts of the overall task as a class assignment. A key benefit for the students is that they learn a great deal simultaneously about sources and research. With carefully designed instructions, it could even be possible for interested citizens outside the university setting to carry out some of the information gathering.

Not long ago a session at the annual meeting of the Southern Historical Association detailed a good example of such crowd-sourcing efforts. The goal of this project was to learn more about slaves who ran away during the Civil War. The source of information on runaways was defined for this project as advertisements placed in newspapers by slaveholders. Professors and students from more than one university could contribute as each group examined the advertisements that appeared in a specific newspaper or particular years from that paper. When finally constructed, this kind of database could be exhaustive for newspapers of a single state or could cover various states. After information from newspapers has been gathered, other types of records may potentially provide further information about runaways.[3]

Learning more about runaway slaves deepens our understanding of actions that undermined the Confederacy and led to significant strengthening of the Union war effort. In this runaway-slave project, a host of variables, or pieces of information, about the escaped slaves became the targets for data gathering. There were nineteen relevant variables for which the newspaper advertisements often provided information. Among the nineteen were the runaway's age; the runaway's gender; his or her complexion; the date of his or her escape; whether he or she traveled alone or in a group;

the size of the group; location of his or her plantation; characteristics of that plantation; what portion of the plantation's slaves had escaped; whether a reward was offered; the size of the reward; how the reward changed over time; and so on. The potential value of such a project is obvious, and Professor Robert Kenzer of the University of Richmond reported that the project also was an interesting learning exercise for his students.[4]

The possibility of expanding our knowledge about runaway slaves through data collected from other types of sources is clear from a project undertaken by Max Grivno, a professor at the University of Southern Mississippi. He focused on Alabama and Mississippi and looked at newspapers not just to find advertisements about runaways but also notices about those who were captured and put in local jails. There were many notices of incarceration, and this kind of information could obviously expand the territorial coverage of the project being undertaken at the University of Richmond, although Professor Grivno had different priorities. In this particular case, he used the data to study mobility—how far and how rapidly slaves were traveling and how they may have gathered information that helped them escape. He used an open-source platform called Drupal to help him manage his data and to display it in a way that would highlight the distance traveled and where runaways' paths coincided.[5]

One more example of the use of crowd-sourcing to create a database is the Mapping the Fourth project of the Virginia Center for Civil War Studies at Virginia Tech. Designed primarily as a teaching tool, this project invites participation from other professors and other schools to create a digital archive on the way Northerners celebrated July 4 during the Civil War years. In the process of contributing to the archive, professors can assign their students a short exercise that will introduce them to research or could make the project the basis for a longer research paper. "Newspaper articles, letters, and diaries from a wide variety of perspectives" are the intended sources of information, and in the initial stages of the project Paul Quigley and his associates offered "customized guidance" and produced a project website for Mapping the Fourth (http://www.july4.civilwar.vt.edu). This effort has support from Virginia Tech and from the National Historical Records and Publications Commission of the National Archives.

Of course, bringing a coordinated approach to the analysis of separate databases is not dependent on crowd-sourcing, and historians are merging or coordinating different sources to gain a much fuller picture of particular people, developments, or events. One example is the large-scale project that

William G. Thomas undertook on railroads before and during the Civil War. Thomas combined data on the year-by-year expansion of railroad lines with census data on cotton production, slaveholding, farm values, investment in manufacturing, and other aspects of economic development and with information from military records, corporation documents, newspapers, and other publications to produce a number of online maps that show important changes over time.[6]

Some of Thomas's results contradicted what may have seemed conventional wisdom to those who assumed that industrial development and slavery were antithetical. For example, in Georgia heavy cotton production and railroads went hand in hand, and southeastern slave owners proved to be most numerous in belts served by the railroads. During the war years, Thomas also looked at guerrilla attacks and movement by slaves in conjunction with the railroads. Many of his findings are available online (http://railroads.unl.edu), and his project also produced a useful list (although it is now several years old) of digital projects around the nation (http://digitalhistory.unl.edu).[7]

The Nau Center for Civil War History at the University of Virginia has launched a digital project on the lives of African American men from Albemarle County. One of its strengths is bringing together information from many different sources. The project focuses on black men from that county who served in the US Army, and the goal is to develop a picture of their lives before, during, and after their military service. More than two hundred of these individuals have been identified so far, and because the goal of the project is so encompassing, it casts a wide and varied net for information. Records from the Adjutant General's Office, combined military service and pension records, letters and newspaper articles written by some of these black soldiers, records of later officeholding, and even Federal Writers' Project Slave Narratives are contributing to the first products of this initiative. There will be a website for the project to document the researchers' progress as findings accumulate.[8]

The variety of records that are being used to study Albemarle County's black soldiers suggests another kind of digital project that is useful. This type of project could be called a "total study" of a particular area (or, more colloquially, a "data dump")—an ambitious if geographically focused aggregation of data. We have already seen a fine example of this type of digital study in Edward Ayer's Valley of the Shadow project. Ayers and his coworkers collected government data (such as military records and both population and agricultural censuses) and an array of civilian sources (such as diaries, letters, newspapers, and even photographs) from the Shenandoah Valley in both Union and Confederate territory and used these many types of records to create a digital archive from which they produced books and articles and furthered their own research. But they also made this material available online to many others. The larger the aggregation of data, the greater the number of valuable studies that can be produced from multiple users of such a digital archive.[9]

Longitudinal studies can benefit greatly from the new opportunities for digitization. Analyzing change over time is a common definition of the historian's task, and there are many questions worth pursuing even in the relatively short period of the Civil War era. How did the age at first marriage, for example, change from the 1850s to the war years? How did marriage rates or the proportion of unmarried women change over time? Aggregated data that now are easier to search can help answer that kind of question. Dealing with an abundance of local records would have been difficult and discouraging in the past, but now it can be more manageable. How did landholdings and wealth, as measured by real and personal property in tax records, change in key areas, North and South, during the decades that bracket the Civil War? What happened to certain categories of people as the Civil War changed their lives and their futures?

Answering the latter question is a characteristic goal of longitudinal studies, and Stephen Berry and his collaborators are undertaking an ambitious study of the life histories of former slaves interviewed in the Federal Writers' Project Slave Narratives. Those Depression-era records have well-recognized value both for what we can learn about the experience of slavery and for what the former slaves said about events in their lives after the war. Recognizing that fact, the Library of Congress digitized the Slave Narratives collection and made it available online. But no systematic effort has been made to learn more about the individuals in that collection. Professor Berry points out that text mining, mapping technologies, and crowd-sourcing have created the possibility to learn much more about the former slaves—individuals who were part of "one of the most emblematic groups of Americans"—and even about their interviewers. With such an effort, it may be possible to illuminate the history and culture of Southern blacks as well as to learn about residential patterns in their postwar black communities and to create a database of historical place-names for future development.[10]

Using the addresses given for the interviewees, this project aspires to collect all the information possible about them, both through collaborative effort by scholars investigating traditional documentary sources and through crowd-sourced information from relatives, descendants, and interested citizens. The roughly 2,300 former slaves who were interviewed for the Slave Narratives project are too many for a single historian to study but a workable number for an ongoing, collaborative effort. The Slave Narratives project has given scholars more to work with than is usually the case: for millions of slaves, we have little more than a first name that may appear in plantation record books or the manuscript census. Many citizens are interested in the former slaves, and some of the grandchildren of these men and women are still alive and may be eager to share information. Thus, there is a good chance to learn more about the whole pattern of these former slaves' lives. By using the addresses given in the Federal Writers' Project interviews, the project can see not only how far the former slaves moved from their plantations but also what patterns may exist in terms of where they lived and worked.[11]

On that point, a particular advantage of digitization comes into play. Geospatial data from one project can be used in conjunction with other data sets, and it is easy to "layer" different sets of spatial information on top of each other. That is, information about residences or locations or economic activity, though drawn from different projects, can be superimposed upon the same map of a city or neighborhood. The spatial relationships inherent in such data then become clear, and the layering reveals new patterns from the aggregation of data. "Where cliometricians wanted to aggregate data to (definitively) answer old questions," Professor Berry observes, "today's digital humanists assemble spatial data in the hopes of asking new ones." By building some common elements into the design of the project, Berry will be able to use information from other projects undertaken for other purposes.[12]

Among the other projects that are already under way for the 1930s, there is one that seeks to map the location of Union veterans who joined the Grand Army of the Republic. Another, different project is using *The Negro Motorist Green Book* to map black business districts. Still a third project is charting the urban neighborhoods that were "redlined" or identified as poor risks for loans by the Home Owners' Loan Corporation in the 1930s. By superimposing those maps upon maps of the former slaves' residence at that time, Berry's project will be able to see if black and white veterans lived close together or far apart and whether the former slaves lived in the heart of a black district or more distant from it, in a redlined area or outside it. Without the layering of maps, it would be nearly impossible to acquire such information in any other way, and Berry identifies this ability to layer as a particular advantage of digital methodologies.

Mapping is a dramatic way to bring our visual faculties into play, and I feel that the visual results of projects are going to make a special contribution. Just as we are accustomed to the concept of various learning styles, we can appreciate different approaches for assimilating information. Visual information has an impact that is different from the impact of the written word, and in some ways it can be more intuitive, instructive, or powerful. When we say that a slave ran away from his plantation and reached a certain contraband camp, we have the basic facts about that journey. But when we see a map that places that trip in reference to state or county boundaries or geographical features, we sense the distance in a stronger way. For me, this seems to be true even if the escape is represented merely by a straight line connecting two points (rather than by the longer, more roundabout route that reality required). The powerful impact of visualization also is evident when a succession of maps reveals the change that occurred over time—change in population density or economic production or troop levels or support for a politician, for example.

Historians and software designers are finding new, effective ways to present information visually. The older conventions that relied on different levels of shading or various patterns of cross-hatching now seem quite old-fashioned, even quaint, and we probably will see new ideas for visual representation of data. Populations are being represented by circles of different size, each size corresponding to a quantity given on the legend. Events have been mapped effectively as dots or little starbursts or explosions, and varying the size of those markers can be used to indicate different levels of participation or injury or death. Depending on what needs to be indicated on a map, researchers can use today's technology to create irregular shapes that reveal the area in which a given phenomenon occurred. Visual markings of these types also can be combined with shadings on the map that indicate county-by-county levels of a relevant variable, whether it be voting or cotton production or epidemic illness. It is especially impressive when such maps, created for different months or years, are combined in a program that allows the viewer to move along a time line and *see* the changes that occurred as time passed. Following such changes has a different, less-dynamic quality when it is based solely on the reading of documents. It also is more difficult to sense from documents the geographical dimension of the change.

In earlier chapters, I have noted the importance of guerrilla violence during the Civil War. The aspect of guerrilla war that strikes us most strongly is usually its savage violence; guerrillas are remembered for their envenomed infliction of suffering or death in comparison to the organized killing en masse that took place when large armies confronted each other. But one historian, Andrew Failka, has argued that perhaps we overemphasize the irregular aspect of this kind of "irregular" warfare because we have not visualized it. We usually have focused on the cruelty of individual acts, he believes, rather than visualizing and seeing patterns within a larger spatial context.

Focusing on Missouri—a state that was famous, or infamous, for its guerrilla violence during the Civil War—Failka developed animated maps "created in ArcGIS and Neatline" to view the violence there over time. His software also allowed him to employ "synchronized timelines, zoom functions capable of transcending multiple scales, and the ability to embed packages of information onto the map." It was crucial to his study that he combined data about the activities of the guerrillas with information documenting the location and activities of Union occupiers during the war. The combination of data about opposing forces, when displayed in a visual way, revealed patterns where previously our interpretive emphasis had been on unpatterned and senseless violence.

Failka found that the instances and duration of Union occupation varied during the war. That variation was important because temporary or inconsistent occupation of towns and counties tended to destabilize the areas, whereas a permanent or continuous occupation by Union forces created pacified districts. At the beginning of the Civil War, most occupations were permanent rather than temporary, but as the war continued, more and more Union troops were transferred to other theaters of war. Temporary occupations then became much more frequent and, in fact, were the dominant pattern. Pro-Confederate guerrillas—however improvised or anarchical their actions seemed in a local context—targeted their violence at the Union army. Moreover, the spatial picture shows that they focused especially on areas of temporary occupation where Union troops were less numerous and on areas where Union policy had allowed the burning of homes or other acts affecting female family members in pro-Confederate households. What has seemed anarchical to some scholars followed an overall pattern: "instances of irregular violence occurred in predictable locations and against expected targets."

Failka's published spatiotemporal maps use different shadings by county to show the frequency of Union occupation or the number of instances of guerrilla violence in Missouri's counties. Circles of different sizes locate individual or multiple guerrilla attacks. The shading of counties in the state gives his maps a rather traditional look because we have often seen county-level maps that indicate which party won a particular election. But the overlap of Union occupations and Confederate guerrilla violence in the mapped counties is revealing and convincing. It visually illustrates his conclusion about the overall pattern of guerrilla violence. In a further argument against the perception of guerrilla violence as uncontrolled or senseless, he points out that most guerrillas, in contrast to the well-known exceptions such Jesse and Frank James, surrendered once the Confederate army no longer existed to offer support or hope for a victorious outcome.[13]

Different spatiotemporal maps with a more unusual and innovative look appear in another project dealing with the Union army's presence in the South, Mapping Occupation: Force, Freedom, and the Army in Reconstruction, by Gregory P. Downs and Scott Nesbit. It is a very large-scale, web-mounted piece of research, covering the entire South and the years of Reconstruction, and the valuable information in it is available for other researchers to use as they create their own narratives with the curated data. Professor Downs gathered an immense amount of information on the Union army and its presence in the Southern states. The website where the study is described (http://mappingoccupation.org) provides that information in an expanded and downloadable form along with visual estimates of where troops might have been able to make their presence known in a reasonable time period and where freed people would have been able to reach the potentially supportive Union forces. (The two spatial estimates are different because former slaves usually walked, whereas soldiers might be mounted on horseback or traveling at times by train.) Information on the website specifies the assumptions made in order to develop these estimates.

The scope of this project is large and impressive. The maps contain information about the number of US troops, whether they were infantry or cavalry, and the race of the units; the location of railroad lines; the percentage of blacks in the population by county for 1870 and 1880; the way counties voted in four elections; and the reach of army influence and its accessibility to African Americans. Information technology experts at the

University of Georgia guided and assisted in developing interactive capabilities in the maps, using "the Esri [Environmental Systems Research Institute] suite of software products, especially ArcGIS online and the StoryMap software." As a result, the visual information is very rich. The user can enlarge maps for closer scrutiny of a particular area or shrink them to grasp more clearly an overall pattern. He or she also can choose what information to display or to hide and—perhaps most revealing of all—can move a pointer along a time line from May 1865 to December 1880 and note visually how all the information about US troops changes. Thus, it is easy to see how and where the military presence increased or decreased during the Reconstruction years *and* how that presence reflected or departed from the location and density of the black population. With data mapped in this way over time, the generalizations that we all have read about "military reconstruction" suddenly seem overly general and imprecise. Moreover, the changes visible on the maps suggest questions to pursue or new directions for research.[14]

Because the data for this project are available to all and can be downloaded, and because Professor Downs explains the assumptions underlying his estimates about the scope of US troop influence and the access of freed people to US assistance, other scholars can scrutinize or dispute or confirm his interpretations. The effective visual presentation of this website inspires further research, and the wealth of data available through it makes undertaking new research much easier. In these respects, it is a model for future digital humanities mapping projects, along with the earlier Visualizing Emancipation project, of which Scott Nesbit is codirector along with Edward Ayers.

Visualizing Emancipation focuses on the places and time periods in which emancipation actually occurred during the Civil War. Whereas our verbal descriptions tend to treat emancipation as a single event and to lump together all the ways in which it occurred, this website (http://dsl.richmond.edu/emancipation/) makes it very plain to the user that the end of slavery came about haltingly and unevenly throughout the South. The project collects and displays an enormous amount of data, but by placing data on a map and giving the user the ability to choose what types of data are displayed, Visualizing Emancipation is a very usable website.

Aided by undergraduate researchers, the project started by amassing data from standard sources such as *The War of the Rebellion,* Ira Berlin's multivolume collection *Freedom: A Documentary History of Emancipation,*

Frederick Dyer's *A Compendium of the War of the Rebellion,* and the Making of America project begun by the University of Michigan and Cornell University. It also built upon earlier digital humanities efforts (such as the Edward Ayer's Valley of the Shadow project). After collecting information on more than 3,000 emancipation events in various locations, the project classified each event as one of ten different types. These types ranged from positive experiences, such as runaways who reached Union lines, to negative ones, such as abuse of African Americans or their recapture by Confederates. As is true for the Downs/Nesbit project Mapping Occupation, use of this website can encourage further research by other scholars, and Nesbit invites other historians and the general public to contribute additional information about emancipation events.

Such sophisticated and impressive websites depend on a significant amount of support and expertise. The Visualizing Emancipation project benefited from information technology experts at the University of Richmond and used both open-source applications and technology and the services of a private company that specializes in creating geographic web software. Other help came from work that had been done at Tufts University, which digitized Dyer's *Compendium,* and from Harvard University, whose Center for Geographic Analysis made available the mapped location of Civil War–era railroads. The project also needed significant amounts of money, which came from grants from the National Endowment for the Humanities and the University of Richmond, and it is clear that such large-scale, ambitious efforts cannot go forward without external financial support and the cooperation of scholars who are ready to share both information and finished digital humanities projects.[15]

As exciting as these websites that have mapped human actions and movement are, they do not represent the totality of valuable digital work in the humanities. It is very likely that we are going to see additional research that focuses on the results of human activity rather than the actions of people themselves. Economic developments and changes are unquestionably important, and all sorts of economic information is being digitized. It thus becomes available for researchers to use, however the results of their investigations might be presented. A revealing way to evaluate the results of human activity is to focus on land use. Historians who want to study population changes, urbanization, environmental effects, and agricultural patterns will be able to exploit the abundant data now available on land use through time.

Although much of this chapter has focused on some of the most ambitious and visually impressive digital humanities projects, it remains true that digitization is going to aid Civil War historians in many less-noticeable but nevertheless important ways. Perhaps the best example of a less-visible but valuable technique made possible by digitization is text mining or text analytics. In the business world and in national security organizations, the tools of text analytics have become very sophisticated, and perhaps such tools will aid future historical research. But it also is true that simple aspects of text mining can prove very helpful to historians. One of the greatest advantages of digitization is that it is putting at our computer keyboards a doorway to many large and valuable collections of documents, such as long runs of newspapers or year-by-year debates of legislative bodies. In addition, the better-funded libraries of the nation are putting the text of manuscript collections online for use in historical studies. This expansion of readily available primary materials is a great boon, but it could take months or years for a person to read through large collections of documents. With text mining, though, even the simplest techniques can be very helpful. By tagging certain names or noun phrases, one can quickly obtain a kind of index that will greatly simplify the search for material relevant to a given research problem. Tagging names can take the researcher to historical actors under study, and noun phrases, if well chosen, can aid research on concepts that mattered. Moreover, such text mining promises to be more complete and accurate than some of the indexes that were prepared years ago by human beings for, say, a newspaper such as the *New York Times.*

Somewhat more advanced uses of text mining or text analytics are already proving useful to historians. With appropriate software, it is possible to search large databases for mention of key actors *and* those persons to whom they were connected. Such a search will lead to identification of networks within which the individuals whom we want to study actually worked and communicated. In this way, the research broadens from a single individual to the associates in his or her endeavors. The historian's analysis thus may encompass a larger group, illuminate its role, and become more deeply based. Other relationships can be probed through text analytics, and even the feelings of those who wrote about a topic can be identified by computer programs. Software for all of these functions is available both from private vendors and in open-source formats. Such free applications will encourage greater use by historians.

I will be surprised if the various tools of digital humanities research are not put to work in the future to study Civil War soldiers in greater depth. The public's fascination with soldiers and military history does not seem to be diminishing, and the national government and the states have published rosters, service records, and much additional useful material about troops and their units. These abundant collections of data can be studied in conjunction with census records, tax records, election results, price data, and other information to give us a more complete and interesting picture of soldiers and the challenges that they and their families faced. What characteristics describe early volunteers in both the North and the South or deserters in the various armies? Does the assumed influence of membership in a unit composed of one's neighbors stand up to thorough analysis? What effect did the experience of moving about the country as a soldier have on a man's later decisions about where to live and how to make a living?

The potential advantages of digital humanities are great, and it may prove to be the case that the next generation of Civil War historians will publish many kinds of studies that simply did not exist twenty years ago. This area is growing and building momentum, but it seems obvious that a few key practices or principles need to guide the expansion of digital humanities research if we are to see the maximum benefits. I think a list of desirable practices would include at least the following:

- *Cooperation and sharing among historians involved in digital research.* In some of the most impressive projects that have already been completed, we have seen that scholars have been able to use the base maps or digitized documents originally produced by other historians. This has greatly simplified and speeded their work, and it makes good sense for everyone. The leaders in the field have set a fine example by inviting contributions of data and by sharing digitized products with others. The generosity of scholars in the field of history is one of the finest aspects of our profession, and by continuing this practice, everyone will encourage progress in areas of digital humanities.
- *Voluntary standardization of key databases and tools.* Sharing depends on the compatibility of base maps, platforms, and some tools or software. At present, a great many ideas and products are being developed, and some of the most desirable, useful software may not yet have been developed. But as the field matures, it will be highly desirable for researchers to settle upon and use the same kind of databases or tools as much as possible in order to speed progress for everyone.

- *A registry of digital humanities projects.* This is a vital means to enhance cooperation. Some of our best researchers have set out to design projects and then found that other researchers are at work in ways that can be beneficial. This phenomenon is particularly evident in the layering that works so well in mapping historical data. To design the best project, wouldn't it be helpful to know what other scholars are doing? If some university or organization would offer to be the record keeper for a comprehensive list of projects, it would benefit everyone.
- *A repository for digitized documents, databases, and projects.* Having such a repository would facilitate the adoption and incorporation of earlier work. Fortunately, there is already in existence an excellent candidate to fulfill this role: the Inter-university Consortium for Political and Social Research at the University of Michigan. It has long been helpful and interested in curating and maintaining computerized research.
- *Increased digitization by libraries, universities, and other organizations.* Greater digitization seems to be happening as a widely accepted practice, but we should continue to encourage it, and fund-raising will often be necessary to support expansion of services into this area.
- *Development of open-source software.* Not every scholar or project will have the ability to purchase useful software for digital research, and therefore it is important that open-source tools continue to develop and advance. Many of these tools may come from information technology staff at universities, but one hopes that participation will be widespread.
- *Increased funding for digital humanities research.* The major grant-giving agencies have already recognized the importance of digital research. To encourage the growth of digital humanities grants, we need to advocate not only for historical and humanities research but also for research in all areas of knowledge. We cannot assume that the politicians are going to recognize and act upon the importance to society of giving broad-based support to research.

Surely with progress along these lines, the prospects are bright for digital research on the Civil War era.

6

Environmental Approaches to the Civil War

Like the new research in digital humanities, environmental history has created excitement among scholars and offers approaches that can be highly valuable for Civil War studies. For a long time, historians have been aware that the military contest had an impact on the physical environment, although in the past they generally did not pursue all the implications of such an impact. In other ways, scholars have sometimes noted the role of the environment in influencing and affecting civilians or soldiers. Practitioners of environmental history now challenge us to pursue more energetically the interactions of people and the environment and not merely in an obvious or superficial manner. Environmental historians insist that the physical world is an actor in historical events. In fact, they sometimes broaden the definition of the term *environment* to embrace much of the traditional stuff of history. For example, Douglas Sackman writes, "In some of the most illuminating studies, the environment is viewed not as a thing but as a set of relationships under ongoing construction; matters of perception, political economy, and the dynamics of living ecosystems are viewed together, using interdisciplinary approaches."[1]

However we define the limits of environmental history, it is clear that this approach can benefit study of the Civil War in many ways, for the consequences of the interactions between people and environment radiated in many directions during the war. There is much to be gained by investigating the ways in which the environment affected human activities in wartime, and there is no doubt that people affected the physical environment, usually in a destructive fashion. We can also probe how these interactions had additional direct and indirect effects.

For example, there were direct effects on the economy, on people's perceptions and attitudes, and on agriculture and livestock. Less directly, but still in an important manner, there were effects on such things as patterns of economic development and government policies toward the West. Scholars have noted that reactions to the environmental damage of the Civil War encouraged the birth of preservation efforts. This chapter surveys, with examples, some of the work that can be done or is under way through an environmental approach to the Civil War.

Seeing the environment as an actor in events has been common in military history in some respects. Geography and terrain often played a decisive role in certain battles. One obvious example was the battle of Fredericksburg, where Union troops who were trying to advance uphill against entrenched Confederates on Marye's Hill suffered such enormous and predictable casualties that some called it butchery. The defenders of Cemetery Ridge at Gettysburg similarly profited from a very advantageous position against General George Pickett's charging Confederates, and near Richmond in 1862 Union forces enjoyed the high ground against their Confederate foes at Malvern Hill. After the battle for Malvern Hill, General Daniel Hill described the heavy Confederate losses by saying, "It was not war. It was murder." Military historians usually are attentive to the effects of geography.[2]

But weather, too, is an important part of the environment, as some scholars have shown. Kenneth Noe studied eighty-two battles with an eye to identify the effects of weather—heat, cold, rain, floods, and other factors. He found that in sixteen of the eighty-two encounters, weather played a decisive role, and in thirty-three other battles its effect was significant. Civil War soldiers also suffered from drought, and sometimes thirsty units ran into each other while they were searching for sources of water. Tim Silver has shown that rain and drought and other weather conditions contributed to suffering and the spread of disease in camps of induction in North Carolina. Commanders committed a serious error if they did not take into account the impact of weather conditions.[3]

Nor should we overlook the effect of weather and climate on the fighting men's psychological condition and battle readiness. No less a military expert than Robert E. Lee believed that the torrid heat and humidity of the lower Mississippi Valley would frustrate or delay Union efforts against Vicksburg. Combined with disease, such weather could be both mentally and physically debilitating. Union general Samuel Curtis, commanding the Department of the Missouri, tried to aid the capture of Vicksburg by sending expeditions along the Arkansas River and the Mississippi River and its tributaries. His soldiers accomplished little because the locale and its weather defeated them in both energy and spirit. "Curtis's soldiers," writes Daniel Sutherland, "already in a vile mood, cursed the swampy Arkansas delta unsparingly: the foulest place on earth, they called it. Flies, gnats, and mosquitoes tormented them. Bad drinking water bred sickness. Malaria, typhoid, and chronic diarrhea left no more than two-thirds of the army available for duty between August 1862 and February 1863."[4]

Disease was a potent part of the environment's influence on the Civil War, as shown by the fact that in both armies more men died of disease than from wounds suffered in battle. Army surgeons spread infection through lack of sanitation and use of unclean scalpels and saws, but still more men died from bacteria-induced illness. In camps of instruction, soldiers unwittingly shared diseases from their home counties, and infantry encampments often became incubation centers for communicable diseases. Dysentery, typhoid fever, and other water-borne illnesses took a heavy toll and caused much suffering among those who survived them. Malaria, spread by mosquitoes in the South, was also a serious problem that afflicted thousands of Northern and Southern soldiers. These men carried this debilitating condition with them once the war was over.

The lack of understanding of what became the germ theory of disease and the failure to require proper sanitary conditions in camps caused many deaths and left large portions of both armies in a weakened condition. Parts of Virginia, including the beautiful Shenandoah Valley, became in 1862 "more like sprawling latrines to the hundreds of thousands of humans who hunkered down to make war. Regiments and their horses rapidly fouled the water supplying encampments, and, in the worst cases, piled trash high between the rows of their tents, forming transitory urban slums." The fact that both armies brought large numbers of men together in camps almost inevitably caused the spread of disease. Measles and mumps "rendered nearly half of some newly-formed Confederate regiments unfit for battle in 1861." The dirt and hardships of soldiering caused most men to suffer from body lice, which could be the hosts for typhus and other fevers. Many soldiers also took advantage of opportunities to visit the prostitutes who congregated around army camps, and Union army records show that venereal disease affected at least eighty-two of every thousand soldiers.[5]

Despite the appearance of a number of recent studies focused on disease and medical care, there is room for further investigation of the role of disease in the Civil War. The wives and families of those soldiers who contracted venereal disease found that their lives, too, were affected by the war's health crisis. The suffering and deaths of civilians in general has been an understudied topic. Yet we know that many noncombatants lived near mass graves or obtained their water supply from streams that flowed by military camps or received the runoff from such areas. The spread of disease due to wartime events deserves more attention, as does its postwar impact on both the men who fought and their families.

In a similar fashion, other environmental factors affected civilian society in important ways and had a major impact on the outcome of the Civil War. The South fought the war during a period of extended drought that had serious effects on crop yields. A number of Confederate governors pleaded repeatedly with the Richmond administration to suspend conscription or to send aid to parts of their state where the crops were "short" due to drought. That shortage meant hunger, which became a serious problem in Confederate society before the end of 1862, and weather-related problems of crop production contributed to bread riots and suffering, which had important consequences for morale and politics. For the South, the onset of war also meant that important supplies of meat that traditionally came from the Midwest were not going to be available. When extreme cold in the winter of 1863–1864 killed up to 50 percent of the cattle in Texas, Southern civilians and soldiers had to live with another major blow to their supply of meat. Thus, weather proved very important to the region's serious shortage of food.[6]

There may be a greater appreciation of the fact that human beings affected the environment during the Civil War because we remember striking facts, such as the way that soldiers' bullets cut through trees in some intense battles. But few of us have grasped the extent of human damage to the environment. Consider, for example, the effect on forests. Soldiers in the field had many uses for wood—to build forts, fires, and breastworks or to construct winter quarters, bridges, and corduroy roads—and they didn't hesitate to take wood wherever they found it. The attitude of the men whom war had snatched from their normal lives and thrown into dangerous surroundings seemed to be that they had every right to take whatever they needed. Both Northern and Southern troops stole fence rails to use as firewood, and the collective scale of such action was shocking. "In November 1862," Joan Cashin writes, "Private Anthony W. Ross estimated that each man in his regiment of ten thousand, the Seventy-third Ohio Volunteer Infantry, burned an average of five rails daily, or a total of fifty thousand rails every day." Wherever armies traveled, they seized wood in every direction and could completely strip large areas. "For a distance of two miles along the Tennessee River near Nashville, and a mile and a half into the interior on each bank, [F]ederal troops cut down every tree and tore down every fence for fire wood."[7]

From the start of the war, both the Union and Confederate armies "practiced what is now called 'clear-cutting'" because it was most efficient for them to chop down every tree to gain the wood they needed. Sometimes they denuded large areas in order to build forts or winter quarters or to create an open space that deprived the enemy of cover. When "the U.S. army cleared land to build Fort Rosecrans," states Cashin, it destroyed a forest "some two hundred acres in size, located north of Murfreesboro, Tennessee." To protect themselves from winter weather, troops cut down trees in order to build huts or cabins and to gain firewood. One Federal soldier whose unit "camped near Fredericksburg, Virginia, estimated that the army used up to two hundred acres of pine that winter [1862–1863] to build their quarters and fuel their camp fires." In Louisiana, troops who wanted more comfortable accommodations stripped the boughs from trees to carpet their tents. When units left their winter quarters to resume campaigning, the soldiers often burned the wooden buildings they had constructed. All of this was in addition to the fact that in major battles "the armies wreaked tremendous damage on the forest in a single day."[8]

By the beginning of 1863, writes Cashin, "outright deforestation was under way in many parts of the" South. A journalist "described Stafford County as a wasteland with no forest and no vegetation, only blackened, well-trodden earth," due to the Union army's construction of forts in Virginia. At the end of the war, "long stretches of land in North Carolina were stripped of pine forests, the fields empty, without a fence in sight, according to a Yankee journalist who called the landscape 'awful' to behold." Such deforestation had many effects. It "killed off wildlife—mammals, birds, amphibians, and fish," and if clear-cutting occurred in hilly or mountainous areas, it led to extensive erosion. Near Chattanooga, Tennessee, "the [F]ederal army cut down most of the timber in the fall of 1863," with the result that topsoil silted up many streams.[9]

The erosion caused by deforestation damaged the land's fertility by carrying away valuable topsoil. Cashin points out that deforestation also "created the perfect conditions for oceans of mud. Since mature trees of different species can suck up a hundred gallons of water from the soil daily, the destruction of thousands of trees left the earth saturated with moisture. From the first winter of the war, mudbaths appeared wherever large number of soldiers camped." When more rain fell, human beings and draft animals could become lodged in the mire. In some places, horses "sank up to their shoulders in mud holes, and mules drowned in [the holes] as shocked onlookers watched."[10]

Deforestation and destruction on such a scale merit further analysis. It is true, of course, that trees will eventually grow back, and in the postwar period some observers were pleased to see how soon some damage seemed to disappear. But there remain questions about what species of trees or plants replaced the original vegetation and what difference that may have made for the use of the land and the diversity of the ecosystem. Human beings also may have altered their plans or practices after armies changed the landscape, and changing human activity would have had an impact on both the environment and economic output.

Another question that deserves attention is the environmental damage caused by pollution of water sources. The poor sanitation of army encampments and the rapid burials of slain soldiers, horses, and mules created the conditions for serious health and environmental problems. Kathryn Shively Meier found that battle-scarred areas of Virginia in 1862 "looked and felt ominous" as "the bodies of men and animals slain in battle polluted soil and air" as well as water.[11] As erosion fed into streams, it probably had a serious impact on fish, amphibians, and other animals that lived in or depended on the water courses. How this pollution affected the ecology of southern regions has not been studied. Although it might be difficult, it would be important to try to assess the effect of polluted water supplies on the noncombatant population as well. The scope and cause of civilian deaths in the Civil War is a little-understood topic that needs more attention. We know that water-borne diseases took a heavy toll in the nineteenth-century United States, so the impact of soldiers' treatment of forests and streams most likely had far-reaching consequences.

Troops usually cut down trees without more purpose than to meet an immediate need, but at times the armies undertook ambitious plans to change nature. Some Union commanders initially assumed that "to defeat the South it was necessary to master its nature, to dominate, control, and comprehend its landscapes." Experience with nature on the lower Mississippi River in 1862 forced some alteration of these attitudes as "two Union armies tried to change the course of the river, but failed." General John Pope's men dug a canal around Island Number 10, which enabled them to move farther south, encircle the Confederates, and force them to surrender. Admiral David Farragut and General Benjamin Butler had no such luck when they tried to divert the Mississippi away from Vicksburg. Although they put eleven hundred African American laborers to work for weeks cutting down trees and digging a path through a bayou, cave-ins and falling water frustrated their plans. Then General Ulysses S. Grant tried to cut a new waterway around Vicksburg, but nature also frustrated his efforts. The power of the Mississippi waterway and its environment was such that commanders had to learn how to work with it instead of against it.[12]

The power of nature also challenged military operations along the Confederate coastline. Southern commanders had to put large numbers of their men and impressed laborers to work constructing earthen forts that in many places were enormous in size. The amount of soil and sand that men moved was tremendous in places such as Fort Fisher in North Carolina. Perhaps similar projects took place all along the coast, from Charleston to Mobile and westward. These man-made alterations of the coastline could affect the action of currents and tides, washing away barriers or changing the shore still more. The environmental effects of the scores of ships that were sunk, on purpose or in battle, in coastal rivers and estuaries also need to be considered.

In a crucial area necessary for human survival, the armies interfered deeply with the power of nature. Soldiers and commanders dealt a heavy blow to the South's already threatened food supply, both through individuals' decisions and sometimes according to strategic plans.

As Joan Cashin's work and earlier studies have demonstrated, there quickly developed in the Confederacy an ominous competition between soldiers and civilians for food. Armies, it is said, march and fight on their stomachs, and the men in both armies seemed to believe that they had a right to be adequately fed. The South proved unable to supply its troops effectively, but it is less well recognized that the Union's supply system also was inefficient and unreliable. As a result, Civil War soldiers began to seize food from the residents of areas where either army was operating. In both armies, men ignored regulations that barred the taking of food except under conditions of absolute necessity. When Union general John Pope gave an order in 1862 to seize food from Virginia residents, Southern politicians loudly protested about a turn to barbarous treatment of civilians.

But Joan Cashin shows that Southern commanders paid little attention to the controversy because both armies were already accustomed to doing that very thing in practice.[13]

Seizures of food by the armies became a constant and increasingly heavy burden on civilians. Even in the first winter of the war, many Southerners were worrying about having enough to eat, but the Southern military had to impress food to feed its troops. The Confederacy eventually passed an impressment law designed to provide for reimbursement of food that was taken. It also enacted a tax in kind, claiming 10 percent of farmers' nonperishable crops in a desperate effort to reinforce its faltering supply system. Despite these efforts, Confederate soldiers frequently went hungry, and civilians' suffering grew. One factor that made the taking of food especially problematic was the reality that armies were not evenly spread over the landscape; fighting often tended to concentrate in certain areas, and those neighborhoods suffered renewed demands on the food supply.

By the fall of 1862, soldiers began reporting food deserts—areas where the food supply was exhausted. The Confederate army also reduced the daily rations for its soldiers. It was clear by that point that agriculture was not going to be the enormous strength for the Confederacy that white Southerners had expected. In addition to confiscation of food by both armies, high prices, short supplies, loss of territory, transportation problems, and unfavorable weather were among the problems that only increased as the war dragged on. The relationship between agriculture and military strength was one of the most crucial ties between the battlefield and the home front.[14]

A shortage of food obviously would have serious repercussions not just for the army but for civilian society and its politics as well. Local and state governments in the South tried to find ways to relieve suffering in the population, and the programs they undertook were based on the recognition that a substantial minority of the white population was in need. But the Confederate government never provided much aid and, in fact, competed with local relief efforts. The army simply was demanding too much food. Southern civilians stopped cooperating with their soldiers and resorted to hiding the food supplies. Resentment among ordinary people increased as word spread that food that was meant for the armies oftentimes rotted alongside railroad depots and never reached the troops. By 1863, soldiers began to talk of starvation, and the mayor of Columbia, South Carolina, estimated that 150 people died of starvation after his town was burned in 1865. Although we have no reliable studies of starvation in the Confederacy, and although historians may have ignored or de-emphasized this topic, Cashin notes that "instances of actual starvation . . . appear in the historical record."[15]

As the Union's "hard war" became more intense in the last two years of the conflict, the environmental effects were striking. During his operations against Vicksburg, General Ulysses S. Grant learned that his forces could live off the land, which encouraged him and General William Tecumseh Sherman to think of raids on a large scale. With the March to the Sea, Sherman carried out an assault on the environment of the South with the aim of destroying the physical as well as psychological resources that sustained the Southern war effort. His army tore up railroad lines and dismantled factories, but what may have been even more important was that it devastated Georgia's "agroecological system." Sherman's troops left behind them a wide burned district where they had destroyed crops and slaughtered livestock. By turning farms into a "waste," Sherman "attacked and destroyed the agroecological system on which the Confederacy and its citizens relied and hastened the end of the conflict."[16]

Animals are another important dimension of the environmental story of the Civil War. Some of the first landmark studies in environmental history emphasized the importance of the interchange of nonhuman living things when cultures or civilizations collide. Alfred Crosby's book *The Colombian Exchange: Biological and Cultural Consequences of 1492* is by now a famous example of a study of the transfer and spread of plants, animals, and microbes. Human explorers and colonizers of the Western Hemisphere changed the biological environment and thus changed people and societies. Stephen Berry has pointed out that the same phenomenon occurred in the Civil War as soldiers carried into unfamiliar regions not only their germs but also the horses and mules that provided transportation as well as the cattle and hogs that supplied them with meat. "The Civil War was a massive stir of the biotic soup," writes Berry, "and in many ways *that stir,* more than the battles themselves was the story of the war."[17]

Therefore, it is important to examine the animal side of this environmental story, and historians are beginning to find not only that the effects on animal life were enormous but also that these effects had far-reaching implications for human society. Hogs, horses, and cattle suffered from the war's "stir of the biotic soup" when communicable diseases had devastating effects on these animal populations. What affected the animals then had some deep or lasting impacts on the human population and society.

Cattle fever was an ancient disease that came to North America in the seventeenth century. Spanish explorers and colonists imported cattle from the West Indies to Mexico, and the disease came with the newly introduced animals. Subsequently it spread to parts of the United States. Cattle fever is caused by a parasite that attacks the red blood cells of its host, and it was not understood until after the Civil War that this parasite was transmitted by ticks. When cattle today are "dipped" or forced to go through a bath at stockyards, the purpose is to kill any ticks they may be carrying. Because the South's supply of beef was modest to begin with and then reduced when midwestern supplier states remained in the Union, cattle fever could severely threaten the Confederacy's sources of meat. It did exactly that. The disease arrived in eastern parts of the Confederacy from Texas and soon began to have a severe effect on herds. By the end of the war, it, along with hog cholera, "may have killed half the livestock in Virginia."[18]

The threat to horses came from a disease known as glanders. Caused by a bacterium, glanders is a highly infectious disease that can affect donkeys and mules as well as horses—thus, all the thousands of pack animals used by the armies were at risk. Glanders affects the mucous membranes and respiratory tract and can lead to death in a matter of days. Because it is spread through infected water or feed, the conditions of wartime aided its transmission and spread. Both armies brought together horses from many sources and stabled them or penned them up in close quarters. Thus, one sick animal was soon able to spread the disease to others. As early as 1861, this disease was becoming a problem for the military.

Though glanders affected horses in the Union army as well as those in Confederate forces, its impact on the South was much greater. A large portion of the horses and mules of slaveholding states were in the border states that did not join the Confederacy. Thus, Southerners had fewer horses from the beginning, and they also found fewer suppliers from which to buy horses. As a result, the army often took animals from Southern farms, where they were vital for plowing. That policy had a negative effect on the productivity of Southern agriculture, which aggravated the food shortage. Then glanders began to reduce the number of horses that the army had obtained, which made it more difficult to carry supplies with a marching army or to equip cavalry units. The shortage of horses contributed directly to the declining effectiveness of the Confederate cavalry, which most observers feel was superior to its Union counterpart at the beginning of the war. "For want of animals and provisions," however, "the Confederate cavalry slowly withered away. By the time of the southern surrender, Grant had more horses in the field than Lee had men."[19]

To discuss the impacts of these animal diseases as a wartime phenomenon alone ignores the long-term problems they caused. Once established in various regions of the South, cattle fever and glanders were not easy to eradicate. Agriculturists in the nineteenth century did not have a cure for these diseases. The nature of some of the bacteria or viruses that killed livestock allowed them to persist in the environment for months, even without a host. Decades would pass before modern science understood these animal diseases and found ways to restrict or wipe them out. In the meantime, Southern agriculture continued to suffer in the postwar years.

Hog cholera was a prime example of all these difficulties, and it may have had the most extensive, long-lasting effect on Southern agriculture, farm families, and even a key aspect of the organization of Southern agriculture—the open range or "commons." Virtually unknown in the antebellum South outside of Kentucky and Tennessee, hog cholera (or classical swine fever in modern terminology) was a devastating, highly contagious hemorrhagic fever. Its cause is an RNA virus that affects many types of tissues—from skin and lungs to kidneys and intestines—simultaneously. After a fairly short incubation period, the disease can kill up to 70 percent of infected animals, and "if a hog survives, lifelong immunity is conferred although seldom do the pigs return to full health." In the United States, this dangerous malady was not eradicated until 1978, and agricultural experts still fear its possible reemergence.[20]

The introduction and spread of deadly hog cholera had a clear connection to the two armies' movements and practices. In both cases, the military collected hogs from various locations and brought them together with other animals in order to have meat for the soldiers. By mixing many animals together, either in depots or wagon trains or aboard trains, the armies unwittingly provided the conditions in which one infected animal could spread the disease to others through blood, secretions, or excretions. In addition to direct contact, the virus spread through the soil, where it could persist for several months even without contact with a new host. Union soldiers had a more organized system of depots and stockyards that sometimes held thousands of animals, but the more informal Confederate practice of gathering up animals and taking them on the march had the same unfortunate result.

There is abundant evidence to indicate that it was military procurement of the animals that spread hog cholera. In 1861, for example, Confederate sympathizers in southern Missouri rounded up hogs from local farms and drove them to a Confederate supply depot near Batesville, Arkansas. That depot in 1862 was the origin of an epidemic of hog cholera "that devastated herds throughout that state." Similarly, General Kirby Smith, on his transfer from the Army of East Tennessee to the Trans-Mississippi Department, "took a wagon train southward from Kentucky that allegedly stretched 40 miles and contained over 8,000 live hogs." Before long, farmers in Mississippi and Louisiana were blaming infected swine from Kentucky for a serious outbreak in their states. In one Louisiana county, three-fourths of the hogs died. Northwest Georgia experienced an outbreak in 1863 "brought in by a shipment of hogs for the support of the Confederate Army." All Confederate armies on the march tended to seize hogs from one area and take them to another. This practice simply multiplied the chances of spreading the infection to new areas. Erin Mauldin has noted the irony that "in the Confederacy the acquisition of hogs and their transport actually *harmed* livestock production over the course of the war."

Hog cholera's impact on agriculture and the environment was severe during the war, when Southerners in and out of uniform went hungry. In 1965, Paul Gates concluded that this disease, by reducing Southerners' supply of meat, had a larger impact than all other diseases that affected people or animals. In addition, it severely affected agriculture for decades thereafter. "Because of the war, hog cholera became endemic in the South." In many states long after the war, epidemics occurred every two years. This recurrence stimulated later scientific researchers to try to find the cause and cure of the disease, but it also contributed to a major change in Southern agricultural practice—the closing of the open range.[21]

Although the North had adopted a livestock industry based on the fencing or containment of animals grown for food, Southern tradition was different. From first settlement in the Chesapeake, Southerners had allowed their pigs and other animals to roam free, feeding themselves in the forests or the "commons"—any uncultivated, unfenced area. Only crops were fenced in to protect them from animals. The traditional practice of an open range was valued by many landless whites, nonslaveholders, and small farmers, who also liked to hunt in the woods. But as some Southern areas moved toward a more intensive commercial agriculture, fencing crops began to be more expensive and time consuming, and by the 1840s some older areas were discussing fence laws to end the open range. Such laws were attractive to wealthy farmers but not to their poorer neighbors, who benefited from allowing their livestock to feed on other people's land. Thus, a conflict developed over fence laws and the closing of the commons, as Steven Hahn discusses in *The Roots of Southern Populism.*[22]

That conflict played out over a few decades, reaching into the postwar period, and a number of factors aided the advocates of fence laws. But one influence was the problem of hog cholera that the Civil War had introduced into the Southern environment. Outbreaks of hog cholera had followed upon the transport of hogs from other areas to places such as Arkansas, Louisiana, and Georgia, and reformers assumed that closing the Southern commons could break the thread of transmission. Thus, "hog cholera clearly provided a 'medical' reason for penning stock," which also meant "the destruction of a key subsistence practice in the South." The closing of the open range was a fundamental change in Southern social and agricultural practice. Erin Mauldin has pointed out that it is related to the environmental history of the Civil War.[23]

In this way, the wartime disease environment among livestock was connected to a series of changes in agriculture that deeply affected society. The closing of the open range added pressure on Southern farmers to enter the market and become commercial farmers, which, in turn, had implications for agricultural practices and the environment. As participants in the market economy, small farmers had to vary their crop mix. Instead of producing first for the needs of their families and as a second priority growing a modest amount of something marketable in order to obtain some cash, farmers now gave priority to a market crop. Giving up their family-first strategy meant that they became dependent for subsistence on the earnings from those crops they sold. In a few regions, their principal market crop may have been wheat or some other foodstuff, but in most of the South it was cotton. To grow more cotton, many agriculturists turned to the use of fertilizers, thus changing the use of the land and the previous mix of crops. Moreover, as postwar prices of cotton fell, the individual farmer usually decided to boost his income by growing more cotton, only to find that the price fell further.

Thus, a wartime, war-produced livestock disease, such as hog cholera, became part of a connected string of developments that affected the environment while also contributing to important social and political changes. The closing of the open range affected the lifestyles and economic strategies of many Southerners, and their subsequent immersion in the market economy led to problems of debt and tenancy. Those problems were among the sources of the Populist revolt, which had its own important political and racial legacies. Environmental history here became part of a long, varied, and large story.

In addition, we should note that livestock diseases of the war period, taken together, had a major impact on Southern agriculture and social classes. For nonslaveholders, the drastic losses in livestock were a financial disaster because much of their financial security and family sustenance had been tied up with the health of their animals. Slaveholders lost a great deal of their wealth due to emancipation, but the economic reverses suffered by ordinary Southern whites were of equal importance. The decline in their well-being had potential impacts for the Southern class system and its discontents. In this way, we can see that an environmental issue became relevant to many other topics and had repercussions in many directions.

In this sense, Douglas Sackman's sweeping definition of the environment has suggestive value. Instead of viewing the environment as a place or a physical setting with associated weather conditions, animal life, and natural processes, Sackman describes it as "a set of relationships under ongoing construction." He then extends that idea to include "matters of perception, political economy, and the dynamics of living ecosystems."[24] If we take the prewar environment as our starting point and then consider how wartime events changed relationships among all the parts of the environment, we can identify possible changes in perceptions, attitudes, and human practices related to politics and economics. Such an approach would open up new areas for scholarly exploration.

A number of historians have already begun exploring the war's influence on attitudes about nature, progress, and the environment. On the one hand, many Americans were shaken by the vast amount of destruction inflicted on the physical environment. Aaron Sachs has argued that the loss of life and the damage to the land darkened prevailing ideas about progress. Human beings had not moved forward, and their assault on nature undermined a previously held faith in the ability of wilderness to heal spiritual wounds. Lisa Brady concludes that a new and negative understanding of wilderness came into being—wilderness as a wasteland devastated by the war's operations, an area where there was no longer any evidence of improvement through human efforts. Megan Kate Nelson, in her volume titled *Ruin Nation,* agrees that war's destruction changed attitudes, causing people to wonder how so much damage could serve to save the Union and raising "concerns about how the nature of war shaped the nature of humanity."[25]

Yet these historians tend to agree that there was also a more positive backlash against the environmental damage caused by the war. American farmers had often exploited the land, using it up and moving on. But with the shocking destruction of the war, the attitude toward nature changed, and people began to place a higher value on the natural endowment. "Increasingly," write Judkin Browning and Tim Silver, "so called unspoiled landscapes or wilderness—especially in the West—served as a cultural antidote for eastern fields and forest ravaged by war." Ideas of conservation and protection of the natural wilderness gained strength. Shortly after the war, John Muir traveled in the South, and he, along with Frederick Law Olmsted, began to advocate preservation. A bill creating what would be called Yosemite National Park passed Congress and was signed by Abraham Lincoln in 1864. Reverence for the sacrifice made by thousands of fallen soldiers also inspired people to preserve and protect battlegrounds. Thus, the modern preservation movement had some of its roots in the damage caused by the Civil War.[26]

William Thomas sees another influence on attitudes, one connected with the large-scale railroad operations of the Federal army as well as General Sherman's March to the Sea. The Union built or repaired hundreds of bridges and miles and miles of railroad track as part of its offensives against the Confederacy. In the minds of top commanders by 1864, he writes, "the Civil War became a far-reaching attempt to reshape the social and physical environment of the Confederacy—and to demonstrate the reach of the American nation-state." The success of Union railroad operations and Sherman's success in reconfiguring "the environmental and social geography in front of him" as he marched to Savannah bolstered desires to develop the West. For leaders who were looking westward, that success increased confidence in their identification of the North with progress and civilization. Because the Confederate states were no longer represented in Congress, it was easy for lawmakers to implement their plans to organize the western territories on the model of northern farms. Similarly, they moved ahead with legislation to build the long-debated transcontinental railway. Northern capitalists took advantage of the changed legislative environment to push for industrial forestry and mining in western lands. An enhanced desire to master or control the environment and extract wealth from it probably contributed to a readiness to dominate and control the Native Americans of the West.[27]

We should investigate other ways in which the wartime interaction of soldiers and civilians with the environment might have changed attitudes. There was considerable enthusiasm among many Southerners for railroad development in the years right after the war. How much of that enthusiasm might have been a reaction to the advantages that northern railroad development had given the Union in the war? Were defeated Confederates now concluding that "the iron way" was the way to regain power and recover prosperity? The embrace of industrialization that came with New South ideas also seems related to the war; textile pioneer D. A. Tompkins cited the South's defeat as one of his motives for gaining economic power.[28] In this manner, environmental experiences during the war may have fostered rapacious approaches to the environment in subsequent decades. Was the later attitude governing Southern exploitation of timber and coal resources something that grew out of the wartime environment?

Seeing the environment as "a set of relationships" involving human beings, society, and nature also opens up lines of inquiry for the North. Adam Dean has shown the potential of exploring relationships between agriculture, antislavery politics, and nature parks in this era.[29] Leaders of the US Sanitary Commission certainly acted upon a new awareness of the connections between people, their environment, and disease, but we can consider less-obvious relationships as well. Economic historians have developed an extensive literature focused on the question whether the Civil War stimulated or retarded Northern industrialization. But we also might ask in what ways the relationships of wartime changed the direction of or the emphases in the Northern economy. What was needed and produced in wartime differed from the realities of the peacetime economy. Did new emphases and new investments advance some parts of the economy over others? How much of a boost did the war give to the adoption of farm machinery in Northern agriculture? Did this begin to have an influence on the size or organization of Northern farms? Was there a greater trend toward monoculture after the Civil War than there had been before? Because monoculture, mechanized cultivation, and use of chemicals have become characteristic of American farming, we might ask how much of this pattern was furthered by the environment of war.

Another salient characteristic of the wartime experience was the uprooting of huge numbers of people from the regions they knew and their movement into new and unfamiliar environments. Greater attention needs to be given to the experience and environmental effects of the tens of thousands of refugees driven from their homes in search of greater security elsewhere. By fleeing from their homes, they left a gap in their original environment and home economy. What happened to their homes, their livestock, and their fields and crops? Upon their arrival in another county, city, or state, it is certain that they often had a great impact on that location. Overcrowding may have contributed to disease and social disorganization. Sudden population booms in towns and cities changed the built environment, burdened the infrastructure, and probably altered patterns of development for the future. We need to know more both about the human challenges and suffering of refugees and about the ways such population shifts affected the natural and social environment.[30]

In respect to disease, we have seen that the movement and uprooting of civilians had serious, deleterious consequences. But we might also ask how the change in people's location and environment may have had other effects, such as on attitudes and practices. Years ago, in a study focused on North Carolina, Robert Kenzer showed that service in the Confederate army made many veterans more mobile after the war. Instead of staying in localities dominated by relatives and kin, some Tar Heels chose to live in other parts of the state or outside North Carolina. We likewise know that some Northern soldiers decided to live in the warmer states of the South after the war or to pursue economic opportunities there. What did the extensive movement of troops, aid workers, and volunteer teachers do to their outlooks and their views of the North and the South? How did ideas about the nation change when they moved South or when some former Confederates developed careers in New York or cities in the North?[31]

A final possibility is connected to gender. Susan Schrepfer and Douglas Sackman have pointed out that people view the natural world through the gendered concepts that they hold of themselves. Different "strands of masculinity and femininity," they assert, "have been wrought into the wilderness idea—and into all visions of nature." In the settlement of the West, for example, men thought of seizing the land and wringing wealth or a living from it, whereas women thought more about creating a garden and fitting into the landscape. By 1900, "an anxiousness and unease with prescribed or received gender roles both shaped and propelled environmentalism."[32] This perspective prompts us to ask whether the reactions to environmental damage in the Civil War differed according to gender. Did Northern women have attitudes toward nature, the South, and emancipation that differed from those held by Northern men? Did Southern women bring gendered attitudes toward rebuilding their lives and supporting wounded husbands, while personal and environmental damage accented a crisis of masculinity for Southern veterans? Such differences lead us from the environmental to the social realm and can prove their value while showing the diverse uses of an environmental perspective, considered broadly. Such environmental approaches to Civil War history demonstrate the manifold ways in which the environment shaped the Civil War while warfare was affecting the environment.

7

Consequences and Continuities

The Civil War has claimed a prominent place in US history in part because it was such a massive, destructive conflict. But the scope of the war has never been more than part of the explanation. The significance of the war to our nation's story has always rested largely on its consequences—the changes that it brought to society, government, law, and values. For many years, there has been a consensus around the idea that the consequences of the Civil War were profound. It was a war that settled and determined things, a culmination or outcome that made a large mark on the future. Even a modern-day southerner with cultural sympathies for rebel warriors, such as Shelby Foote, could proclaim in the popular television series by Ken Burns that the war made us who we are.[1]

In its earlier, simple formulations, what the war decided was plain. *United States* became a singular noun; its people would live in one nation, not two. State rights at long last had to give way to the more weighty constitutional powers of the central government. And emancipation put an end to enslavement. The institution of slavery no longer could exist in the postwar nation, which now could make its claim to being a land of freedom without shame or qualification.

Even in previous generations there was a recognition that these statements had a sweeping, summary character that oversimplified some facts on the ground. But until quite recently key elements of the traditional description of the war's consequences remained in place. In an essay published in 2009, James McPherson described the war's transformation in familiar terms: it settled that the United States would be one nation and a free nation rather than half slave; it determined that the federal government would have more power to protect citizens; Southerners no longer would control the government; and free-labor entrepreneurial capitalism would dominate instead of a slave-based plantation society and its ideologies. In addition, constitutional amendments would provide a basis for later progress by African Americans. Another influential scholar, Richard Bensel, concluded that "a strong national state emerged in the middle of the nineteenth century."[2]

Now, however, we have entered a period of far-reaching reevaluations and reconceptualizations of the consequences of the Civil War. This period is producing stimulating and provocative ideas that make discussion of the significance of the war just as exciting as any of the issues discussed in previous chapters. To describe this developing scholarly landscape and to offer suggestions are the goals of this chapter.

The new ideas and approaches derive in part from a deeper, more searching look at what long were recognized as shortcomings in outcomes or the incomplete resolution of wartime issues. But they also have new sources, especially a number of questions deriving from the following: new scholarship on the wartime and postwar history of the West; new ways of looking at Reconstruction and establishing its boundaries in time; and awareness that the Western world saw a variety of conflicts over national consolidation in the nineteenth century. With this renewed questioning, many issues are up for discussion. Did the Civil War create a strong central government or one that was unable to defend citizens' rights? Did the war inaugurate a period of laissez-faire or of potent state building? Was it a culmination of key issues and social conflicts or a period of transition? In terms of periodization, should we stop talking about the Civil War era and instead view those years as part of a Greater Reconstruction? Were the Civil War years dominated by the North–South conflict, or should they be seen as an earlier phase in the westward imperial thrust that eventually would go beyond California?

Let us consider first some questions that we have known were not entirely settled by the Civil War. There are good reasons to look more closely at these questions, and chief among them concerns the status of African Americans. In a recent essay, Gregory Downs has shown how much we can learn by taking seriously the issue of when and how emancipation occurred. The reality of emancipation for enslaved Southerners was not established through a presidential proclamation or by the passage of a constitutional amendment. The Emancipation Proclamation and the Thirteenth Amendment merely announced rights in the abstract. In the daily lives of Southern blacks in 1865, emancipation frequently did not arrive until weeks or months after the war ended. Actual freedom usually depended on the presence of Federal troops. Not until Union soldiers arrived in Southern neighborhoods did many slave owners have to loosen their grip on human "property," and not until then could slaves begin to explore the opportunities of freedom. After 1865, as Downs reminds us, for many blacks gaining freedom still depended on the army or the Freedmen's Bureau *restraining* the freedom of others—that is, countering what Southern whites saw as their rights. Emancipation thus was a piecemeal, complicated process that required active intervention to become real. Meaningful freedom for former slaves meant "defensible rights," and with a federal government whose attorney general had a staff consisting of only two clerks, "there was no mechanism of enforcement" once the army was gone.[3]

These facts suggest the importance of penetrating deeper into Southern neighborhoods to learn when and how real freedom developed. Generalizations cannot capture the shifting reality of a freedom that remained tenuous for the former slaves; only further, careful research can do that. For the entire region, the challenge is to map the progress of liberty, understood as the gaining (and subsequent losing) of "defensible rights."

Laura Edwards has made a similar point through her analysis of the functioning of the legal system. Federal laws did not guarantee change at the local level, for in the South especially local courts, churches, organizations, and communities had a great deal to say about what the law meant in practice. What people understood as rights continued to be shaped by community assumptions about slavery, racial subordination, and male supremacy over women. Slavery had given owners power over their slaves and whites power over blacks, just as white men enjoyed power over their women and children. For decades, these powers had been fundamental elements of the local community "peace." In the context of these traditional social patterns, giving equal rights to a former slave or to a woman meant taking rights away from whites or from men.[4]

The Civil War did not settle these questions of rights and status so much as it unleashed a contest over them. The legal consequences of emancipation promised to overturn what local communities understood as the basis of the "peace" and the social order. The former slaves spoke up and worked to claim their rights, and although they had the support of a few Republicans, they ran into widespread opposition in the white community. Pressing their claims in the legal system was a long and difficult process, for if local courts were unsympathetic, appeals had to go through various levels even to reach the federal courts. Edwards sees the legal and social contest over rights as one of the reasons there was so much violence in the South after the war ended. After years of change and conflict during the war, and with radically different values now proclaimed in Reconstruction, the legal system could not carry out its most basic function: the preservation of the peace in local communities. Thus, violence was in part whites' response to their loss of the previous legal consensus and an effort to reestablish past practices.[5]

Edwards and other scholars have pointed to another serious shortcoming in emancipation, if emancipation and the era's constitutional amendments were supposed to give rights to African Americans. Most Republican leaders in Washington and the North did not support the kind of rights understood and sought by black men and women (or in later years by many workers). Republican leaders instead defended property rights and blocked land redistribution for the former slaves. Interestingly, confiscation of property had characterized both the American Revolution and the actions of the Confederate government. But Northern legislators had come to have a different idea of the powers of government in regard to private property. In Congress, some New England Republicans joined with Democrats and border-state legislators to defeat any broad confiscation by the North. Their ideas, argues Daniel Hamilton, had changed from the era of the revolution, influenced in part by the legal theories of justices James Kent, Joseph Story, and John Marshall. Over the course of the nineteenth century, confiscation became a legal "relic, enforceable only by courts, and only for the life of an offender." The Constitution became the "ultimate protector of the natural rights of individual property." Social as well as legal currents of thought undoubtedly contributed to this change, which deserves further study and understanding, for this outlook would have important consequences as the nation industrialized and as corporate power grew.[6]

The nation's courts, argues Edwards, upheld a narrow, individualized view of civil rights, a view that was much less expansive than many citizens—blacks, women, and workers—wanted. The federal judiciary soon adopted and maintained a concept of rights based on an abstraction—"the ideal legal individual, self-interested, unencumbered, and fully empowered." Such an "individualized view" of citizens and their rights "ignored the social context that described actual Americans' lives." Sharecropping laws and labor relations favored not the laborer, who was economically and socially disadvantaged in terms of power, but rather the rights of the idealized individual. Whereas "structural inequalities" required "collective solutions[,] . . . the era's individualized definition of rights made it extremely difficult for the American people to harness the federal government's power to realize collective visions of social change." Instead, "the rights of property owners took precedence, in law, over the interests of the public." Edwards's argument here centers on the federal courts, but it would be worthwhile to scrutinize the effects of these values in state courts as well.[7]

The shortcomings related to emancipation, black freedom, and rights are not the only drivers of scholarly reevaluations. New ideas about the significance of the Civil War also have arisen from different ways of looking at the big picture—different ways of conceptualizing how the war changed society and the direction of national development, different ways of imagining how the Civil War fit in the trajectory of nineteenth-century US history. In a great deal of rethinking of these questions, the West plays a prominent role.

Steven Hahn has argued that the effects of the war on Pacific and international developments need greater attention and that the standard framework of a North–South conflict needs to be discarded. In his interpretation, the United States was not a nation-state before the Civil War. There was only a little industrial development in the Northeast and the Midwest, and slavery, which he feels was not another form of capitalism, extended its influence almost everywhere. The real axis of division in the nation's politics, Hahn argues, lay between the Northeast, where industrialization was most advanced, and the Mississippi Valley, where slaveholders had plans for territorial expansion and the conquest of Cuba. But what began as a slaveholders' rebellion "turned into a social and political revolution, bourgeois in nature, that simultaneously made for an imperial nation-state." The war set the course for development in the West, argues Hahn, and changed the character of American capitalism. The transcontinental railroad helped to create a real nation-state and bring about an end to Indian influence. In the changes brought about by the war, he sees the establishment of new patterns that led to corporate dominance and government action against railroad workers and labor strikers in the trans-Mississippi West. Similarly, officials who came to govern subjected Indian peoples later became supervisors of conquered people in the Philippines. The new form of capitalism looked outward to expand its influence in the Caribbean, the Pacific, and Mexico.[8]

This sweeping reconceptualization of the war and later decades raises many interesting issues for scholars to pursue. One might question the new geographical division between the Northeast and what for Hahn clearly is a Southern-influenced Mississippi Valley. Was it functioning as the real axis of division before the war? Southern leaders, it is true, often voiced hopes that the important channels of commerce provided by the Mississippi, Ohio, and Missouri Rivers would tie the Old Northwest to the South. But neither John C. Calhoun in the 1840s nor Confederate leaders during the war had much success in attracting the Old Northwest and uniting the Mississippi Valley behind their interests.

Another challenge posed by Hahn's ideas is also inherent in many discussions of the war's consequences—the challenge of identifying causation. A different country emerged after the Civil War. Clearly, the United States of the 1880s had a different character from the United States of the 1850s. We historians often say without much precision that changes brought by the war led to important later developments, but did the war cause them? Or did other causes, operating after the war ended, result in something new? For example, did the postwar rise of large industrial corporations introduce new factors and influences? That type of question calls for further research, greater specificity, and closer analysis. As I have already argued, it is important to undertake such work, as in the quest to understand exactly when and how a narrow idea of civil rights—based on idealized, independent individuals free to enter into contracts—came to be dominant.

Other historians who specialize in the West have argued as strongly and in greater detail for that region's influence in the Civil War and on subsequent decades. In one respect, it is undeniable that the scale of military operations in the West was small during the war; much larger armies fought the major battles of the war east of the Mississippi River. But both the Union and the Confederacy coveted western territory, and each saw possession of the area as critical to its nation's future. Southern leaders such as Jefferson Davis had always prophesied a bright future for slave interests in the Southwest. Republicans such as Lincoln had insisted that free-labor development of the West was crucial. From the very start of the war, both governments made plans to gain control of the West and authorized military actions toward that end. The Union's military effort was larger and more persistent, but both sides were frustrated as much by the geography and climate of the region as by hostile Indians. Scarce supplies of water hampered Union operations and played a major role in the failure of Confederate efforts.[9]

Nevertheless, the Union army, encouraged by western governors and strengthened by local volunteers, carried out numerous campaigns against Native American peoples such as the Sioux, Cheyenne, Arapahos, Navajos, and Apaches. Summer campaigns in 1863–1864, "followed by volunteer operations to protect vital roads in 1865, served notice to the Sioux, Cheyenne, Arapahos, and other Plains Indians that the United States would use all available means to extend federal power over their homelands." Colonels James Carleton and Christopher "Kit" Carson spearheaded operations against Apaches and Navajos in the Southwest. As Carson explained his goal, "When they [the Navajos] become convinced that destruction will follow on resistance, they will gladly avail themselves . . . of peace and plenty under the fostering care of the Government [on reservations]." Meanwhile, back in Washington the Republican Party took important steps to implement its "vision of the future West developed with farms, ranches, businesses, and towns" by passing the Homestead Act in 1862 and legislation for the transcontinental railroad. Using the telegraph, railroads, repeating rifles and pistols, and army columns, Union volunteers "delivered the imperial power of their nation with fire, lead, and steel."[10]

Noting the connections between small but important military actions in the West during the Civil War and major directions of policy that shaped subsequent decades, historians of the West "have long insisted on the region's centrality to understanding critical questions of federal power and governance at the heart of the Civil War era." Richard White comments that the West "served as the kindergarten of the American state." He writes less colorfully elsewhere that "in some basic ways the federal government created itself in the West." In both instances, the point is that institutions such as the army, the Land Office, and the Bureau of Indian Affairs came out of the war and then channeled later development. Stacey Smith argues that "the Civil War and the Indian wars were interrelated processes of state-building and citizen-making rather than separate and disparate regional phenomena." She also has written that "the 'accouterments of a powerful state,' which would be integral to the consolidation of federal control in the twentieth century, had their roots not only in the Civil War but in westward expansion."[11]

The West's influence, these scholars argue, was part of an imperialistic drive by a Federal government that was gaining power, and they include that westward thrust among similar international developments that were part of nation building in the nineteenth century. What the Federal government did in the West, says Stacey Smith, was "part of a broader national effort to solidify the territorial sovereignty of the United States and impose a particular vision of liberal citizenship and free labor market relations on diverse, resistant peoples, North, South, and West." In this sense, the Civil War was part of "a multi-front struggle among multiple, competing sovereignties across the continent." The Federal government was fighting not just Confederates but also Indians and Mexicans in the West and the Southwest. The resistance of these diverse groups to government policies shows that Southerners' bid for independence was merely "one of many rebellions against federal authority that wracked the U.S. nation-state in the last half of the century." By 1900, a more cohesive, modern nation had emerged. Elliott West describes the government's various military and bureaucratic efforts as a "powerful drive toward national consolidation . . . the integration of a divided America into a whole."[12]

The work of these historians of the West questions the idea that the Civil War created a powerful or dominant nation that easily got its way. Although the Union defeated the Confederacy, its victory was not so swift or sure in the West. If one sees "the Civil War as a multi-front struggle among multiple, competing sovereignties across the continent," some failures in the West pointed to Federal weakness, not strength. In the West, "Indian nations, residents of colonized territories, and state governments . . . resisted the rapidly expanding power of the U.S. federal government and fought for home rule and local control." The power of the government was partial, incomplete, and frequently challenged. A variety of local resisters sometimes won in their struggles with Washington as the government had trouble in three areas: establishing its sovereignty; instituting "liberal notions of citizenship"; and imposing "free wage labor on western communities that relied heavily on coercive labor systems." It encountered resistance not only from Indian nations but also from former Mexicans who relied on coercive labor systems and from Californians who used federal rights legislation to serve anti-Chinese policies.[13]

Such a view diminishes the finality usually attached to Union victory over the Confederacy and instead asserts that the war left many things unsettled. The Civil War then becomes, according to Elliott West, one part of the long "drive toward national consolidation" and integration. He proposes scrapping "the Civil War era" as an organizing term and replacing it with the "Greater Reconstruction." In the more comprehensive Greater Reconstruction, writes Smith, "the war between North and South [w]as just one of many conflicts over the limits of federal power and the boundaries of citizenship that rocked the entire nation." Though the Union defeated the Confederacy, its larger project of "state-building" in the western part of the continent, says Stacey Smith, was "a longer and more ambiguous project . . . in which federal authority was often contested, nonexistent, or ineffectual."[14]

This perspective finds an echo in the concept of the "Stockade State," proposed by Gregory Downs and Kate Masur. In relation to how the Civil War affected the power of the nation-state, they see the outcome of the war quite differently from James McPherson and Richard Bensel, both of whom described a much more powerful federal government. Similarly, they differ from Eric Foner, who wrote that the war created "a national state possessing vastly expanded authority and a new set of purposes." To Downs and Masur, "what defined the era" was the ability of many different people to defy the government's new reach. Applying their perspective to the often successful resistance by former Confederates in the Reconstruction South as well as to the West, they point out that "violence and enduring local power relations" remained "crucial aspects" of social reality. Accordingly, they suggest that the United States remained "fundamentally inchoate, its regions anarchic and chaotic." The war did not yield a "modern, consolidated nation"; many citizens were still not "free and independent individuals capable of entering into contracts, owning land, and raising families." The postwar society was one of much violence interrupted by flashes of rights rather than a world in which citizens could enjoy equal rights amid stable conditions. The nation-state could guarantee rights only in certain areas or "stockades."[15]

The work of Downs and Masur calls our attention to a fact of great human importance—the failure of the Civil War and Reconstruction to bring full freedom to emancipated slaves in the South. Freedom also was often in short supply in the West, but historians of that region have found an ironic pattern. In certain Indian territories, the government used its power to ensure that freed African Americans could enjoy citizenship and gain land and at the same time "eroded the political and legal sovereignty of slave-holding Indian nations." This fact suggests, argues Smith, "that the Civil War was more effective in suppressing the independence of Indian nations in the West than [of] white secessionists in the South." Where the power of the government was directed "against indigenous peoples," it sometimes did more for the rights of African Americans than in the South, where most former slaves lived.[16]

This irony reveals an important insight about the Stockade State and the outcomes of the Civil War. Race was the most important factor in determining the result of all the conflicts of national consolidation, whether in the South or in the West. Resistance in the South came from stubborn, white former Confederates, whereas in the West the opponents of government policies were Indians, certain whites, and former Mexicans. What made the difference in the outcome from one region to the other was race. The federal government and the white voting public were determined to defeat and colonize the Indians. That task wasn't easy, but the will to prevail was firm and enduring. Where white people formed the opposition, however, the central government had less will. White Southerners soon controlled the racial outcome of the war, white Californians found ways to discriminate against the Chinese, and even former Mexicans (though not considered completely white) in the Southwest continued to use traditional forms of coerced labor. A white-dominated society and government always proved to be less determined and more lenient with whites than with Indians. Similarly, it proved more willing to accept limitations on black people's liberty. The Stockade State showed its weakness where whites were the opponents, but it showed its power in "protracted and bloody internal wars against indigenous peoples."[17] This fact returns us to a perspective on race that has been central to the "Civil War era" and suggests that this perspective should be equally important with respect to the "Greater Reconstruction."

One of the ways in which the Stockade State flexed its muscles and demonstrated its power during the Greater Reconstruction was through cultural legislation. Here, too, the privileged treatment for whites' traditional racial and cultural patterns emerged. Whites did not hesitate to impose their will on those who were culturally different as all levels of government passed laws in the realm of "morals, sexuality, marriage, and race relations." The national government and federal courts found ways to suppress plural marriage among Mormons. It strongly encouraged or required former slaves to marry, and it insisted that Indian peoples accept allotments of land and adopt the agricultural lifestyle and gender roles practiced by whites. States joined in the process, passing antimiscegenation laws, defining race, and legislating against alcohol, vice, and obscenity. The postwar decades, as Gaines Foster and Susan Pearson have shown, were not a period of strict laissez-faire. They were instead characterized by hundreds of laws that, according to Pearson, "reached deep into the most intimate spheres of social and personal life in order to shape a social order organized around Protestant morals and hierarchies of race and gender."[18]

In assessing the "state of the State," Pearson uses these facts to point the argument about the Stockade State in the opposite direction. She argues that one could "characterize the years after the Civil War as a period of state building" rather than as a period in which the state was weak, limited in its reach, and unable to act. Organized groups of citizens and politicians were calling for a larger government role in the area of morals and social and cultural behavior. At the same time, governments passed many laws to try to regulate corporations and various business activities, even though these laws often proved ineffective or were limited by the courts. In 1888, the British visitor James Bryce found that Americans were "eager for state interference." In a challenge to the Stockade State concept's picture of a state that had not consolidated and could not control multiple challenges, Pearson argues that the Civil War "amplified the role of police powers and regulation in ordering the citizenry."[19] It seems clear that there is merit in both interpretations. Racism and the role of ethnocentric cultural attitudes can reconcile the two approaches. Thus, we have a post–Civil War government that exercised more power, but it persisted or was successful only in areas that were compatible with the values and prejudices of the white Protestant majority. A WASP majority and its values or biases proved to be dominant.

What do these new concepts mean for future study of the Civil War? The same question applies to the topic of the Stockade State versus a powerful national government and to the topic of the Greater Reconstruction versus Reconstruction. Eric Foner sees the new concepts and the broader periodization as "positive" but asks, "Will expanding to a national focus displace the South, and the emancipated slaves, from a central role in the story?" He answers, "I hope not."[20] In an analogous way, I believe that slavery, emancipation, and issues of race should continue to be central themes for the Civil War. Slavery versus free labor (in all their aspects—economic, social, and ideological) drove the prewar contests over power and the nation's future. Emancipation and what it should mean were vitally important to the war years in a multitude of ways. These key issues exercised a dominant influence that tied the events of the period together. Similarly, the consequences of emancipation and questions of rights and racial equality carried over directly into Reconstruction, logically creating a Civil War "era." In both periods, the nation was grappling with the same fundamental issues. It seems to me that the complicated politics of Reconstruction in the

South can justify separate treatment of postwar political developments. But where it is workable to carry wartime themes into the Reconstruction years, the effort will prove valuable and surely will continue.

The concepts "Civil War era," the "Greater Reconstruction," and "national consolidation" in the nineteenth century all have their special utility. For the historian, they should not be seen as incompatible because they represent different perspectives and pursue different questions. Most studies of the Civil War era have assumed as a starting point the perspective of those who lived the era and experienced its conflicts, crises, and changes. Competing visions of the future mattered to them, but the controversies and conflicts of their time were intensely real, demanding, and deadly. The goal generally has been to understand more fully the society and the forces that produced a great war, Union victory, and Confederate defeat. There is a unity to this periodization, a unity that derives from the fact of war itself.

The concept of the Greater Reconstruction or process of national consolidation, in contrast, seeks to identify connections or unifying patterns over a longer span of years and as part of a larger, multipart process. It deals with periods previously seen as separate, eras in which the society admittedly had become different, as perceived by the people living then. Its focus is on "a larger historiographic development," on "transregional and globally integrated forces," and on larger processes that took place over decades and through the action of various and sometimes unrelated forces.[21] There is greater diversity in the kaleidoscope of factors that eventually brought the Greater Reconstruction to an end point—a nation of continental dimensions, imperial projection, and modern economic and political power. The potential of this longer periodization lies in identifying and analyzing the forces that pushed toward this end point. Where did they get their strength, and how did they persist? The Civil War era has a stronger coherence and interaction among forces that were intimately connected with secession, war, Union victory, and reunion. Both perspectives can be useful without being mutually exclusive.

What about the areas in the Civil War era that deserve exploration across the war's end, exploration that bridges from the prewar or war years into Reconstruction in order to pursue important connections or development? One area that needs to be explored is the nature and evolution of conservative thought. In the North, an important center of conservative ideas and worldview was the Democratic Party. Its conservatism had roots in the Democrats' understanding of the Constitution, a state-based federalism, and liberty that derived from small government. But there also were Burkean elements to the Democratic Party leaders' outlook, and George Fredrickson in an earlier study identified conservative currents among Northern intellectuals and Republicans. He found a wartime movement toward greater organization, bureaucratization, and elite control. Surely those intellectuals were not alone in being affected by the changes that the war brought to society and to individuals' outlooks. In the South, the question of what happened to conservatism certainly is relevant. Slavery had enshrined values of paternalism and had stamped on social theory a strong emphasis on hierarchy and order. Leading clergymen had devoted themselves to giving the principal of hierarchy a religious justification. God, they preached, had ordained gradations of power so that there would be order and stability in the society, the family, and gender relations. Antidemocratic ideas were thus not just politically supportive of slavery—they also were God's teaching and design for all of society. Southern clerical leaders condemned the madness and fanaticism of reformers in the North, where only a few apologists for the South and religious figures held these same conservative ideas.[22]

Decades have elapsed since Fredrickson's important work in the 1960s, and although critical perspectives on it have developed, we still lack a new or revisionist approach to the subjects he examined. It is natural, too, to wonder how Northern Democrats reacted to the Union victory and their failure to end the Republican Party's control of government. The fundamental changes of the war years must have had some impact on their political ideas and on Northern conservative ideology and thought. For Southerners, the challenge must have been greater still because defeat in itself would require some adjustment of wartime convictions. In addition, the same clergymen who had preached a God-ordained hierarchy and condemned the reform movements of Northern society as a turning away from God had tied the Confederacy's fate to God's will. They had assured their congregations that the outcome of the war was in God's hands. For a while, they could explain battlefield reverses as God's attempt to chastise his chosen people, to make them more pious and deserving. But ultimate defeat of the Southern cause logically implied a judgment by God against the Confederates. What were the implications of this judgment for the structure of conservative ideas? As Leslie Butler has argued, "The development of ideas in the Reconstruction South deserves greater attention" and could shed light on "the distinct varieties of American conservatism that developed."[23]

Ministers and intellectuals were not the only figures for whom the Civil War era saw or encouraged a change of ideas. The psychology of the Northern public changed dramatically from the war years to the postwar years. What began only as a war to preserve the Union became a war for emancipation, and the government reversed itself to welcome black men into the army as soldiers. Black leaders sometimes marveled that so much progress was taking place in so short a time. Progress that had previously required decades now seemed to be occurring in a matter of months. Prominent Republicans and even some members of Lincoln's cabinet looked back in surprise at how rapidly policies had changed. As the Union turned toward a "hard war" to defeat the rebellion, the public accepted measures that few had contemplated only a short time earlier. The crisis of the Union created an emergency situation in which ideas changed rapidly.

Yet it is striking how rapidly the attitudes that had fueled the Northern war effort and supported the adoption of stronger measures faded away in the postwar years. An early hint of that change was visible in 1866, during the first months of Andrew Johnson's presidency. After the shocking assassination of Abraham Lincoln, many Northerners (at least in the judgment of many newspapers) seemed ready to trust that Johnson would right the ship and govern sensibly. The intransigent defiance of Southern whites and Johnson's growing conservatism then revived a determination in Congress to press forward with change. Spurred by white Southerners' resistance, political leaders continued to legislate change. But it was evident in their debates that many congressmen took these further steps reluctantly, even unwillingly, and some of them feared that the public was fast losing interest in the governance of the former Confederacy. By 1869, Carl Schurz summed up the alteration in Northern attitudes, though he was probably a bit tardy in doing so: "The civil war, which once absorbed all our thoughts, is day after day receding into a deeper past." The public had turned away from key wartime issues to focus instead on "new wants, new problems."[24]

Much has been written about the retreat from Reconstruction, which was also a retreat from the recently evolved attitudes of the Civil War, and many scholars have tried to explain the conservative rulings of a Republican-dominated Supreme Court. But the changing psychology of the Northern public demands a deeper understanding. Surely part of the explanation lies in the fact that the North was never committed to racial equality and therefore unwilling to defend it in the South when problems arose after the war. Susan-Mary Grant also makes a sensible point when she observes that nationalist thinking paused with the end of the war because people were ready for a respite from the pressures of the war years, and Mark Summers argues that after four long years of war the public's priority was reunion. But the evaporation of wartime support for strong measures seemed surprisingly swift among everyone except the congressmen who felt directly challenged by Johnson's Southern governments. Considering the extent to which state rights had caused problems, the willingness to defend those rights can be surprising. Here is an area in which research in letters, diaries, family papers, and periodicals could yield more understanding.[25]

We also should do more to investigate changes in Southern attitudes across the years from war to postwar. As Leslie Butler observes, "The process of moving from Civil War to a civil peace required mental adaptation," and that was true not just for politics but equally for issues of identity and daily life. For example, how did white Southerners feel about themselves in the immediate postwar years, once the war was over and they had to live with defeat and widespread destruction? The answer probably differed according to one's social class, status as a soldier or civilian, and gender. For religious Southerners, there was the added challenge of accepting a divine judgment against the Confederate cause. Sincere and pious believers would have to come to terms with the idea that they had been profoundly mistaken. Enthusiastic Confederates also would have to ask themselves some hard questions. Had they done enough? Their own leaders during the war made many statements clearly suggesting that they had not. Toward the end of the war, in an effort to revive morale in the face of discouraging defeats, Southern leaders and newspapers delivered many thunderous declarations: to allow Atlanta to fall would be a "burning disgrace"; "shame, shame forever" if the Georgia militia did not "rally to the defence of Atlanta"; and "it will be an everlasting stigma upon [Georgians'] character" if they allowed Sherman "to march with impunity through their territory." After Sherman did precisely those things, did some Confederates have to face an uncomfortable judgment of themselves?[26]

How, also, were anti-Confederate Southerners going to live with their pro-Confederate neighbors after the war? How would the two groups fashion some kind of "civil peace"? Because recent work has shown how deep and bitter were the wartime conflicts among white Confederates, the process of coming together after the war must have been very difficult. A few scholars have addressed this question in particular localities and usually with a focus on politics, but it must have been a broadly preoccupying one during the immediate period after the war. Most Southerners lived in face-to-face rural communities, and the hostilities bred of war surely were impossible to overlook. How did wartime foes worship together in the same church on Sunday? Or did they? Did rural patterns of cooperation or swapping of labor return? Rancor surely persisted, yet some kind of social equilibrium had to be reestablished. On another level, how did Southern Unionists or critics of the Confederacy carry their beliefs and pro-Union identity into social life and politics? Given the tenacity with which they had held onto their ideas during the war, more studies of these dissenters' lives after the war would be useful.[27]

Southern Unionists surely felt that their belief in the nation had been vindicated, but what did defeat mean for the former Confederates' ideas of nationalism? Jefferson Davis tried to shift Southerners' reverence for the Founding Fathers of the American Revolution to the Confederacy, but the war must have required various modifications to their beliefs about nationalism. Charles Wilson tells us that the Confederates' nationalism had a religious character, in which freedom "became a *sacred* right." The nation, ever since the American Revolution, had "a special destiny under God witnessing for political democracy." Southern Confederates had seen themselves as having a covenanted identity under God as they pursued independence.[28] Yet their nation failed, and what Confederates had seen as an act of self-government—secession—now was branded as illegitimate. Was there any remaining sense of nationalism among defeated Southern whites after the war? How had the Confederate experience, in which the central government had played a totally unexpected and dominant role, affected former Confederates' ideas about the proper character of a nation?

Another path to studying nationalism in the Civil War era lies with a focus on immigrants and their ideas. The experience of immigrants is attracting much new attention, and these groups deserve attention in themselves and for wider reasons both social and religious. But immigrant populations also offer an intriguing opportunity to study nationalism and what the nation meant during and after the war. Immigrants are naturally impressionable and receptive to their new environment. Those of the Civil War era would soak up the prevailing ideas and feelings of the society as they came to learn about the United States and its culture. The research could be difficult, but in the writings of literate immigrants there must be many clues to what Americans believed about their nation during the war or after it was reunited. Their impressions can serve as a gauge to determine how much nationalism in the North had changed over the Civil War years. We also can learn how much the concept of the Union resonated with the values that motivated their immigration in the first place. The experience of the immigrants becomes a valuable window on society.

A final and very promising way to bridge from the war years to postwar life and to capture the significance of the war lies in long-term community studies. Due to its enormous scope, the Civil War had effects that reached far beyond the battles and the men who fought them. Soldiers were affected by their wounds and psychological scars and by the adjustments required when they resumed civilian life, and we need closer study of veterans' struggles to reestablish themselves socially and economically. But still more can be gained by focusing over time on the communities from which they came. The soldiers' families had to deal with the men's absence during war, with their deaths on the battlefield, and with the trauma and changes that the veterans brought back with them. The men's absence during four years changed whole communities, and their deaths made those changes lasting. The war created gaps in the economic and social life of towns and districts in both North and South. It affected communities' businesses, organizations, and social infrastructure. In some cases, large percentages of the young men from an area never returned to take up their former roles. Many villages or towns were not the same as they moved into the Reconstruction and postwar decades.

The repercussions of the war on soldiers and their communities were economic, social, psychological, and political. Long-term, detailed studies of men, their families, and their home towns can help us to see in a new way the wider dimensions of the war's impact. Judkin Browning has begun a study that can illustrate the promise of this approach to research. As noted in chapter 4, he has identified two regiments, one from Michigan and one from North Carolina, that confronted each other at Gettysburg with enormous casualties. "Each regiment lost nearly 80% of its force," and the fact that hundreds of young men were killed, wounded, or disabled meant that their towns or farming districts would not be the same. By studying both the men and their communities over decades, Browning is finding how the war's impact reached into the twentieth century.[29]

We are aware of the many ramifications of war on those who recently fought in Iraq and Afghanistan. Research focused on Union and Confederate soldiers and their home communities can bring the long-term repercussions of the Civil War to light and illuminate its costs and legacies in a new way. Such community studies may prove to be one of the most valuable of new approaches to the field of Civil War history.

Acknowledgments

Beyond my thanks for the stimulating work by many scholars, I owe a particular debt to a number of individuals. Jeffrey J. Crow again provided valuable comments and criticisms, as he has done throughout my career. I am very grateful for his help and friendship. I also want to offer my sincere thanks and gratitude to those who have shared their work or their plans with me. In alphabetical order, they are: Stephen Berry, Judkin Browning, Brian Fennessy, Max Grivno, Robert Kenzer, Melinda Lawson, Chandra Miller Manning, and Erin Mauldin. The helpful comments from two anonymous evaluators were an important part of the professionalism and efficiency of the staff of the University Press of Kentucky.

Notes

Preface

1. Yael Sternhell, *Routes of War: The World of Movement in the Confederate South* (Cambridge, MA: Harvard University Press, 2012), 5; Daniel Sutherland, *American Civil War Guerrillas: Changing the Rules of Warfare* (Santa Barbara, CA: Praeger, 2013), xi, xii; Megan Kate Nelson, *Ruin Nation: Destruction and the American Civil War* (Athens: University of Georgia Press, 2012), 136, 152–53, 176.

2. Among the best works produced by such literary figures are Robert Penn Warren, *The Legacy of the Civil War* (1961; reprint, Lincoln: University of Nebraska Press, 1998), and Edmund Wilson, *Patriotic Gore: Studies in the Literature of the American Civil War* (New York: Oxford University Press, 1962).

3. Frank Towers, "Partisans, New History, and Modernization: The Historiography of the Civil War's Causes, 1861–2011," *Journal of the Civil War Era* 1, no. 2 (June 2011): 237–64.

4. Carl Becker, "Everyman His Own Historian," annual address of the president of the American Historical Association, Minneapolis, December 29, 1931, *American Historical Review* 37, no. 2 (1931): 221–35, at https://www.historians.org/about-aha-and-membership/aha-history-and-archives/presidential-addresses/carl-l-becker, with the quoted passage near the very end of the address.

1. Understanding the Roots of War

1. David M. Potter, *The Impending Crisis, 1848–1861* (New York: Harper Colophon, 1976).

2. The quotations come from Bertram Wyatt-Brown, *The Shaping of Southern Culture: Honor, Grace, and War, 1760s–1880s* (Chapel Hill: University of North Carolina Press, 2001), 177, 154. Wyatt-Brown's basic work on Southern honor is, of course, *Southern Honor: Ethics and Behavior in the Old South* (New York: Oxford University Press, 1982).

Among studies that focus closely on the friction points and events leading to war and on the Southerners' path to secession, William W. Freehling's work has equaled the enduring contribution of scholars such as Potter. Freehling's impressive and illuminating volumes are *The Road to Disunion: Secessionists at Bay, 1776–1854* (New York: Oxford University Press, 1990) and *The Road to Disunion: Secessionists Triumphant, 1854–1861* (New York: Oxford University Press, 2007).

3. Paul Quigley, review of Michael Woods, *Emotional and Sectional Conflict*

in the Antebellum United States (New York: Cambridge University Press, 2014), *Journal of the Civil War Era* 5, no. 3 (September 2015): 440.

4. Chandra Miller [Chandra Manning], "'Title Page to a Great Tragic Volume': The Impact of the Missouri Crisis on Slavery, Race, and Republicanism in the Thought of John C. Calhoun and John Quincy Adams," *Missouri Historical Review* 94, no. 4 (July 2000): 365–88, quotation on 371.

5. See John Craig Hammond, "'Uncontrollable Necessity': The Local Politics, Geopolitics, and Sectional Politics of Slavery Expansion," in John Craig Hammond and Matthew Mason, eds., *Contesting Slavery: The Politics of Bondage and Freedom in the New American Nation* (Charlottesville: University of Virginia Press, 2011), 138–60, and Brian Schoen, *The Fragile Fabric of Union: Cotton, Federal Politics, and the Global Origins of the Civil War* (Baltimore: Johns Hopkins University Press, 2009).

6. James L. Huston, *Calculating the Value of the Union: Slavery, Property Rights, and the Economic Origins of the Civil War* (Chapel Hill: University of North Carolina Press, 2003), 25, 27–30. Gavin Wright's book *The Political Economy of the Cotton South: Households, Markets, and Wealth in the Nineteenth Century* (New York: Norton, 1978) remains another landmark study essential to an understanding of the cotton South.

7. Huston, *Calculating the Value of the Union,* xiv, 119.

8. See Edward E. Baptist, *The Half Has Never Been Told: Slavery and the Making of American Capitalism* (New York: Basic Books, 2014); Edward Bartlett Rugemer, *The Problem of Emancipation: The Caribbean Roots of the American Civil War* (Baton Rouge: Louisiana State University Press, 2008), 222–57.

9. Timothy Mason Roberts, *Distant Revolutions: 1848 and the Challenge to American Exceptionalism* (Charlottesville: University of Virginia Press, 2009).

10. See Edward Bartlett Rugemer, "Caribbean Slave Revolts and the Origins of the Gag Rule: A Contest between Abolitionism and Democracy, 1797–1835," in Hammond and Mason, eds., *Contesting Slavery,* 94–116. See also Yonatan Eyal, "A Romantic Realist: George Nicholas Saunders and the Dilemmas of Southern International Engagement," *Journal of Southern History* 78, no. 1 (February 2012): 107–30.

11. Sven Beckert, *Empire of Cotton: A Global History* (New York: Vintage, 2014), 85, 117, 171. Beckert, through reliance on his truly global perspective, is also able to offer a new way of thinking about the collision between Northern and Southern interests. The United States, he notes, was "the only country in the world divided between war and industrial capitalism, a unique characteristic that would eventually spark an unprecedentedly destructive civil war" (171).

12. See Matthew Pratt Guterl, "Slavery and Capitalism: A Review Essay," *Journal of Southern History* 81, no. 2 (May 2015): 405–20.

13. Beckert, *Empire of Cotton,* 171; Gavin Wright, foreword to Susanna Delfino and Michele Gillespie, eds., *Technology, Innovation, and Southern Industrialization: From the Antebellum Era to the Computer Age* (Columbia: University of Missouri Press, 2008), xi, ix, xii.

14. Frank J. Byrne, *Becoming Bourgeois: Merchant Culture in the South, 1820–1865* (Lexington: University Press of Kentucky, 2006), 16, 75, 3, 40, appendix.

15. Aaron Marrs, *Railroads in the Old South: Pursuing Progress in a Slave Society* (Baltimore: Johns Hopkins University Press, 2009), 6–10; William G. Thomas, *The Iron Way: Railroads, the Civil War, and the Making of Modern America* (New Haven, CT: Yale University Press, 2011), prologue, database, and chap. 1, especially 22, 20, 24, 26.

16. John Majewski, *Modernizing a Slave Economy: The Economic Vision of the Confederate Nation* (Chapel Hill: University of North Carolina Press, 2009), 3, 12, 17, 21.

17. For example, see Edward Bartlett Rugemer, "Why Civil War? The Politics of Slavery in Comparative Perspective: The United States, Cuba, and Brazil," in David T. Gleeson and Simon Lewis, eds., *The Civil War as Global Conflict* (Columbia: University of South Carolina Press, 2014), 14–35. See also the essays in Don Doyle, ed., *Secession as an International Phenomenon: From America's Civil War to Contemporary Separatist Movements* (Athens: University of Georgia Press, 2010). In "Napoleon Is Coming! Maximilian Is Coming!" (in Robert E. May, ed., *The Union, the Confederacy, and the Atlantic Rim* [Gainesville: University Press of Florida, 2013], 115–44), Thomas Schoonover reveals why Southern leaders' assumptions were mistaken.

18. Beckert, *Empire of Cotton,* 244–45. In regard to regional differences in attitude and industrial investment, Georgia may be an interesting state to study. Before the Civil War, state leaders at times were extremely optimistic about potential revenue from the state-owned railway, and during the war the Confederate government gave a substantial boost to manufacturing. Some aspects of these issues in Georgia are discussed in Chad Morgan, *Planters' Progress: Modernizing Confederate Georgia* (Gainesville: University Press of Florida, 2005).

19. William Freehling, *The South vs. the South: How Anti-Confederate Southerners Shaped the Course of the Civil War* (New York: Oxford University Press, 2001).

20. Aaron Astor, *Rebels on the Border: Civil War, Emancipation, and the Reconstruction of Kentucky and Missouri* (Baton Rouge: Louisiana State University Press, 2012), 244–45; Stanley Harrold, *Border War: Fighting over Slavery before the Civil War* (Chapel Hill: University of North Carolina Press, 2010).

21. Harrold, *Border War,* 212, 11–12, 177.

22. Astor, *Rebels on the Border.* Here I am taking the liberty of extending Astor's argument beyond the two states to which he gives careful consideration.

23. Ibid., 247.

24. Clay's declaration, made on February 5 and 6, 1850, during debate over the compromise measures of that year, can be found in Richard Hofstadter, ed., *Great Issues in American History,* 2 vols. (New York: Vintage, 1958), 1:346.

25. Astor, *Rebels on the Border,* 245, 247.

26. Robert William Fogel and Stanley L. Engerman, *Time on the Cross: The*

Economics of American Negro Slavery (Boston: Little, Brown, 1974); Paul D. Escott, *Paying Freedom's Price: A History of African Americans in the Civil War* (Lanham, MD: Rowman and Littlefield, 2016), 39–41.

27. Susan O'Donovan is one of the scholars pursuing an interest in the slaves' political ideas, and we can look forward to new findings in this area.

28. For the debate over who deserves credit for freeing the slaves, see articles by James McPherson in the *New York Review of Books,* April 21, 1994, and June 13, 2002, and Ira Berlin, "Who Freed the Slaves? Emancipation and Its Meaning," in David W. Blight and Brooks D. Simpson, eds., *Union and Emancipation: Essays on Politics and Race in the Civil War Era* (Kent, OH: Kent State University Press, 1997), 105–22. See also David Williams, *I Freed Myself: African American Self-Emancipation in the Civil War Era* (New York: Cambridge University Press, 2014).

29. Steven A. Channing, *Crisis of Fear: Secession in South Carolina* (New York: Simon and Schuster, 1970); Donald A. Reynolds, *Texas Terror: The Slave Insurrection Panic of 1860 and the Secession of the Lower South* (Baton Rouge: Louisiana State University Press, 2007), 213, 96, 98.

30. David Grimsted, *American Mobbing, 1828–1861: Toward Civil War* (New York: Oxford University Press, 1998), 86, 101.

31. See, for example, the sermons that appear online in the Documenting the American South project of the Southern Historical Collection at the University of North Carolina, Chapel Hill.

32. Larry E. Tise, *Proslavery: A History of the Defense of Slavery in America, 1701–1840* (Athens: University of Georgia Press, 1987).

33. See Susan-Mary Grant, "'How a Free People Conduct a Long War': Sustaining Opposition to Secession in the American Civil War," in Doyle, ed., *Secession as an International Phenomenon*, 132–50. Grant credits Phillip Paludan for the idea of "localism as nationalism." In *Calculating the Value of the Union,* Huston also stresses the importance of Northern village society.

2. Understanding Societies in War

1. Michael R. Bradley has called attention to the Provost Marshal Records of the United States Army, arguing that they are rich but rarely used and shed light on irregular war in areas such as Tennessee. See his essay "'I Shoot the Men and Burn Their Houses'': Home Fires in the Line of Fire," in Kent T. Dollar, Larry H. Whiteaker, and W. Calvin Dickinson, eds., *Sister States, Enemy States: The Civil War in Kentucky and Tennessee* (Lexington: University Press of Kentucky, 2009), 168–87. Catherine Clinton sees the need to examine the records of military tribunals and the medical corps. Such records, she argues, can tell us much about race, sex, and gender through analysis of military campaigns to regulate prostitution and penalize rape. See her essay "'Public Women' and Sexual Politics during the American Civil War," in Orville Vernon Burton, Jerald Podair, and Jennifer L. Weber, eds., *The Struggle for Equality: Essays on Sectional Conflict, the Civil War, and the Long Reconstruction* (Charlottesville: University of Virginia Press,

2011), 119–36. In *Southern Rights: Political Prisoners and the Myth of Confederate Constitutionalism* (Charlottesville: University of Virginia Press, 1999), Mark Neely corrects a generations-old misconception by finding evidence for thousands of civilians imprisoned by Confederate authorities in the large collection Letters Received, Confederate Secretary of War, Microfilm Record M 437, National Archives, Washington, DC. Also see in chapter 5 the discussion of new possibilities created by digitization.

2. Emory M. Thomas opened new vistas with *The Confederacy as a Revolutionary Experience* (Englewood Cliffs, NJ: Prentice-Hall, 1970). A few examples of studies that reversed the emphasis include Paul D. Escott, *After Secession: Jefferson Davis and the Failure of Confederate Nationalism* (Baton Rouge: Louisiana State University Press, 1978); Richard E. Beringer, Herman Hattaway, Archer Jones, and William N. Still Jr., *Why the South Lost the Civil War* (Athens: University of Georgia Press, 1986); and David Williams, Teresa Crisp Williams, and David Carlson, *Plain Folk in a Rich Man's War: Class and Dissent in Confederate Georgia* (Gainesville: University Press of Florida, 2002).

3. Again, for a few examples, see Gary W. Gallagher, *The Confederate War* (Cambridge, MA: Harvard University Press, 1997); Aaron Sheehan-Dean, *Why Confederates Fought: Family and Nation in Civil War Virginia* (Chapel Hill: University of North Carolina Press, 2007); Bradley Clampitt, *Confederate Heartland: Military and Civilian Morale in the Western Confederacy* (Baton Rouge: Louisiana State University Press, 2011); and Jason Phillips, *Diehard Rebels: The Confederate Culture of Invincibility* (Athens: University of Georgia Press, 2007).

4. I have argued elsewhere for the importance of the government's measures of coercion and control, both legal and military. See Paul D. Escott, *Military Necessity: Civil–Military Relations in the Confederacy* (Westport, CT: Praeger Security International, 2006).

5. Margaret M. Storey, *Loyalty and Loss: Alabama's Unionists in the Civil War and Reconstruction* (Baton Rouge: Louisiana State University Press, 2004), 59–64; Daniel W. Hamilton, *The Limits of Sovereignty: Property Confiscation in the Union and the Confederacy during the Civil War* (Chicago: University of Chicago Press, 2007); Stephen Berry, ed., *Weirding the War: Stories from the Civil War's Ragged Edges* (Athens: University of Georgia Press, 2011); Rodney Steward, *David Schenck and the Contours of Confederate Identity* (Knoxville: University of Tennessee Press, 2012); John C. Inscoe and Robert C. Kenzer, eds., *Enemies of the Country: New Perspectives on Unionists in the Civil War South* (Athens: University of Georgia Press, 2001). See also Jeffrey J. Crow and Paul D. Escott, "The Social Order and Violent Disorder: An Analysis of North Carolina in the Revolution and the Civil War," *Journal of Southern History* 52, no. 3 (August 1986): 373–402; William T. Auman, *Civil War in the North Carolina Quaker Belt* (Jefferson, NC: McFarland, 2014); and Victoria E. Bynum, *The Free State of Jones* (Chapel Hill: University of North Carolina Press, 2001).

6. Daniel Sutherland, "Memories of a Rooted Sorrow: The Legacy of the

Guerrilla War," *Civil War History* 62, no. 1 (March 2016): 13, introduction to *American Civil War Guerrillas,* and *A Savage Conflict: The Decisive Role of Guerrillas in the American Civil War* (Chapel Hill: University of North Carolina Press, 2009); Robert Mackey, *The Uncivil War: Irregular Warfare in the Upper South, 1861–1865* (Norman: University of Oklahoma Press, 2004), 6–8, 19–21. Sutherland concludes in *American Civil War Guerrillas* that guerrilla warfare is "*as* decisive as any other factor, including battlefield defeats," in causing the defeat of the Confederacy (87, emphasis in original).

7. Mackey, *The Uncivil War,* 48–49.

8. Sutherland, *American Civil War Guerrillas*, chaps. 2 and 8, and *A Savage Conflict,* 54, 27.

9. See Brian D. McKnight, "'Time by the Forelock': Champ Ferguson and the Borderland Style of Warfare," in Dollar, Whiteaker, and Dickinson, eds., *Sister States, Enemy States,* 140–67.

10. Barton A. Myers, *Rebels Against the Confederacy: North Carolina's Unionists* (New York: Cambridge University Press, 2014), 13, 125, 57.

11. Sutherland, *A Savage Conflict,* 278.

12. Laura Edwards, *A Legal History of the Civil War and Reconstruction: A Nation of Rights* (New York: Cambridge University Press, 2015), 44, 56, 57, 62.

13. Sternhell, *Routes of War,* 94, 108, 113; Lorien Foote, "'They Cover the Land Like the Locusts of Egypt': Fugitive Federal Prisoners of War and the Collapse of the Confederacy," *Journal of the Civil War Era* 6, no. 1 (March 2016): 30–55, data on 31.

14. Grimsted, *American Mobbing,* 89, 90, 98. Grimsted defines the prewar South as "a society where status and character were tied to mastery, to the numbers of people over whom one wielded unquestioned domination" (98).

15. Edwards, *Legal History of the Civil War and Reconstruction,* 47, 43, 60. A thought-provoking analysis of Northern differences can be found in Phillip S. Paludan, "The Civil War Considered as a Crisis in Law and Order," *American Historical Review* 77, no. 4 (October 1972): 1013–34.

16. George Rable, "Rebels and Patriots in the Confederate 'Revolution,'" in William J. Cooper Jr. and John M. McCardell Jr., eds., *In the Cause of Liberty: How the Civil War Redefined American Ideals* (Baton Rouge: Louisiana State University Press, 2009), 86. Such traits make one think of the violent, fiercely independent characters in William Faulkner's trilogy about the Snopes clan.

17. Edwards, *Legal History of the Civil War and Reconstruction,* 60, 62. See also Escott, *After Secession,* chap. 4.

18. Gerard Delanty and Krishan Kumar, eds., *The Sage Handbook of Nations and Nationalism* (London: Sage, 2006).

19. George C. Rable, *God's Almost Chosen People: A Religious History of the American Civil War* (Chapel Hill: University of North Carolina Press, 2010); Harry S. Stout, *Upon the Altar of the Nation: A Moral History of the American Civil War* (New York: Viking, 2006); Chandra [Miller] Manning, "Wartime National-

ism and Race: Comparing the Visions of Confederate, Black Union, and White Union Soldiers," in Cooper and McCardell, eds., *In the Cause of Liberty,* 87–104; Grant, "'How a Free People Conduct a Long War.'" In *Freedom National: The Destruction of Slavery in the United States, 1861–1865* (New York: Norton, 2012), James Oakes also has emphasized the importance of emancipation as an inspiring goal.

20. Melinda Lawson, *Patriot Fires: Forging a New American Nationalism in the Civil War North* (Lawrence: University of Kansas Press, 2002), 11, 160–75.

21. Heather Cox Richardson, *The Greatest Nation of the Earth: Republican Economic Policies during the Civil War* (Cambridge, MA: Harvard University Press, 1997), 6–7; Potter's view is cited in Lawson, *Patriot Fires,* 160.

22. On German American assimilation, see Christian B. Keller, *Chancellorsville and the Germans: Nativism, Ethnicity, and Civil War Memory* (New York: Fordham University Press, 2007).

23. Sean A. Scott, *A Visitation of God: Northern Civilians Interpret the Civil War* (New York: Oxford University Press, 2011).

24. Ibid., 4, 185, and chaps. 2, 4, and 6.

25. Ibid., chaps. 8 and 9.

26. "Northern Democrats in the Civil War Era," a roundtable discussion at the Biennial Meeting of the Society of Civil War Historians, June 12–14, 2014, Baltimore; Mark E. Neely Jr., *The Union Divided: Party Conflict in the Civil War North* (Cambridge, MA: Harvard University Press, 2002), 177.

27. Neely, *The Union Divided,* 193.

28. Jennifer Weber, "The Political Culture of the North: Party Politics of Nation and State," in Stephen D. Engle, ed., *The War Worth Fighting: Abraham Lincoln's Presidency and Civil War America* (Gainesville: University Press of Florida, 2015), 91–109; Robert M. Sandow, "Damnable Treason or Party Organs? Democratic Secret Societies in Pennsylvania," in Andrew L. Slap and Michael Thomas Smith, eds., *"This Distracted and Anarchical People": New Answers for Old Questions about the Civil War–Era North* (New York: Fordham University Press, 2013), 42–59; Matthew Warshauer, "Copperheads in Connecticut: A Peace Movement That Imperiled the Union," in Slap and Smith, eds., *"This Distracted and Anarchical People,"* 60–79; Matthew Isham, "'A Press That Speaks Its Opinions Frankly and Openly and Fearlessly': The Contentious Relationship between the Democratic Press and the Party in the Antebellum North," in Slap and Smith, eds., *"This Distracted and Anarchical People,"* 11–28; Neely, *The Union Divided,* 179–83. Michael Vorenberg gives some attention to the possibility of rapprochement following the elections of 1864 in *Final Freedom: The Civil War, the Abolition of Slavery, and the Thirteenth Amendment* (Cambridge: Cambridge University Press, 2001).

29. Adam I. P. Smith, *No Party Now: Politics in the Civil War North* (New York: Oxford University Press, 2006), 68, 78.

30. Sean Nalty, "Come Weal, Come Woe, I Am with the Anti-slavery Party:

Federalism and the Formation of the Pennsylvania Union Party, 1860–1864," in Gary W. Gallagher and Rachel A. Shelden, eds., *A Political Nation: New Directions in Mid-Nineteenth-Century American History* (Charlottesville: University of Virginia Press, 2012), 143–66; Michael F. Holt, "Abraham Lincoln and the Politics of Union," in *Political Parties and American Political Development from the Age of Jackson to the Age of Lincoln* (Baton Rouge: Louisiana State University Press, 1991), 330; Ludwell Johnson, "Lincoln's Solution to the Problem of Peace Terms, 1864–1865," *Journal of Southern History* 34, no. 4 (November 1968): 576–86.

31. Oakes, *Freedom National*; Daniel Crofts, *Lincoln and the Politics of Slavery: The Other Thirteenth Amendment and the Struggle to Save the Union* (Chapel Hill: University of North Carolina Press, 2016); Paul D. Escott, *"What Shall We Do with the Negro?": Lincoln, White Racism, and Civil War America* (Charlottesville: University of Virginia Press, 2009); Phillip W. Magness and Sebastian N. Page, *Colonization after Emancipation: Lincoln and the Movement for Black Resettlement* (Columbia: University of Missouri Press, 2011).

32. Eric Foner, *Free Soil, Free Labor, Free Men: The Ideology of the Republican Party before the Civil War* (Oxford: Oxford University Press, 1970). See also, among other works, T. Harry Williams, *Lincoln and the Radicals* (Madison: University of Wisconsin Press, 1972); Holt, *Political Parties and American Political Development;* Magness and Page, *Colonization after Emancipation.*

33. Neely, *The Union Divided,* 193.

34. Forrest Wood, *Black Scare: The Racist Response to Emancipation and Reconstruction* (Berkeley: University of California Press, 1968). Chandra Manning is among those who have analyzed soldiers' attitudes toward emancipation—for example, in her essay "Wartime Nationalism and Race."

35. Leslie A. Schwalm, *Emancipation's Diaspora: Race and Reconstruction in the Upper Midwest* (Chapel Hill: University of North Carolina Press, 2009), 101, 104, 3, chap. 3.

36. Nina Silber, *Gender and the Sectional Conflict* (Chapel Hill: University of North Carolina Press, 2008), especially the second chapter; Stanton quoted in Rachel Filene Seidman, "Monstrous Doctrine? Northern Women on Dependency during the Civil War," in Paul A. Cimbala and Randall M. Miller, eds., *An Uncommon Time: The Civil War and the Northern Home Front* (New York: Fordham University Press, 2002), 188.

37. J. Matthew Gallman, *Northerners at War: Reflections on the Civil War Home Front* (Kent, OH: Kent State University Press, 2010), 172; Morton Keller, *Regulating a New Society: Public Policy and Social Change in America, 1900–1933* (Cambridge, MA: Harvard University Press, 1994); Lyde Cullen Sizer, *The Political Work of Northern Women Writers and the Civil War, 1850–1872* (Chapel Hill: University of North Carolina Press, 2000), 4.

38. Gallman, *Northerners at War,* 172; Stephanie McCurry, *Confederate Reckoning: Power and Politics in the Civil War South* (Cambridge, MA: Harvard University Press, 2010), 138, 215.

39. See J. Matthew Gallman, "The President as Pedagogue: Teaching Citizenship in Time of War," in Engle, ed., *The War Worth Fighting,* 37–61, and *Defining Duty in the Civil War: Personal Choice, Popular Culture, and the Union Home Front* (Chapel Hill: University of North Carolina Press, 2015), 14, 16, 194, 251–52; Phillip Paludan, "The America Civil War Considered as a Crisis in Law and Order," *American Historical Review* 77, no. 4 (1972): 1030–34, and *A People's Contest: The Union and the Civil War, 1861–1865* (New York: Harper and Row, 1988), 10–15; Lawson, *Patriot Fires,* 11. In a different way, one could ask how much the idea of citizenship was affected by efforts to wrap the nation-state in the "mystical aura" mentioned by Lawson. Such a mystical aura would presumably tend to create notions of duty rather than of free choice.

40. Richardson, *The Greatest Nation of the Earth*; Daniel Walker Howe, interview, *Historically Speaking* 9, no. 4 (March–April 2008): 30–32.

41. See, for example, Robert E. May, *Slavery, Race, and Conquest in the Tropics: Lincoln, Douglas, and the Future of Latin America* (New York: Cambridge University Press, 2013) and *The Southern Dream of a Caribbean Empire, 1854–1861* (Gainesville: University of Florida Press, 2002); Paul D. Escott, *Lincoln's Dilemma: Blair, Sumner, and the Republican Struggle over Racism and Equality in the Civil War Era* (Charlottesville: University of Virginia Press, 2014); and Magness and Page, *Colonization after Emancipation.* Additional work on this topic is being produced by Sebastian Page and Michael Douma. For example, see Sebastian Page, "'A Knife Sharp Enough to Divide Us': William H. Seward, Abraham Lincoln, and Black Colonization," *Diplomatic History* 41, no. 2 (2017): 362–91, at https://doi.org/10.1093/dh/dhw039, and Michael Douma, "The Lincoln Administration's Negotiations to Colonize African Americans in Dutch Surinam," *Civil War History* 61, no. 2 (June 2015): 111–37. In addition, President Ulysses S. Grant's interest in annexation of the Dominican Republic should be studied to see in what way colonizationists' ideas led to that postwar initiative.

3. African Americans in the Civil War Years

1. Jim Downs, "The Future of Civil War Era Studies: Race," *Journal of the Civil War Era* 2, no. 1 (March 2012), at http://journalofthecivilwarera.org/forum-the-future-of-civil-war-era-studies/the-future-of-civil-war-era-studies-race/.

2. In some nonacademic circles, debate continues about whether there were black Confederate soldiers. It is clear that on occasion black people who were accompanying Confederate soldiers found themselves under fire and that some were described by Northern soldiers or observers as returning fire. There is no evidence, however, that the Confederate government ever decided to accept or enroll black soldiers before the final weeks of 1865. In North Carolina, careful research by Henry Jordan, who prepared the North Carolina Civil War Roster, turned up one or two free blacks who were enrolled, at least briefly, although at least one of these men was discharged when his race became known. I thank Jeffrey J. Crow for the latter piece of information.

3. James H. Brewer, *The Confederate Negro: Virginia's Craftsmen and Military Laborers, 1861–1865* (Durham, NC: Duke University Press, 1969); Jaime Amanda Martinez, *Confederate Slave Impressment in the Upper South* (Chapel Hill: University of North Carolina Press, 2013).

4. See Ira Berlin, Barbara J. Fields, Thavolia Glymph, Joseph P. Reidy, and Leslie S. Rowland, eds., *Freedom: A Documentary History of Emancipation,* series 1, vol. 1: *The Destruction of Slavery* (Cambridge: University of Cambridge Press, 1985), 703; James M. McPherson, *The Negro's Civil War* (1965; reprint, New York: Ballantine Books, 1991), 25–28.

5. Pinkerton quoted in McPherson, *The Negro's Civil War,* 149. See also statements by General Abner Doubleday and escaped Union soldier Hannibal Johnson on the helpfulness of the slaves in McPherson, *The Negro's Civil War,* 151, 153–54. The general tendency to aid the Union does not deny the fact that with millions of individuals living in varying circumstances, there were slaves who cooperated with the Confederacy and for a variety of reasons. See Ervin L. Jordan, *Black Confederates and Afro-Yankees in Civil War Virginia* (Charlottesville: University Press of Virginia, 1995).

6. McCurry, *Confederate Reckoning,* 285, including the quote from the Confederate official.

7. See Ira Berlin, Barbara J. Fields, Steven F. Miller, Joseph P. Reidy, and Leslie S. Rowland, eds., *Free at Last: A Documentary History of Slavery, Freedom, and the Civil War* (New York: New Press, 1992), 289; planter Jon'a Pearce quoted in ibid., 114.

8. See ibid., 701–2, 96–97, 107–9, 112.

9. The text of General Cleburne's proposal can be found at http://web.utk.edu/~mfitzgel/docs/374/GCM1864.pdf; Charles Roland, "The Generalship of Robert E. Lee," in Lawrence Lee Hewitt and Thomas E. Schott, eds., *Lee and His Generals: Essays in Honor of T. Harry Williams* (Knoxville: University of Tennessee Press, 2012), 20; Sternhell, *Routes of War,* 94.

10. Astor, *Rebels on the Border,* conclusion, 247, 245; Harrold, *Border War,* 211; Stephanie McCurry, "War, Gender, and Emancipation in the Civil War South," in William A. Blair and Karen Fischer Younger, eds., *Lincoln's Proclamation: Emancipation Reconsidered* (Chapel Hill: University of North Carolina Press, 2009), 120–50, esp. 137. Although slavery was legal in Kentucky, the law allowed recruitment of slaves from disloyal owners. Recruitment officers who needed more troops often decided that they could not determine that a black man was the "property" of a loyal or disloyal slaveholder, and so they went ahead with enrollment in the army.

11. Steven Hahn, *The Political Worlds of Slavery and Freedom* (Cambridge, MA: Harvard University Press, 2009), 76, 80; statement about the effectiveness of the slave grapevine quoted in McPherson, *The Negro's Civil War,* 66.

12. Elizabeth Regosin and Donald R. Shaffer, *Voices of Emancipation: Understanding Slavery, the Civil War, and Reconstruction through the U.S. Pension Files* (New York: New York University Press, 2008). In her book *Loyalty and Loss,* Margaret Storey also found these records to be very informative when she studied the

family and neighborhood relationships among Alabama Unionists. She also found in such records information about cooperation between white Unionists and slaves (see, for example, 45–46 and 51–54).

13. See Edwards, *Legal History of the Civil War and Reconstruction,* chap. 4. Susan O'Donovan is working in this area, and two recent studies that shed significant light on black Southerners' wartime political thinking and activity are David S. Cecelski, *The Fire of Freedom: Abraham Galloway and the Slaves' Civil War* (Chapel Hill: University of North Carolina Press, 2012), and Catherine Bishir, *Crafting Lives: African American Artisans in New Bern, North Carolina, 1770–1900* (Chapel Hill: University of North Carolina Press, 2013).

14. Cleburne proposal; see also the chapter "Did We Miss the Greatest Slave Rebellion in Modern History?" in Hahn, *Political Worlds of Slavery and Freedom,* 55–114. Many examples of descriptions of the slaves' activities can be cited here. The phrases "insurrectionary activities" and "the enemy within" come from McCurry, *Confederate Reckoning,* 262, 291, though she also endorses the phrase "massive slave rebellion" (259).

15. Freehling, *The South vs. the South.*

16. Hahn, *Political Worlds of Slavery and Freedom,* 55; Steven Hahn, *A Nation under Our Feet: Black Political Struggles in the Rural South from Slavery to the Great Migration* (Cambridge, MA: Harvard University Press, 2005). Eugene D. Genovese developed his concept of protonationalism in *Roll, Jordan, Roll: The World the Slaves Made* (New York: Pantheon, 1974).

17. Chandra Manning, "Working for Citizenship in Civil War Contraband Camps," *Journal of the Civil War Era* 4, no. 2 (June 2014): 172–204, quotation on 187; McPherson, *The Negro's Civil War,* 113; Christopher Span, *From Cotton Field to Schoolhouse: African American Education in Mississippi, 1862–1875* (Chapel Hill: University of North Carolina Press, 2009), 42. In a different context, Gregory Downs and Kate Masur have observed that people's actions are often guided not by "any single ideological framework but by their best calculation of what would work to preserve their lives, families, and communities" ("Civil War Sesquicentennial. Reconstruction: Retrospect and Prospects," *Civil War Book Review,* Summer 2015, at http://www.cwbr.com/index.php?q=6049&field=ID&browse=yes&record=full&searching=yes&Submit=Search).

18. Remond's comments are given in C. Peter Ripley, ed., *The Black Abolitionist Papers,* vol. 5, *The United States, 1859–1865* (Chapel Hill: University of North Carolina Press, 1992), 322.

19. Martin Delany, *The Condition, Elevation, Emigration, and Destiny of the Colored People of the United States* (New York: Arno Press, 1968); letter to the *Weekly Anglo-African,* April 13, 1861, in McPherson, *The Negro's Civil War,* 81; the comment on the petition to Congress is included in Ira Berlin, Thavolia Glymph, Steven F. Miller, Joseph P. Reidy, and Leslie S. Rowland, eds., *Freedom: A Documentary History of Emancipation,* series 1, vol. 3: *The Wartime Genesis of Free Labor* (Cambridge: University of Cambridge Press, 1991), 28.

20. Quotations from Robert Purvis and Frederick Douglass in McPherson, *The Negro's Civil War,* 97–98, 17–18; quotations from Henry Highland Garnet (quoted by Robert Hamilton) and from Robert Hamilton are from the *Weekly Anglo-African,* January 3, 1863, in Ripley, ed., *The Black Abolitionist Papers,* 5:176.

21. National Convention of Colored Men, Syracuse, October 1864, address and proceedings, at http://coloredconventions.org/files/original/91057571556d50 3505e8e86e8474d923.pdf; Hugh Davis, *"We Will Be Satisfied with Nothing Less": The African American Struggle for Equal Rights in the North during Reconstruction* (Ithaca, NY: Cornell University Press, 2011), 23–25.

22. Rock quoted in McPherson, *The Negro's Civil War,* 83; see also Stephen Kantrowitz, *More Than Freedom: Fighting for Black Citizenship in a White Republic, 1829–1889* (New York: Penguin, 2012). In addition to Kantrowitz's fine book, see Manisha Sinha's exhaustive study *The Slave's Cause: A History of Abolition* (New Haven, CT: Yale University Press, 2016).

23. Pennington quoted in McPherson, *The Negro's Civil War,* 17, 76, full capitalization given in the original.

24. H. Ford Douglas, addressing the Western Anti-Slavery Society, September 23, 1860, in Ripley, ed., *The Black Abolitionist Papers,* 5:94; National Convention of Colored Men, address, 56; McPherson, *The Negro's Civil War,* 275.

25. Statement by the chief of police in Philadelphia, in McPherson, *The Negro's Civil War,* 35, emphasis in original; letter from R. H. V. (probably Robert H. Vandyne) in the *Weekly Anglo-African,* September 1861, in Ripley, *The Black Abolitionist Papers,* 5:118; Davis, "*We Will Be Satisfied with Nothing Less,*" 11.

26. McPherson, *The Negro's Civil War,* 51–52.

27. National Convention of Colored Men, address and proceedings. See also Escott, "*What Shall We Do with the Negro?,*" chapter 4, for a more detailed examination of the events described in this paragraph and the next three paragraphs of the chapter text as well as for the material quoted in those paragraphs (emphasis as given there). For background on the black convention movement, see Howard Holman Bell, *A Survey of the Negro Convention Movement, 1830–1861* (New York: Arno Press, 1969).

28. Quotations from Escott, "*What Shall We Do with the Negro?";* National Convention of Colored Men, address, 51–52, 50, 48; and Escott, *Paying Freedom's Price,* chap. 4, emphasis in original.

29. National Convention of Colored Men, proceedings, 34, 36; *Proceedings of the First Annual Meeting of the National Equal Rights League* (Philadelphia: Markley and Son, 1865), 28, 4, at http://babel.hathitrust.org/cgi/pt?id=hvd .hnvpf5;view=1up;seq=10.

30. Editor's notes in Ripley, ed., *The Black Abolitionist Papers,* 5:84, 287.

31. Davis, *"We Will Be Satisfied with Nothing Less,"* 29, 16.

32. Schwalm, *Emancipation's Diaspora,* chap. 3.

33. Davis, *"We Will Be Satisfied with Nothing Less,"* 15, 29; Schwalm, *Emancipation's Diaspora,* introduction. Jean Yellin's biography *Harriet Jacobs: A Life* (New

York: Basic Civitas Books, 2004) is informative and useful in learning more about the lives of African American women at this time.

34. Crystal Feimster, "'What If I Am a Woman?': Black Women's Campaigns for Sexual Justice and Citizenship," in Gregory P. Downs and Kate Masur, eds., *The World the Civil War Made* (Chapel Hill: University of North Carolina Press, 2015), 249–68; Edwards, *Legal History of the Civil War and Reconstruction,* 152–62.

35. Jim Downs, *Sick from Freedom: African American Illness and Suffering during the Civil War and Reconstruction* (New York: Oxford University Press, 2012), 18, 5, 22; see also Margaret Humphreys, *Intensely Human: The Health of the Black Soldier in the American Civil War* (Baltimore: Johns Hopkins University Press, 2008).

36. Joseph T. Glatthaar, *Forged in Battle: The Civil War Alliance of Black Soldiers and White Officers* (New York: Free Press, 1990), 160.

37. See Bruce Tap, *The Fort Pillow Massacre: North, South, and the Status of African Americans in the Civil War* (London: Routledge, 2014), and Michael Bennett, "The Black Flag and Confederate Soldiers: Total War from the Bottom Up?" in Slap and Smith, eds., *"This Distracted and Anarchical People,"* 142–59.

38. Bob Luke and John David Smith, *Soldiering for Freedom: How the Union Army Recruited, Trained, and Deployed the U.S. Colored Troops* (Baltimore: Johns Hopkins University Press, 2014), 83–84; George Stephens to the *Weekly Anglo-African,* August 1, 1864; Richard M. Reid, *Freedom for Themselves: North Carolina's Black Soldiers in the Civil War Era* (Chapel Hill: University of North Carolina Press, 2008); Glatthaar, *Forged in Battle;* Thomas, *The Iron Way,* 121.

39. Editorial in the *Weekly Anglo-African* in November 1862 and statement by Henry McNeal Turner in October 1862, emphasis in original, both quoted in McPherson, *The Negro's Civil War,* 297–98, 136; final quotation from Robert Hamilton in the *Weekly Anglo-African,* January 3, 1863, in Ripley, ed., *The Black Abolitionist Papers,* 5:176–77.

40. Information on labors among the freed people appears in records of some individuals—for example, Harriet Jacobs. See Jean Fagan Yellin, Joseph M. Thomas, Kate Culkin, and Scott Korb, eds., *The Harriet Jacobs Family Papers,* 2 vols. (Chapel Hill: University of North Carolina Press, 2008), and Yellin, *Harriet Jacobs.*

41. Charlotte Forten Grimké, *The Journals of Charlotte Forten Grimké,* ed. Brenda Stevenson (New York: Oxford University Press, 1988), 388, 393, 402.

4. Military History

1. See, for example, Gary W. Gallagher, "'The Progress of Our Arms': Whither Civil War Military History?" Forty-Fourth Fortenbaugh Lecture, Civil War Institute, Gettysburg College, 2005; and Richard McMurray, personal communication, c. 2005.

2. Gary W. Gallagher, *Becoming Confederates: Paths to a New National Loyalty,* Mercer University Lamar Memorial Lectures no. 54 (Athens: University of

Georgia Press, 2013); Joseph T. Glatthaar, *General Lee's Army: From Victory to Collapse* (New York: Free Press, 2008).

3. Barton Myers, "The Future of Civil War Era Studies: Military History," *Journal of the Civil War Era* 2, no. 1 (March 2012), at http://journalofthecivilwarera.org/forum-the-future-of-civil-war-era-studies-military-history/; Myers, *Rebels against the Confederacy;* Gallagher, "'The Progress of Our Arms'"; Gary Gallagher, "Disaffection, Persistence, and Nation: Some Directions in Recent Research on the Confederacy," *Civil War History* 55, no. 3 (September 2009): 329–53.

4. Myers, "The Future of Civil War Era Studies: Military History." Myers has also pointed out that the number of nations whose emigrants fought for the North is very large. See his comments in "Roundtable Discussion: The Legacy of the U.S. Civil War, 150 Years Later," *FifteenEightyFour,* Cambridge University Press blog, April 9, 2015, at http://www.cambridgeblog.org/2015/the-legacy-of-the-u-s-civil-war-150-years-later/.

5. Myers, "The Future of Civil War Era Studies: Military History"; William C. Davis, *The Cause Lost: Myths and Realities of the Confederacy* (Lawrence: University Press of Kansas, 1996). See also Rick Atkinson, *An Army at Dawn: The War in North Africa, 1942–1943* (New York: Holt, 2002), *The Day of Battle: The War in Sicily and Italy, 1943–1944* (New York: Holt, 2007), and *The Guns at Last Light: The War in Western Europe, 1944–1945* (New York: Holt, 2013).

6. See the fine study by Archer Jones, *Civil War Command and Strategy: The Process of Victory and Defeat* (New York: Free Press, 1992).

7. Donald Stoker, *The Grand Design: Strategy and the U.S. Civil War* (New York: Oxford University Press, 2010), 122, 130–31, 159, 208, 229, 310–12.

8. James M. McPherson, *Embattled Rebel: Jefferson Davis as Commander in Chief* (New York: Penguin, 2014), 248, 28, 30–37; Paul D. Escott, *The Confederacy: The Slaveholders' Failed Venture* (Santa Barbara, CA: Praeger/ABC-CLIO, 2010).

9. Stoker, *The Grand Design,* 11.

10. Steven E. Woodworth, *Davis and Lee at War* (Lawrence: University Press of Kansas, 1995); Escott, *Military Necessity*, chaps. 3 and 6; Stoker, *The Grand Design,* 186–88, 280.

11. Robert E. May, contribution in "Roundtable Discussion: The Legacy of the U.S. Civil War."

12. Roland, "The Generalship of Robert E. Lee," 20, 31.

13. Stoker, *The Grand Design,* 120; J. F. C. Fuller, *Grant and Lee: A Study in Personality and Generalship* (Bloomington: Indiana University Press, 1957), 39–40; Mark Weitz, *More Damning Than Slaughter* (Lincoln: University of Nebraska Press, 2005), 27; Roland, "The Generalship of Robert E. Lee," 21.

14. Stoker, *The Grand Design,* 26–27. I have argued that the departmental system seemed to work adequately early in the war but poorly later on (see Escott, *Military Necessity*). A thorough analysis of the reasons for that difference would be useful.

15. Earl J. Hess, *The Civil War in the West: Victory and Defeat from the Appalachians to the Mississippi* (Chapel Hill: University of North Carolina Press, 2012), 1–6.

16. Ibid.; Mackey, *The Uncivil War,* 22.

17. Thomas L. Connelly and Archer Jones, *The Politics of Command: Factions and Ideas in Confederate Strategy* (Baton Rouge: Louisiana State University Press, 1973).

18. Marx's opinion is given in *Die Presse* (Vienna), March 27, 1862. For more discussion of Beauregard, see Connelly and Jones, *The Politics of Command;* Roland's argument is in "The Generalship of Robert E. Lee," 24.

19. Sherman quoted in Michael Fellman, *Citizen Sherman: A Life of William Tecumseh Sherman* (New York: Random House, 1995), 177, 179, 181, 182, ix; Richard Wheeler, *Sherman's March* (New York: Crowell, 1978), 42, 52, 53; "Reply of Major General Sherman to the Mayor of Atlanta," Library of Congress, at https://archive.org/details/replyofmajgenshe00sher; Lisa Tendrich Frank, *The Civilian War: Confederate Women and Union Soldiers during Sherman's March* (Baton Rouge: Louisiana State University Press, 2015); Jacqueline Glass Campbell, *When Sherman Marched to the Sea: Resistance on the Confederate Home Front* (Chapel Hill: University of North Carolina Press, 2003).

20. Frank, *The Civilian War.*

21. Thomas, *The Iron Way,* chap. 5.

22. Stoker, *The Grand Design,* 8–9, 412–13; Brian Holden-Reid, *America's Civil War: The Operational Battlefield, 1861–1863* (Amherst, NY: Prometheus Books, 2008).

23. Stoker, *The Grand Design,* 78. In 1862, General Hunter, with the knowledge of the secretary of war but contrary to Lincoln's policy, started raising and training black troops.

24. Duvergier de Hauranne quoted in Andrew M. Fleche, *The Revolution of 1861: The America Civil War and the Age of Nationalist Conflict* (Chapel Hill: University of North Carolina Press, 2012), 152.

25. Timothy J. Orr, "'All Manner of Schemes and Rascalities': The Politics of Promotion in the Union Army," in Slap and Smith, eds., *"This Distracted and Anarchical People,"* 81–103.

26. Jonathan White, "'For My Part I Dont Care Who Is Elected President': The Union Army and the Elections of 1864," in Slap and Smith, eds., *"This Distracted and Anarchical People,"* 104–22; see John H. Eicher and David J. Eicher, *Civil War High Commands* (Stanford, CA: Stanford University Press, 2001), for a list of commanders in both armies who served in Congress.

27. Stoker, *The Grand Design,* 122, conclusion.

28. Maris Vinovskis, quoted in Diane Miller Sommerville, "'Will They Ever Be Able to Forget?' Confederate Soldiers and Mental Illness in the Defeated South," in Berry, ed., *Weirding the War,* 322; Brian Craig Miller, *Empty Sleeves: Amputation in the Civil War South* (Athens: University of Georgia Press, 2015), 117, 124.

See also Ansley Herring Wegner, *Phantom Pain: North Carolina's Artificial Limb Program for Confederate Veterans* (Raleigh: North Carolina Department of Cultural Resources, 2004).

29. Sommerville, "'Will They Ever Be Able to Forget?'" 322; David Silkenat, *Moments of Despair: Suicide, Divorce, and Debt in Civil War Era North Carolina* (Chapel Hill: University of North Carolina Press, 2014); Judkin Browning, personal communication, October 18, 2014.

30. Miller, *Empty Sleeves,* 107, chap. 3. Two recent studies argue that we may have overestimated the effects of battlefield deaths on social patterns. See J. David Hacker, Libra Hilde, and James Holland, "The Effect of the Civil War on Southern Marriage Patterns," *Journal of Southern History* 79, no. 1 (February 2010): 39–70, and Nicholas Mitchell, "The Great Exaggeration: Death and the Civil War," *Journal of the Civil War Era* 4, no. 1 (March 2014): 3–27.

31. Thomas, *The Confederacy as a Revolutionary Experience.*

5. New Techniques, New Opportunities

1. J. Morgan Kousser, *The Shaping of Southern Politics: Suffrage Restriction and the Establishment of the One-Party South, 1880–1910* (New Haven, CT: Yale University Press, 1974); Fogel and Engerman, *Time on the Cross.*

2. Sara M. Gregg, "Cultivating an Agro-Environmental History," in Douglas Cazaux Sackman, ed., *A Companion to American Environmental History* (Chichester, UK: Wiley-Blackwell, 2010), 438.

3. "Workshop: Digital Collaborations across Institutions: Using *Visualizing Emancipation* to Teach the End of Slavery," Southern Historical Association Annual Meeting, November 13–16, 2014, Atlanta, GA. Such a runaway slave–newspaper advertisement project obviously adds new dimensions to previous works such as Loren Schweninger and John Hope Franklin, *Runaway Slaves: Rebels on the Plantation* (New York: Oxford University Press, 1999). Schweninger and Franklin wisely placed their work online to benefit other scholars.

4. "Information on Runaway Slaves and Their Masters," document compiling data gathered in a class taught by Robert Kenzer, who shared this document with the author. This research was a contribution to the Visualizing Emancipation project sponsored by the University of Richmond, which is discussed at greater length later in this chapter. See also the Documenting Runaway Slaves project website at http://aquila.usm.edu/drs/.

5. Max Grivno, "Mapping the Runaways: Digital Humanities and the Landscape of Slavery," paper presented at the Southern Historical Association Annual Meeting, November 13–16, 2014, Atlanta, GA, copy in the author's files, courtesy of Professor Grivno.

6. The book that came out of this research project is Thomas, *The Iron Way.*

7. A list of digital projects reviewed by the *Journal of American History* is available at http://historymatters.gmu.edu/webreviews/. The list grows every day, but here I mention two projects focused on the movement of runaway slaves: Docu-

menting Runaway Slaves, n.d., at http://aquila.usm.edu/drs/, and Freedom on the Move: A Database of Fugitives from North American Slavery, n.d., http://freedom onthemove.org/.

8. A blog post by William Kurtz on the H-CivWar daily digest, October 4, 2016, announced this project from the Nau Center for Civil War Studies at the University of Virginia and included the paper by Jonathan W. White of Christopher Newport University. See also United States Colored Troops, Men of Albemarle County Digital Project, Nau Center for Civil War History, University of Virginia, Charlottesville, at https://networks.h-net.org/node/4113/discussions/146677/introducing-nau-centers-usct-men-albemarle-county-digital-project.

9. The Valley of the Shadow project, which was a model for others, can be found at http://valley.lib.virginia.edu/.

10. The Born Unfree project, founded by Professor Stephen Berry and Professor Claudio Saunt of the University of Georgia, was described to the author in detail in an email from Stephen Berry, August 28, 2014. It is also described online at http://www.ehistory.org/projects/born-unfree.html.

11. For a discussion of the many types of information found in the Federal Writers' Project Slave Narratives, see Paul D. Escott, *Slavery Remembered: A Record of Twentieth Century Slave Narratives* (Chapel Hill: University of North Carolina Press, 1978), appendix A.

12. Berry, email description of the Born Unfree project, August 28, 2014. See also Mark A. Moore, Michael Hill, and Jessica A. Bandel, *The Old North State at War: The North Carolina Civil War Atlas* (Chapel Hill: University of North Carolina Press, 2015), for a study begun somewhat earlier that demonstrated the value of using geospatial data to provide greater insight into events of the Civil War.

13. Andrew Failka, "Controlled Chaos: Spatiotemporal Patterns within Missouri's Irregular Civil War," in Joseph Beilein, ed., *The Civil War Guerrilla: Unfolding the Black Flag in History, Memory, and Myth* (Lexington: University Press of Kentucky, 2015), 43–69, quotations on 44, 46. Among the helpful sources on digital mapping that Failka discusses in his footnotes is David J. Bodenhamer, John Corrigan, and Trevor M. Harris, eds., *The Spatial Humanities: GIS and the Future of Humanities Scholarship* (Bloomington: Indiana University Press, 2010).

14. Information about the software used and the expertise contributed by the University of Georgia appears in the Mapping Occupation website's credits tab. Other valuable information about major spatial, electoral, or railroad data sets that formed the basis of the mapping effort appears under the data tab.

15. For more detail, see the credits tab of the Visualizing Emancipation website, https://dsl.richmond.edu/emancipation/credits/.

6. Environmental Approaches to the Civil War

1. Douglas Cazaux Sackman, "Introduction," in Sackman, ed., *Companion to American Environmental History,* xv.

2. General Hill quoted in Judkin Browning and Timothy Silver, book pro-

posal for an environmental history of the Civil War, shared with the author on October 18, 2014, courtesy of Professor Browning.

3. Kenneth W. Noe, "Fateful Lightning: The Significance of Weather and Climate to Civil War History," and Timothy Silver, "Yancey County Goes to War: A Case Study of People and Nature on Home Front and Battlefield, 1861–1865," in Brian Allen Drake, ed., *The Blue, the Gray, and the Green: Toward an Environmental History of the Civil War* (Athens: University of Georgia Press, 2015), 16–33 and 52–66; Browning and Silver, proposal.

4. Sutherland, *A Savage Conflict,* 133–34.

5. Kathryn Shively Meier, *Nature's Civil War: Common Soldiers and the Environment in 1862 Virginia* (Chapel Hill: University of North Carolina Press, 2013); Browning and Silver, proposal; Downs, *Sick from Freedom;* Humphreys, *Intensely Human;* Margaret Humphreys, *Marrow of Tragedy: The Health Crisis of the American Civil War* (Baltimore: Johns Hopkins University Press, 2013), 73.

6. Noe, "Fateful Lightning," 25; Escott, *After Secession;* Browning and Silver, proposal.

7. The examples and quotations in the next few paragraphs in the text come from a new manuscript by Joan Cashin currently titled "War Stuff: The Struggle for Resources in the American Civil War." I had an opportunity to read this valuable study and to correspond with Cashin by email.

8. Ibid., chap. 4.

9. Ibid., final chapter.

10. Ibid., chap. 4.

11. Meier, *Nature's Civil War,* 1.

12. Thomas, *The Iron Way,* 149; Lisa M. Brady, *War upon the Land: Military Strategy and the Transformation of Southern Landscapes during the American Civil War* (Athens: University of Georgia Press, 2012), chap. 1.

13. Cashin, "War Stuff," chap. 3.

14. Ibid. Two books by R. Douglas Hurt on the interconnected problems of Southern agriculture suggest new directions for research and analysis: *Agriculture and the Confederacy* (Chapel Hill: University of North Carolina Press, 2015) and *Food and Agriculture during the Civil War* (Santa Barbara, CA: Praeger, 2016).

15. Cashin, "War Stuff," chap. 3 and conclusion.

16. Brady, *War upon the Land,* 92, chaps. 2 and 4.

17. Alfred Crosby, *The Colombian Exchange: Biological and Cultural Consequences of 1492* (Westport, CT: Praeger, 2003); Berry quoted in Browning and Silver, proposal.

18. Browning and Silver, proposal.

19. Ibid.

20. The discussion of and associated quotations dealing with hog cholera in this paragraph and the next two paragraphs come from Erin Mauldin, "The Stockman's War: Hog Cholera, Agricultural Reform, and the Fight to Maintain

the Commons during the Civil War Era," paper presented at the meeting of the Society of Civil War Historians, summer 2014, Baltimore. I am very grateful to Mauldin for sharing her research with me.

21. Paul Gates, *Agriculture and the Civil War* (New York: Knopf, 1965), 90, cited in Mauldin, "The Stockman's War."

22. Steven Hahn, *The Roots of Southern Populism: Yeoman Farmers and the Transformation of the Georgia Upcountry, 1850–1890* (1983; reprint, New York: Oxford University Press, 2006).

23. Mauldin, "The Stockman's War."

24. Sackman, "Introduction," xv.

25. Aaron Sachs, "Stumps in the Wilderness," in Drake, ed., *The Blue, the Gray, and the Green,* 96–112; Brady, *War upon the Land,* conclusion; Nelson, *Ruin Nation,* 3–4.

26. Browning and Silver, proposal; Sachs, "Stumps in the Wilderness"; Brady, *War upon the Land,* conclusion. See also Adam Wesley Dean, *An Agrarian Republic: Farming, Antislavery Politics, and Nature Parks in the Civil War Era* (Chapel Hill: University of North Carolina Press, 2015).

27. Thomas, *The Iron Way,* 149–50; Browning and Silver, proposal.

28. See Paul D. Escott, *Many Excellent People: Power and Privilege in North Carolina, 1850–1900* (Chapel Hill: University of North Carolina Press, 1985), chaps. 7 and 8.

29. Dean, *An Agrarian Republic.*

30. An exploration of this topic is given in David Silkenat, *Driven from Home: North Carolina's Civil War Refugee Crisis* (Athens: University of Georgia Press, 2016).

31. Robert Kenzer, *Kinship and Neighborhood in a Southern Community: Orange County, North Carolina, 1849–1881* (Knoxville: University of Tennessee Press, 1987).

32. Susan R. Schrepfer and David Cazaux Sackman, "Gender," in Sackman, ed., *Companion to American Environmental History,* 132, 128.

7. Consequences and Continuities

1. Ken Burns, dir., *The Civil War,* PBS, September 23–27, 1990.

2. James M. McPherson, "The Civil War and the Transformation of America," in Cooper and McCardell, eds., *In the Cause of Liberty,* 1–8; Bensel's position is described in Heather Cox Richardson, "North and West of Reconstruction: Studies in Political Economy," in Thomas J. Brown, ed., *Reconstructions: New Perspectives on the Postbellum United States* (New York: Oxford University Press, 2006), 79 (quotation). See also James M. McPherson, *The War That Forged a Nation: Why the Civil War Still Matters* (New York: Oxford University Press, 2015), in which McPherson reiterates key points of his position and argues that the war to preserve the Union created a modern nation.

3. Gregory Downs, "Force, Freedom, and the Making of Emancipation," in

William A. Link and James J. Broomall, eds., *Rethinking American Emancipation: Legacies of Slavery and the Quest for Black Freedom* (New York: Cambridge University Press, 2016), 42–68.

4. Edwards, *Legal History of the Civil War and Reconstruction,* esp. chap. 5, and Laura Edwards, "Reconstruction and the History of Governance," in Downs and Masur, eds., *The World the Civil War Made,* 24–32.

5. Edwards, *Legal History of the Civil War and Reconstruction.*

6. Ibid.; Hamilton, *Limits of Sovereignty,* quotations from 171, 169.

7. Edwards, *A Legal History of the Civil War and Reconstruction,* 168, 173, 170. Edwards's analysis takes us beyond our traditional understanding of decisions that limited the central government's power, decisions such as the Slaughter House cases. She argues that by the time of *Plessy v. Ferguson* in 1896 the Supreme Court was giving to states the same kind of paternalist power (here exercised over women and blacks) that white men possessed in the family and society.

8. Steven Hahn, "What Sort of World Did the Civil War Make?" in Downs and Masur, eds., *The World the Civil War Made,* 337–56, quotation from 340.

9. Kevin Waite, "Jefferson Davis and Visions of Proslavery Empire in the Far West," *Journal of the Civil War Era* 6, no. 4 (December 2016): 536–65; Megan Kate Nelson, "The Civil War from Apache Pass," *Journal of the Civil War Era* 6, no. 4 (December 2016): 510–35.

10. Durwood Ball, "Liberty, Empire, and the Civil War in the American West," in Virginia Scharff, ed., *Empire and Liberty: The Civil War and the West* (Oakland: University of California Press, 2015), 76, 79, 81, 82.

11. Stacey L. Smith, "Beyond North and South: Putting the West in the Civil War and Reconstruction," *Journal of the Civil War Era* 6, no. 4 (December 2016): 571 (quoting White), 584; Richardson, "North and West of Reconstruction," 69 (quoting White).

12. Smith, "Beyond North and South," 567, 571, 573 (quoting Elliott West).

13. Ibid., 571, 567, 574, 580.

14. Ibid., 587, citing West.

15. Eric Foner quoted in Amanda Claybaugh, "Washington Novels and the Machinery of Government," in Downs and Masur, eds., *The World the Civil War Made,* 206; Gregory Downs and Kate Masur, "Introduction: Echoes of War: Rethinking Post Civil War Governance and Politics," in Downs and Masur, eds., *The World the Civil War Made,* 10, 6, 11–13.

16. Smith, "Beyond North and South," 575.

17. Ibid.

18. Gaines Foster, *Moral Reconstruction: Christian Lobbyists and the Federal Legislation of Morality, 1865–1920* (Chapel Hill: University of North Carolina Press, 2002); Susan J. Pearson, "A New Birth of Regulation: The State of the State after the Civil War," *Journal of the Civil War Era* 5, no. 3 (September 2015): 422–39, quotation on 424.

19. Pearson, "A New Birth of Regulation," 424, 436.

20. Eric Foner, "Historians' Forum: Reconstruction," *Civil War History* 61, no. 3 (September 2015): 288–89.

21. Kevin Waite, interview, *Muster* (blog of the *Journal of the Civil War Era*), February 3, 2017, at http://journalofthecivilwarera.org/2017/02/author-interview-kevin-waite/.

22. Jean Baker, *Affairs of Party: The Political Culture of Northern Democrats in the Mid–Nineteenth Century* (1983; reprint, New York: Fordham University Press, 1998); George Fredrickson, *The Inner Civil War: Northern Intellectuals and the Crisis of the Union* (New York: Harper and Row, 1965); Escott, *"What Shall We Do with the Negro?"* chap. 5. Examples of the relatively few Northerners who took this Southern viewpoint can be seen in the works of David Christy and Episcopal bishop John Henry Hopkins.

23. Leslie Butler, "Reconstructions in Intellectual and Cultural Life," in Brown, ed., *Reconstructions,* 204.

24. Schurz quoted in Adam Arenson, "John Gast's *American Progress:* Using Manifest Destiny to Forget the Civil War and Reconstruction," in Scharff, ed., *Empire and Liberty,* 130.

25. Susan-Mary Grant, "Americans Forging a New Nation, 1860–1912," in Don Doyle and Marco Antonio Pamplona, eds., *Nationalism in the New World* (Athens: University of Georgia Press, 2006), 80–98; Mark Wahlgren Summers, *The Ordeal of the Reunion: A New History of Reconstruction* (Chapel Hill: University of North Carolina Press, 2014).

26. Butler, "Reconstructions in Intellectual and Cultural Life," 173. For the declarations quoted here and others, see *Augusta Daily Constitutionalist,* July 14, 15, 20, and 31, 1864, September 6, 1864, September 9, 1864, and November 29, 1864; *Daily Chattanooga Rebel,* July 21 and November 2 and 21, 1864; *Augusta Chronicle and Sentinel,* September 9 and November 25, 1864.

27. Among the better-known works that focus on postwar conflict are Phillip Shaw Paludan, *Victims: A True Story of the Civil War* (Knoxville: University of Tennessee Press, 1981); Victoria Bynum, *The Long Shadow of the Civil War: Southern Dissent and Its Legacies* (Chapel Hill: University of North Carolina Press, 2010); and William McKee Evans, *To Die Game: The Story of the Lowry Gang, Indian Guerrillas of Reconstruction* (Baton Rouge: Louisiana State University Press, 1971). See also Steven Nash, *Reconstruction's Ragged Edge: The Politics of Postwar Life in the Southern Mountains* (Chapel Hill: University of North Carolina Press, 2016), and Jonathan Dean Sarris, *A Separate Civil War: Communities in Conflict in the Mountain South* (Charlottesville: University of Virginia Press, 2016). Margaret Storey offers a strong recent study of Unionists in *Loyalty and Loss.* Brian Fennessy, a doctoral student at the University of North Carolina at Chapel Hill, is studying the postwar political activities of Unionists and Confederate critics in North Carolina.

28. Charles Reagan Wilson, "Religion and the American Civil War in Comparative Perspective," in Randall M. Miller, Henry S. Stout, and Charles Reagan

Wilson, eds., *Religion and the American Civil War* (New York: Oxford University Press, 1998), 395–96.

29. I thank Judkin Browning for sharing a description of his "Reverberations of Battle" project.

Bibliography

Arenson, Adam. "John Gast's *American Progress:* Using Manifest Destiny to Forget the Civil War and Reconstruction." In Scharff, ed., *Empire and Liberty,* 122–39.

Astor, Aaron. *Rebels on the Border: Civil War, Emancipation, and the Reconstruction of Kentucky and Missouri.* Baton Rouge: Louisiana State University Press, 2012.

Atkinson, Rick. *An Army at Dawn: The War in North Africa, 1942–1943.* New York: Holt, 2002.

———. *The Day of Battle: The War in Sicily and Italy, 1943–1944.* New York: Holt, 2007.

———. *The Guns at Last Light: The War in Western Europe, 1944–1945.* New York: Holt, 2013.

Auman, William T. *Civil War in the North Carolina Quaker Belt.* Jefferson, NC: McFarland, 2014.

Baker, Jean. *Affairs of Party: The Political Culture of Northern Democrats in the Mid–Nineteenth Century.* 1983. Reprint. New York: Fordham University Press, 1998.

Ball, Durwood. "Liberty, Empire, and the Civil War in the American West." In Scharff, ed., *Empire and Liberty,* 66–86.

Baptist, Edward E. *The Half Has Never Been Told: Slavery and the Making of American Capitalism.* New York: Basic Books, 2014.

Becker, Carl. "Everyman His Own Historian." Annual address of the president of the American Historical Association, Minneapolis, December 29, 1931. *American Historical Review* 37, no. 2 (1931): 221–35. At https://www.historians.org/about-aha-and-membership/aha-history-and-archives/presidential-addresses/carl-1-becker.

Beckert, Sven. *Empire of Cotton: A Global History.* New York: Vintage, 2014.

Beilein, Joseph, ed., *The Civil War Guerrilla: Unfolding the Black Flag in History, Memory, and Myth.* Lexington: University Press of Kentucky, 2015.

Bell, Howard Holman. *A Survey of the Negro Convention Movement, 1830–1861.* New York: Arno Press, 1969.

Bennett, Michael. "The Black Flag and Confederate Soldiers: Total War from the Bottom Up?" In Slap and Smith, eds., *"This Distracted and Anarchical People,"* 142–58.

Beringer, Richard E., Herman Hattaway, Archer Jones, and William N. Still Jr. *Why the South Lost the Civil War.* Athens: University of Georgia Press, 1986.

Berlin, Ira. "Who Freed the Slaves? Emancipation and Its Meaning." In Blight and Simpson, eds., *Union and Emancipation,* 105–22.

Berlin, Ira, Barbara J. Fields, Thavolia Glymph, Joseph P. Reidy, and Leslie S. Rowland, eds. *Freedom: A Documentary History of Emancipation.* Series 1, vol. 1: *The Destruction of Slavery.* Cambridge: University of Cambridge Press, 1985.

Berlin, Ira, Barbara J. Fields, Steve F. Miller, Joseph P. Reidy, and Leslie S. Rowland, eds. *Free at Last: A Documentary History of Slavery, Freedom, and the Civil War.* New York: New Press, 1992.

Berlin, Ira, Thavolia Glymph, Steven F. Miller, Joseph P. Reidy, and Leslie S. Rowland, eds. *Freedom: A Documentary History of Emancipation.* Series 1, vol. 3: *The Wartime Genesis of Free Labor.* Cambridge: University of Cambridge Press, 1991.

Bernath, Michael. *Confederate Minds: The Struggle for Intellectual Independence in the Civil War South.* Chapel Hill: University of North Carolina Press, 2010.

Berry, Stephen, ed. *Weirding the War: Stories from the Civil War's Ragged Edges.* Athens: University of Georgia Press, 2011.

Bishir, Catherine. *Crafting Lives: African American Artisans in New Bern, North Carolina, 1770–1900.* Chapel Hill: University of North Carolina Press, 2013.

Blair, William A., and Karen Fischer Younger, eds. *Lincoln's Proclamation: Emancipation Reconsidered.* Chapel Hill: University of North Carolina Press, 2009.

Blight, David W., and Brooks D. Simpson, eds. *Union and Emancipation: Essays on Politics and Race in the Civil War Era.* Kent, OH: Kent State University Press, 1997.

Blum, Edward J. "'The First Secessionist Was Satan': Secession and the Religious Politics of Evil in Civil War America." *Civil War History* 60, no. 3 (September 2014): 234–69.

Bodenhamer, David J., John Corrigan, and Trevor M. Harris, eds. *The Spatial Humanities: GIS and the Future of Humanities Scholarship.* Bloomington: Indiana University Press, 2010.

Born Unfree. N.d. At http://www.ehistory.org/projects/born-unfree.html.

Bradley, Michael R. "'I Shoot the Men and Burn Their Houses': Home Fires in the Line of Fire." In Dollar, Whiteaker, and Dickinson, eds., *Sister States, Enemy States,* 168–87.

Brady, Lisa M. Forum: "The Future of Civil War Era Studies: Environmental Histories." *Journal of the Civil War Era* 2, no. 1 (March 2012). At http://journalofthecivilwarera.org/forum-the-future-of-civil-war-era-studies/.

———. *War upon the Land: Military Strategy and the Transformation of Southern Landscapes during the American Civil War.* Athens: University of Georgia Press, 2012.

Brewer, James H. *The Confederate Negro: Virginia's Craftsmen and Military Laborers, 1861–1865.* Durham, NC: Duke University Press, 1969.

Brown, Thomas J., ed. *Reconstructions: New Perspectives on the Postbellum United States.* New York: Oxford University Press, 2006.

Burton, Orville Vernon, Jerald Podair, and Jennifer L. Weber, eds. *The Struggle for Equality: Essays on Sectional Conflict, the Civil War, and the Long Reconstruction*. Charlottesville: University of Virginia Press, 2011.

Butler, Leslie. "Reconstructions in Intellectual and Cultural Life." In Brown, ed., *Reconstructions,* 172–205.

Bynum, Victoria E. *The Free State of Jones*. Chapel Hill: University of North Carolina Press, 2001.

———. *The Long Shadow of the Civil War: Southern Dissent and Its Legacies*. Chapel Hill: University of North Carolina Press, 2010.

Byrne, Frank J. *Becoming Bourgeois: Merchant Culture in the South, 1820–1865*. Lexington: University Press of Kentucky, 2006.

Campbell, Jacqueline Glass. *When Sherman Marched to the Sea: Resistance on the Confederate Home Front*. Chapel Hill: University of North Carolina Press, 2003.

Cecelski, David S. *The Fire of Freedom: Abraham Galloway and the Slaves' Civil War*. Chapel Hill: University of North Carolina Press, 2012.

Channing, Steven A. *Crisis of Fear: Secession in South Carolina*. New York: Simon and Schuster, 1970.

Cimbala, Paul A., and Randall M. Miller, eds. *An Uncommon Time: The Civil War and the Northern Home Front*. New York: Fordham University Press, 2002.

Clampitt, Bradley. *Confederate Heartland: Military and Civilian Morale in the Western Confederacy*. Baton Rouge: Louisiana State University Press, 2011.

Claybaugh, Amanda. "Washington Novels and the Machinery of Government." In Downs and Masur, eds., *The World the Civil War Made,* 206–25.

Clinton, Catherine. "'Public Women' and Sexual Politics during the American Civil War." In Burton, Podair, and Weber, eds., *The Struggle for Equality,* 119–36.

Connelly, Thomas L., and Archer Jones. *The Politics of Command: Factions and Ideas in Confederate Strategy*. Baton Rouge: Louisiana State University Press, 1973.

Cooper, William J., Jr., and John M. McCardell Jr., eds. *In the Cause of Liberty: How the Civil War Redefined American Ideals*. Baton Rouge: Louisiana State University Press, 2009.

Cottrol, Robert J. *The Long, Lingering Shadow: Slavery, Race, and Law in the American Hemisphere*. Athens: University of Georgia Press, 2013.

Crofts, Daniel. *Lincoln and the Politics of Slavery: The Other Thirteenth Amendment and the Struggle to Save the Union*. Chapel Hill: University of North Carolina Press, 2016.

Crosby, Alfred. *The Colombian Exchange: Biological and Cultural Consequences of 1492*. Westport, CT: Praeger, 2003.

Crow, Jeffrey J., and Paul D. Escott. "The Social Order and Violent Disorder: An Analysis of North Carolina in the Revolution and the Civil War." *Journal of Southern History* 52, no. 3 (August 1986): 373–402.

Davis, Hugh. *"We Will Be Satisfied with Nothing Less": The African American Struggle for Equal Rights in the North during Reconstruction.* Ithaca, NY: Cornell University Press, 2011.

Dean, Adam Wesley. *An Agrarian Republic: Farming, Antislavery Politics, and Nature Parks in the Civil War Era.* Chapel Hill: University of North Carolina Press, 2015.

Delanty, Gerard, and Krishan Kumar, eds. *The Sage Handbook of Nations and Nationalism.* London: Sage, 2006.

Delany, Martin. *The Condition, Elevation, Emigration, and Destiny of the Colored People of the United States.* New York: Arno Press, 1968.

Delfino, Susanna, and Michele Gillespie, eds. *Technology, Innovation, and Southern Industrialization: From the Antebellum Era to the Computer Age.* Columbia: University of Missouri Press, 2008.

Documenting Runaway Slaves. N.d. At http://aquila.usm.edu/drs/.

Dollar, Kent T., Larry H. Whiteaker, and W. Calvin Dickinson, eds. *Sister States, Enemy States: The Civil War in Kentucky and Tennessee.* Lexington: University Press of Kentucky, 2009.

Douma, Michael. "The Lincoln Administration's Negotiations to Colonize African Americans in Dutch Surinam." *Civil War History* 61, no. 2 (June 2015): 111–37.

Downs, Gregory. "Force, Freedom, and the Making of Emancipation." In Link and Broomall, eds., *Rethinking American Emancipation,* 42–68.

Downs, Gregory, and Kate Masur. "Civil War Sesquicentennial. Reconstruction: Retrospect and Prospects." *Civil War Book Review,* Summer 2015. At http://www.cwbr.com/index.php?q=6049&field=ID&browse=yes&record=full&searching=yes&Submit=Search.

———. "Introduction: Echoes of War: Rethinking Post Civil War Governance and Politics." In Downs and Masur, eds., *The World the Civil War Made,* 1–21.

———, eds. *The World the Civil War Made.* Chapel Hill: University of North Carolina Press, 2015.

Downs, Gregory P., and Scott Nesbit. Mapping Occupation: Force, Freedom, and the Army in Reconstruction. Website, initially established March 2015. At http://mappingoccupation.org.

Downs, Jim. "The Future of Civil War Era Studies: Race." *Journal of the Civil War Era* 2, no. 1 (March 2012). At http://journalofthecivilwarera.org/forum-the-future-of-civil-war-era-studies/the-future-of-civil-war-era-studies-race/.

———. *Sick from Freedom: African American Illness and Suffering during the Civil War and Reconstruction.* New York: Oxford University Press, 2012.

Doyle, Don, ed. *Secession as an International Phenomenon: From America's Civil War to Contemporary Separatist Movements.* Athens: University of Georgia Press, 2010.

Doyle, Don, and Marco Antonio Pamplona, eds. *Nationalism in the New World.* Athens: University of Georgia Press, 2006.

Drake, Brian Allen, ed. *The Blue, the Gray, and the Green: Toward an Environmental History of the Civil War.* Athens: University of Georgia Press, 2015.

Durden, Robert F. *The Gray and the Black: The Confederate Debate on Emancipation.* Baton Rouge: Louisiana State University Press, 1972.

Edwards, Laura. *A Legal History of the Civil War and Reconstruction: A Nation of Rights.* New York: Cambridge University Press, 2015.

———. "Reconstruction and the History of Governance." In Downs and Masur, eds., *The World the Civil War Made,* 24–32.

Eicher, John H., and David J. Eicher. *Civil War High Commands.* Stanford, CA: Stanford University Press, 2001.

Engle, Stephen D., ed. *The War Worth Fighting: Abraham Lincoln's Presidency and Civil War America.* Gainesville: University Press of Florida, 2015.

Escott, Paul D. *After Secession: Jefferson Davis and the Failure of Confederate Nationalism.* Baton Rouge: Louisiana State University Press, 1978.

———. *The Confederacy: The Slaveholders' Failed Venture.* Santa Barbara, CA: Praeger/ABC-CLIO, 2010.

———. *Lincoln's Dilemma: Blair, Sumner, and the Republican Struggle over Racism and Equality in the Civil War Era.* Charlottesville: University of Virginia Press, 2014.

———. *Many Excellent People: Power and Privilege in North Carolina, 1850–1900.* Chapel Hill: University of North Carolina Press, 1985.

———. *Military Necessity: Civil–Military Relations in the Confederacy.* Westport, CT: Praeger Security International, 2006.

———. *Paying Freedom's Price: A History of African Americans in the Civil War.* Lanham, MD: Rowman and Littlefield, 2016.

———. *Slavery Remembered: A Record of Twentieth Century Slave Narratives.* Chapel Hill: University of North Carolina Press, 1978.

———. *"What Shall We Do with the Negro?": Lincoln, White Racism, and Civil War America.* Charlottesville: University of Virginia Press, 2009.

Evans, William McKee. *To Die Game: The Story of the Lowry Gang, Indian Guerrillas of Reconstruction.* Baton Rouge: Louisiana State University Press, 1971.

Eyal, Yonatan. "A Romantic Realist: George Nicholas Saunders and the Dilemmas of Southern International Engagement." *Journal of Southern History* 78, no. 1 (February 2012): 107–30.

Failka, Andrew. "Controlled Chaos: Spatiotemporal Patterns within Missouri's Irregular Civil War." In Beilein, ed., *The Civil War Guerrilla,* 43–69.

Feimster, Crystal N. "'What If I Am a Woman?': Black Women's Campaigns for Sexual Justice and Citizenship." In Downs and Masur, eds., *The World the Civil War Made,* 249–68.

Fellman, Michael. *Citizen Sherman: A Life of William Tecumseh Sherman.* New York: Random House, 1995.

Fleche, Andrew M. *The Revolution of 1861: The America Civil War and the Age of Nationalist Conflict.* Chapel Hill: University of North Carolina Press, 2012.

Fogel, Robert William, and Stanley L. Engerman. *Time on the Cross: The Economics of American Negro Slavery.* Boston: Little, Brown, 1974.

Foner, Eric. *Free Soil, Free Labor, Free Men: The Ideology of the Republican Party before the Civil War.* Oxford: Oxford University Press, 1970.

Foote, Lorien. "'They Cover the Land Like the Locusts of Egypt': Fugitive Federal Prisoners of War and the Collapse of the Confederacy." *Journal of the Civil War Era* 6, no. 1 (March 2016): 30–55.

Foster, Gaines. *Moral Reconstruction: Christian Lobbyists and the Federal Legislation of Morality, 1865–1920.* Chapel Hill: University of North Carolina Press, 2002.

Frank, Lisa Tendrich. *The Civilian War: Confederate Women and Union Soldiers during Sherman's March.* Baton Rouge: Louisiana State University Press, 2015.

Fredrickson, George. *The Inner Civil War: Northern Intellectuals and the Crisis of the Union.* New York: Harper and Row, 1965.

Freedom on the Move: A Database of Fugitives from North American Slavery. N.d. At http://freedomonthemove.org.

Freehling, William. *The Road to Disunion: Secessionists at Bay, 1776–1854.* New York: Oxford University Press, 1990.

———. *The Road to Disunion: Secessionists Triumphant, 1854–1861.* New York: Oxford University Press, 2007.

———. *The South vs. the South: How Anti-Confederate Southerners Shaped the Course of the Civil War.* New York: Oxford University Press, 2001.

Fuller, J. F. C. *Grant and Lee: A Study in Personality and Generalship.* Bloomington: Indiana University Press, 1957.

Gallagher, Gary W. *Becoming Confederates: Paths to a New National Loyalty.* Mercer University Lamar Memorial Lectures no. 54. Athens: University of Georgia Press, 2013.

———. *The Confederate War.* Cambridge, MA: Harvard University Press, 1997.

———. "Disaffection, Persistence, and Nation: Some Directions in Recent Research on the Confederacy." *Civil War History* 55, no. 3 (September 2009): 329–53.

———. "'The Progress of Our Arms': Whither Civil War Military History?" Forty-Fourth Fortenbaugh Lecture, Civil War Institute, Gettysburg College, 2005.

Gallagher, Gary W., and Rachel A. Shelden, eds. *A Political Nation: New Directions in Mid-Nineteenth-Century American History.* Charlottesville: University of Virginia Press, 2012.

Gallman, J. Matthew. *Defining Duty in the Civil War: Personal Choice, Popular Culture, and the Union Home Front.* Chapel Hill: University of North Carolina Press, 2015.

———. *Northerners at War: Reflections on the Civil War Home Front.* Kent, OH: Kent State University Press, 2010.

———. "The President as Pedagogue: Teaching Citizenship in Time of War." In Engle, ed., *The War Worth Fighting,* 37–61.

Gates, Paul. *Agriculture and the Civil War.* New York: Knopf, 1965.

Genovese, Eugene D. *Roll, Jordan, Roll: The World the Slaves Made.* New York: Pantheon, 1974.

Glatthaar, Joseph T. *Forged in Battle: The Civil War Alliance of Black Soldiers and White Officers.* New York: Free Press, 1990.

———. *General Lee's Army: From Victory to Collapse.* New York: Free Press, 2008.

Gleeson, David T., and Simon Lewis, eds. *The Civil War as Global Conflict.* Columbia: University of South Carolina Press, 2014.

Grant, Susan-Mary. "Americans Forging a New Nation, 1860–1812." In Doyle and Pamplona, eds., *Nationalism in the New World,* 80–98.

———. "'How a Free People Conduct a Long War': Sustaining Opposition to Secession in the American Civil War." In Doyle, ed., *Secession as an International Phenomenon,* 132–50.

Gregg, Sara M. "Cultivating an Agro-Environmental History." In Sackman, ed., *A Companion to American Environmental History,* 425–41.

Grimké, Charlotte Forten. *The Journals of Charlotte Forten Grimké.* Edited by Brenda Stevenson. New York: Oxford University Press, 1988.

Grimsted, David. *American Mobbing, 1828–1861: Toward Civil War.* New York: Oxford University Press, 1998.

Grivno, Max. "Mapping the Runaways: Digital Humanities and the Landscape of Slavery." Paper presented at the Southern Historical Association Annual Meeting, Atlanta, GA, 2014.

Guterl, Matthew Pratt. "Slavery and Capitalism: A Review Essay." *Journal of Southern History* 81, no. 2 (May 2015): 405–20.

Hacker, J. David, Libra Hilde, and James Holland. "The Effect of the Civil War on Southern Marriage Patterns." *Journal of Southern History* 79, no. 1 (February 2010): 39–70.

Hahn, Steven. *A Nation under Our Feet: Black Political Struggles in the Rural South from Slavery to the Great Migration.* Cambridge, MA: Harvard University Press, 2005.

———. *The Political Worlds of Slavery and Freedom.* Cambridge, MA: Harvard University Press, 2009.

———. *The Roots of Southern Populism: Yeoman Farmers and the Transformation of the Georgia Upcountry, 1850–1890.* 1983. Reprint. New York: Oxford University Press, 2006.

———. "What Sort of World Did the Civil War Make?" In Downs and Masur, eds., *The World the Civil War Made,* 337–56.

Hamilton, Daniel W. *The Limits of Sovereignty: Property Confiscation in the Union and the Confederacy during the Civil War.* Chicago: University of Chicago Press, 2007.

Hammond, John Craig. "'Uncontrollable Necessity': The Local Politics, Geopolitics, and Sectional Politics of Slavery Expansion." In Hammond and Mason, eds., *Contesting Slavery,* 138–60.

Hammond, John Craig, and Matthew Mason, eds. *Contesting Slavery: The Politics of Bondage and Freedom in the New American Nation.* Charlottesville: University of Virginia Press, 2011.

Harrold, Stanley. *Border War: Fighting over Slavery before the Civil War.* Chapel Hill: University of North Carolina Press, 2010.

Hess, Earl J. *The Civil War in the West: Victory and Defeat from the Appalachians to the Mississippi.* Chapel Hill: University of North Carolina Press, 2012.

Hettle, Wallace. *The Peculiar Democracy: Southern Democrats in Peace and Civil War.* Athens: University of Georgia Press, 2001.

Hewitt, Lawrence Lee, and Thomas E. Schott, eds. *Lee and His Generals: Essays in Honor of T. Harry Williams.* Knoxville: University of Tennessee Press, 2012.

"Historians' Forum: Reconstruction." *Civil War History* 61, no. 3 (September 2015): 281–301.

Hofstadter, Richard, ed. *Great Issues in American History.* 2 vols. New York: Vintage, 1958.

Holden-Reid, Brian. *America's Civil War: The Operational Battlefield, 1861–1863.* Amherst, NY: Prometheus Books, 2008.

Holt, Michael F. *Political Parties and American Political Development from the Age of Jackson to the Age of Lincoln.* Baton Rouge: Louisiana State University Press, 1991.

Howe, Daniel Walker. Interview. *Historically Speaking* 9, no. 4 (March–April 2008): 30–32.

Humphreys, Margaret. *Intensely Human: The Health of the Black Soldier in the American Civil War.* Baltimore: Johns Hopkins University Press, 2008.

———. *Marrow of Tragedy: The Health Crisis of the American Civil War.* Baltimore: Johns Hopkins University Press, 2013.

Hurt, R. Douglas. *Agriculture and the Confederacy.* Chapel Hill: University of North Carolina Press, 2015.

———. *Food and Agriculture during the Civil War.* Santa Barbara, CA: Praeger, 2016.

Huston, James L. *Calculating the Value of the Union: Slavery, Property Rights, and the Economic Origins of the Civil War.* Chapel Hill: University of North Carolina Press, 2003.

Inscoe, John C., and Robert E. Kenzer, eds. *Enemies of the Country: New Perspectives on Unionists in the Civil War South.* Athens: University of Georgia Press, 2001.

Isham, Matthew. "'A Press That Speaks Its Opinions Frankly and Openly and Fearlessly': The Contentious Relationship between the Democratic Press and the Party in the Antebellum North." In Slap and Thomas, eds., *"This Distracted and Anarchical People,"* 11–28.

Johnson, Ludwell. "Lincoln's Solution to the Problem of Peace Terms, 1864–1865." *Journal of Southern History* 34, no. 4 (November 1968): 576–86.

Jones, Archer. *Civil War Command and Strategy: The Process of Victory and Defeat.* New York: Free Press, 1992.

Jordan, Ervin L. *Black Confederates and Afro-Yankees in Civil War Virginia.* Charlottesville: University Press of Virginia, 1995.

Kantrowitz, Stephen. *More Than Freedom: Fighting for Black Citizenship in a White Republic, 1829–1889.* New York: Penguin, 2012.

Keller, Christian B. *Chancellorsville and the Germans: Nativism, Ethnicity, and Civil War Memory.* New York: Fordham University Press, 2007.

Keller, Morton. *Regulating a New Society: Public Policy and Social Change in America, 1900–1933.* Cambridge, MA: Harvard University Press, 1994.

Kenzer, Robert. *Kinship and Neighborhood in a Southern Community: Orange County, North Carolina, 1849–1881.* Knoxville: University of Tennessee Press, 1987.

Kousser, J. Morgan. *The Shaping of Southern Politics: Suffrage Restriction and the Establishment of the One-Party South, 1880–1910.* New Haven, CT: Yale University Press, 1974.

Lawson, Melinda. *Patriot Fires: Forging a New American Nationalism in the Civil War North.* Lawrence: University of Kansas Press, 2002.

Link, William A., and James J. Broomall, eds. *Rethinking American Emancipation: Legacies of Slavery and the Quest for Black Freedom.* New York: Cambridge University Press, 2016.

Long, Gretchen. *Doctoring Freedom: The Politics of African American Medical Care in Slavery and Emancipation.* Chapel Hill: University of North Carolina, 2012.

Luke, Bob, and John David Smith. *Soldiering for Freedom: How the Union Army Recruited, Trained, and Deployed the U.S. Colored Troops.* Baltimore: Johns Hopkins University Press, 2014.

Mackey, Robert. *The Uncivil War: Irregular Warfare in the Upper South, 1861–1865.* Norman: University of Oklahoma Press, 2004.

Magness, Phillip W., and Sebastian N. Page. *Colonization after Emancipation: Lincoln and the Movement for Black Resettlement.* Columbia: University of Missouri Press, 2011.

Majewski, John. *Modernizing a Slave Economy: The Economic Vision of the Confederate Nation.* Chapel Hill: University of North Carolina Press, 2009.

Manning, Chandra Miller. "Wartime Nationalism and Race: Comparing the Visions of Confederate, Black Union, and White Union Soldiers." In Cooper and McCardell, eds., *In the Cause of Liberty,* 87–104.

———. "Working for Citizenship in Civil War Contraband Camps." *Journal of the Civil War Era* 4, no. 2 (June 2014): 172–204.

Marrs, Aaron. *Railroads in the Old South: Pursuing Progress in a Slave Society.* Baltimore: Johns Hopkins University Press, 2009.

Martinez, Jaime Amanda. *Confederate Slave Impressment in the Upper South.* Chapel Hill: University of North Carolina Press, 2013.

Mauldin, Erin. "The Stockman's War: Hog Cholera, Agricultural Reform, and the Fight to Maintain the Commons during the Civil War Era." Paper presented at the meeting of the Society of Civil War Historians, Summer 2014, Baltimore.

May, Robert E. *Slavery, Race, and Conquest in the Tropics: Lincoln, Douglas, and the Future of Latin America.* New York: Cambridge University Press, 2013.

———. *The Southern Dream of a Caribbean Empire, 1854–1861.* Gainesville: University of Florida Press, 2002.

———, ed. *The Union, the Confederacy, and the Atlantic Rim.* Gainesville: University Press of Florida, 2013.

McCurry, Stephanie. *Confederate Reckoning: Power and Politics in the Civil War South.* Cambridge, MA: Harvard University Press, 2010.

———. "War, Gender, and Emancipation in the Civil War South." In Blair and Younger, eds., *Lincoln's Proclamation,* 120–50.

McKnight, Brian D. "'Time by the Forelock': Champ Ferguson and the Borderland Style of Warfare." In Dollar, Whiteaker, and Dickinson, eds., *Sister States, Enemy States,* 140–67.

McPherson, James M. "The Civil War and the Transformation of America." In Cooper and McCardell, eds., *In the Cause of Liberty,* 1–8.

———. *Embattled Rebel: Jefferson Davis as Commander in Chief.* New York: Penguin, 2014.

———. *The Negro's Civil War.* 1965. Reprint. New York: Ballantine Books, 1991.

———. *The War That Forged a Nation: Why the Civil War Still Matters.* New York: Oxford University Press, 2015.

Meier, Kathryn Shively. *Nature's Civil War: Common Soldiers and the Environment in 1862 Virginia.* Chapel Hill: University of North Carolina Press, 2013.

Miller, Brian Craig. *Empty Sleeves: Amputation in the Civil War South.* Athens: University of Georgia Press, 2015.

Miller, Chandra [Manning]. "'Title Page to a Great Tragic Volume': The Impact of the Missouri Crisis on Slavery, Race, and Republicanism in the Thought of John C. Calhoun and John Quincy Adams." *Missouri Historical Review* 94, no. 4 (July 2000): 365–88.

Miller, Randall M., Henry S. Stout, and Charles Reagan Wilson, eds. *Religion and the American Civil War.* New York: Oxford University Press, 1998.

Mitchell, Nicholas. "The Great Exaggeration: Death and the Civil War." *Journal of the Civil War Era* 4, no. 1 (March 2014): 3–27.

Moore, Mark A., Michael Hill, and Jessica A. Bandel. *The Old North State at War: The North Carolina Civil War Atlas.* Chapel Hill: University of North Carolina Press, 2015.

Morgan, Chad. *Planters' Progress: Modernizing Confederate Georgia.* Gainesville: University Press of Florida, 2005.

Myers, Barton A. "The Future of Civil War Era Studies: Military History." *Journal of the Civil War Era* 2, no. 1 (March 2012). At http://journalofthecivilwarera.org/forum-the-future-of-civil-war-era-studies-military-history/.

———. *Rebels against the Confederacy: North Carolina's Unionists.* New York: Cambridge University Press, 2014.

Nalty, Sean. "Come Weal, Come Woe, I Am with the Anti-slavery Party: Federalism and the Formation of the Pennsylvania Union Party, 1860–1864." In Gallagher and Shelden, eds., *A Political Nation,* 143–66.

Nash, Steven. *Reconstruction's Ragged Edge: The Politics of Postwar Life in the Southern Mountains.* Chapel Hill: University of North Carolina Press, 2016.

National Convention of Colored Men. Syracuse, October 1864. Address and proceedings at http://coloredconventions.org/files/original/91057571556d503505e8e86e8474d923.pdf.

Neely, Mark E., Jr. *The Fate of Liberty: Abraham Lincoln and Civil Liberties.* New York: Oxford University Press, 1991.

———. *Lincoln and the Triumph of the Nation: Constitutional Conflict in the American Civil War.* Chapel Hill: University of North Carolina Press, 2011.

———. *Southern Rights: Political Prisoners and the Myth of Confederate Constitutionalism.* Charlottesville: University of Virginia Press, 1999.

———. *The Union Divided: Party Conflict in the Civil War North.* Cambridge, MA: Harvard University Press, 2002.

Nelson, Megan Kate. "The Civil War from Apache Pass." *Journal of the Civil War Era* 6, no. 4 (December 2016): 510–35.

———. *Ruin Nation: Destruction and the American Civil War.* Athens: University of Georgia Press, 2012.

Noe, Kenneth W. "Fateful Lightning: The Significance of Weather and Climate to Civil War History." In Drake, ed., *The Blue, the Gray, and the Green,* 16–33.

Oakes, James. *Freedom National: The Destruction of Slavery in the United States, 1861–1865.* New York: Norton, 2012.

Orr, Timothy J. "'All Manner of Schemes and Rascalities': The Politics of Promotion in the Union Army." In Slap and Smith, eds., *"This Distracted and Anarchical People,"* 81–103.

Page, Sebastian. "'A Knife Sharp Enough to Divide Us': William H. Seward, Abraham Lincoln, and Black Colonization." *Diplomatic History* 41, no. 2 (2017): 362–91. At https://doi.org/10.1093/dh/dhw039.

Paludan, Phillip Shaw. "The American Civil War Considered as a Crisis in Law and Order." *American Historical Review* 77, no. 4 (October 1972): 1013–34.

———. *A People's Contest: The Union and the Civil War, 1861–1865.* New York: Harper and Row, 1988.

———. *Victims: A True Story of the Civil War.* Knoxville: University of Tennessee Press, 1981.

Pearson, Susan J. "A New Birth of Regulation: The State of the State after the Civil War." *Journal of the Civil War Era* 5, no. 3 (September 2015): 422–39.

Phillips, Jason. *Diehard Rebels: The Confederate Culture of Invincibility.* Athens: University of Georgia Press, 2007.

Potter, David M. *The Impending Crisis, 1848–1861.* New York: Harper Colophon, 1976.

Proceedings of the First Annual Meeting of the National Equal Rights League. Philadelphia: Markley and Son, 1865. At http://babel.hathitrust.org/cgi/pt?id=hvd.hnvpf5;view=1up;seq=10.

Quigley, Paul. Review of Michael Woods, *Emotional and Sectional Conflict in the Antebellum United States* (New York: Cambridge University Press, 2014). *Journal of the Civil War Era* 5, no. 3 (September 2015): 440–42.

Rable, George C. *God's Almost Chosen People: A Religious History of the American Civil War.* Chapel Hill: University of North Carolina Press, 2010.

———. "Rebels and Patriots in the Confederate 'Revolution.'" In Cooper and McCardell, eds., *In the Cause of Liberty,* 63–86.

Regosin, Elizabeth, and Donald R. Shaffer. *Voices of Emancipation: Understanding Slavery, the Civil War, and Reconstruction through the U.S. Pension Files.* New York: New York University Press, 2008.

Reid, Richard M. *Freedom for Themselves: North Carolina's Black Soldiers in the Civil War Era.* Chapel Hill: University of North Carolina Press, 2008.

Reynolds, Donald A. *Texas Terror: The Slave Insurrection Panic of 1860 and the Secession of the Lower South.* Baton Rouge: Louisiana State University Press, 2007.

Richardson, Heather Cox. *The Death of Reconstruction.* Cambridge, MA: Harvard University Press, 2004.

———. *The Greatest Nation of the Earth: Republican Economic Policies during the Civil War.* Cambridge, MA: Harvard University Press, 1997.

———. "North and West of Reconstruction: Studies in Political Economy." In Brown, ed., *Reconstructions,* 66–90.

Ripley, C. Peter, ed. *The Black Abolitionist Papers.* Vol. 5: *The United States, 1859–1865.* Chapel Hill: University of North Carolina Press, 1992.

Roberts, Timothy Mason. *Distant Revolutions: 1848 and the Challenge to American Exceptionalism.* Charlottesville: University of Virginia Press, 2009.

Roland, Charles. "The Generalship of Robert E. Lee." In Hewitt and Schott, eds., *Lee and His Generals,* 19–48.

"Roundtable Discussion: The Legacy of the U.S. Civil War, 150 Years Later." *FifteenEightyFour,* Cambridge University Press blog, April 9, 2015. At http://www.cambridgeblog.org/2015/the-legacy-of-the-u-s-civil-war-150-years-later/.

Rugemer, Edward Bartlett. "Caribbean Slave Revolts and the Origins of the Gag Rule: A Contest between Abolitionism and Democracy, 1797–1835." In Hammond and Mason, eds., *Contesting Slavery,* 94–116.

———. *The Problem of Emancipation: The Caribbean Roots of the American Civil War.* Baton Rouge: Louisiana State University Press, 2008.

———. "Why Civil War? The Politics of Slavery in Comparative Perspective: The United States, Cuba, and Brazil." In Gleeson and Lewis, eds., *The Civil War as Global Conflict,* 14–35.

Sachs, Aaron. "Stumps in the Wilderness." In Drake, ed., *The Blue, the Gray, and the Green,* 96–112.

Sackman, Douglas Cazaux, ed. *A Companion to American Environmental History.* Chichester, UK: Wiley-Blackwell, 2010.

———. "Introduction." In Sackman, ed., *A Companion to American Environmental History,* xiii–xxi.

Sandow, Robert M. "Damnable Treason or Party Organs? Democratic Secret Societies in Pennsylvania." In Slap and Thomas, eds., *"This Distracted and Anarchical People,"* 42–59.

Sarris, Jonathan Dean. *A Separate Civil War: Communities in Conflict in the Mountain South.* Charlottesville: University of Virginia Press, 2016.

Scharff, Virginia, ed. *Empire and Liberty: The Civil War and the West.* Oakland: University of California Press, 2015.

Schoen, Brian. *The Fragile Fabric of Union: Cotton, Federal Politics, and the Global Origins of the Civil War.* Baltimore: Johns Hopkins University Press, 2009.

Schoonover, Thomas. "Napoleon Is Coming! Maximilian Is Coming!" In May, ed., *The Union, the Confederacy, and the Atlantic Rim,* 115–44.

Schrepfer, Susan R., and David Cazaux Sackman. "Gender." In Sackman, ed., *A Companion to American Environmental History,* 116–45.

Schwalm, Leslie A. *Emancipation's Diaspora: Race and Reconstruction in the Upper Midwest.* Chapel Hill: University of North Carolina Press, 2009.

Schweninger, Loren, and John Hope Franklin. *Runaway Slaves: Rebels on the Plantation.* New York: Oxford University Press, 1999.

Scott, Sean A. *A Visitation of God: Northern Civilians Interpret the Civil War.* New York: Oxford University Press, 2011.

Seidman, Rachel Filene. "Monstrous Doctrine? Northern Women on Dependency during the Civil War." In Cimbala and Miller, eds., *An Uncommon Time,* 170–88.

Sheehan-Dean, Aaron. *Why Confederates Fought: Family and Nation in Civil War Virginia.* Chapel Hill: University of North Carolina Press, 2007.

Silber, Nina. *Gender and the Sectional Conflict.* Chapel Hill: University of North Carolina Press, 2008.

Silkenat, David. *Driven from Home: North Carolina's Civil War Refugee Crisis.* Athens: University of Georgia Press, 2016.

———. *Moments of Despair: Suicide, Divorce, and Debt in Civil War Era North Carolina.* Chapel Hill: University of North Carolina Press, 2014.

Silver, Timothy. "Yancey County Goes to War: A Case Study of People and Nature on Home Front and Battlefield, 1861–1865." In Drake, ed., *The Blue, the Gray, and the Green,* 52–66.

Sinha, Manisha. *The Slave's Cause: A History of Abolition.* New Haven, CT: Yale University Press, 2016.

Sizer, Lyde Cullen. *The Political Work of Northern Women Writers and the Civil War, 1850–1872.* Chapel Hill: University of North Carolina Press, 2000.

Slap, Andrew. *The Doom of Reconstruction: The Liberal Republicans in the Civil War Era.* New York: Fordham University Press, 2006.

Slap, Andrew L., and Michael Thomas Smith, eds. *"This Distracted and Anarchical People": New Answers for Old Questions about the Civil War–Era North.* New York: Fordham University Press, 2013.

Smith, Adam I. P. *No Party Now: Politics in the Civil War North.* New York: Oxford University Press, 2006.

Smith, Stacey L. "Beyond North and South: Putting the West in the Civil War and Reconstruction." *Journal of the Civil War Era* 6, no. 4 (December 2016): 566–91.

Sommerville, Diane Miller. "'Will They Ever Be Able to Forget?': Confederate Soldiers and Mental Illness in the Defeated South." In Berry, ed., *Weirding the War,* 321–39.

Span, Christopher. *From Cotton Field to Schoolhouse: African American Education in Mississippi, 1862–1875.* Chapel Hill: University of North Carolina Press, 2009.

Sternhell, Yael. *Routes of War: The World of Movement in the Confederate South.* Cambridge, MA: Harvard University Press, 2012.

Steward, Rodney. *David Schenck and the Contours of Confederate Identity.* Knoxville: University of Tennessee Press, 2012.

Stoker, Donald. *The Grand Design: Strategy and the U.S. Civil War.* New York: Oxford University Press, 2010.

Storey, Margaret M. *Loyalty and Loss: Alabama's Unionists in the Civil War and Reconstruction.* Baton Rouge: Louisiana State University Press, 2004.

Stout, Harry S. *Upon the Altar of the Nation: A Moral History of the American Civil War.* New York: Viking, 2006.

Summers, Mark Wahlgren. *The Ordeal of the Reunion: A New History of Reconstruction.* Chapel Hill: University of North Carolina Press, 2014.

Sutherland, Daniel. *American Civil War Guerrillas: Changing the Rules of Warfare.* Santa Barbara, CA: Praeger, 2013.

———. "Memories of a Rooted Sorrow: The Legacy of the Guerrilla War." *Civil War History* 62, no. 1 (March 2016): 8–35.

———. *A Savage Conflict: The Decisive Role of Guerrillas in the American Civil War.* Chapel Hill: University of North Carolina Press, 2009.

Tap, Bruce. *The Fort Pillow Massacre: North, South, and the Status of African Americans in the Civil War.* London: Routledge, 2014.

Thomas, Emory M. *The Confederacy as a Revolutionary Experience.* Englewood Cliffs, NJ: Prentice-Hall, 1970.

Thomas, William G. *The Iron Way: Railroads, the Civil War, and the Making of Modern America.* New Haven, CT: Yale University Press, 2011.

Tise, Larry E. *Proslavery: A History of the Defense of Slavery in America, 1701–1840.* Athens: University of Georgia Press, 1987.

Towers, Frank. "Partisans, New History, and Modernization: The Historiography of the Civil War's Causes, 1861–2011." *Journal of the Civil War Era* 1, no. 2 (June 2011): 237–64.

United States Colored Troops, Men of Albemarle County Digital Project. Nau Center for Civil War History, University of Virginia, Charlottesville. At https://networks.h-net.org/node/4113/discussions/146677/introducing-nau-centers-usct-men-albemarle-county-digital-project.

The Valley of the Shadow: Two Communities in the American Civil War. N.d. At http://valley.lib.virginia.edu/.

Visualizing Emancipation. N.d. At http://dsl.richmond.edu/emancipation/.

Vorenberg, Michael. *Final Freedom: The Civil War, the Abolition of Slavery, and the Thirteenth Amendment.* Cambridge: Cambridge University Press, 2001.

Waite, Kevin. Interview. *Muster* (blog of the *Journal of the Civil War Era*), February 3, 2017. At http://journalofthecivilwarera.org/2017/02/author-interview-kevin-waite/.

———. "Jefferson Davis and Visions of Proslavery Empire in the Far West." *Journal of the Civil War Era* 6, no. 4 (December 2016): 536–65.

Ward, Brian, Martyn Bone, and William A. Link. *The American South and the Atlantic World.* Gainesville: University Press of Florida, 2013.

Warren, Robert Penn. *The Legacy of the Civil War.* 1961. Reprint. Lincoln: University of Nebraska Press, 1998.

Warshauer, Matthew. "Copperheads in Connecticut: A Peace Movement That Imperiled the Union." In Slap and Thomas, eds., *"This Distracted and Anarchical People,"* 60–79.

Weber, Jennifer. "The Political Culture of the North: Party Politics of Nation and State." In Engle, ed., *The War Worth Fighting,* 91–109.

Wegner, Ansley Herring. *Phantom Pain: North Carolina's Artificial Limb Program for Confederate Veterans.* Raleigh: North Carolina Department of Cultural Resources, 2004.

Weitz, Mark. *More Damning Than Slaughter.* Lincoln: University of Nebraska Press, 2005.

Wheeler, Richard. *Sherman's March.* New York: Crowell, 1978.

White, Jonathan. "'For My Part I Dont Care Who Is Elected President': The Union Army and the Elections of 1864." In Slap and Smith, eds., *"This Distracted and Anarchical People,"* 104–22.

Williams, David. *I Freed Myself: African American Self-Emancipation in the Civil War Era.* New York: Cambridge University Press, 2014.

Williams, David, Teresa Crisp Williams, and David Carlson. *Plain Folk in a Rich Man's War: Class and Dissent in Confederate Georgia.* Gainesville: University Press of Florida, 2002.

Williams, T. Harry. *Lincoln and the Radicals.* Madison: University of Wisconsin Press, 1972.

Wilson, Charles Reagan. "Religion and the American Civil War in Comparative Perspective." In Miller, Stout, and Wilson, eds., *Religion and the American Civil War,* 385–407.

Wilson, Edmund. *Patriotic Gore: Studies in the Literature of the American Civil War.* New York: Oxford University Press, 1962.

Wood, Forrest. *Black Scare: The Racist Response to Emancipation and Reconstruction.* Berkeley: University of California Press, 1968.

Woods, Michael E. *Emotional and Sectional Conflict in the Antebellum United States.* New York: Cambridge University Press, 2014.

Woodworth, Steven E. *Davis and Lee at War.* Lawrence: University Press of Kansas, 1995.

"Workshop: Digital Collaborations across Institutions: Using *Visualizing Emancipation* to Teach the End of Slavery." Southern Historical Association Annual Meeting, November 13–16, 2014, Atlanta, GA.

Wright, Gavin. Foreword to Delfino and Gillespie, eds., *Technology, Innovation, and Southern Industrialization,* vii–xiii.

———. *The Political Economy of the Cotton South: Households, Markets, and Wealth in the Nineteenth Century.* New York: Norton, 1978.

Wyatt-Brown, Bertram. *The Shaping of Southern Culture: Honor, Grace, and War, 1760s–1880s.* Chapel Hill: University of North Carolina Press, 2001.

———. *Southern Honor: Ethics and Behavior in the Old South.* New York: Oxford University Press, 1982.

Yellin, Jean. *Harriet Jacobs: A Life.* New York: Basic Civitas Books, 2004.

Yellin, Jean Fagan, Joseph M. Thomas, Kate Culkin, and Scott Korb, eds. *The Harriet Jacobs Family Papers.* 2 vols. Chapel Hill: University of North Carolina Press, 2008.

Index

New Directions in Southern History

Series Editors
Michele Gillespie, Wake Forest University
William A. Link, University of Florida

The Lost State of Franklin: America's First Secession
Kevin T. Barksdale

The Civil War Guerrilla: Unfolding the Black Flag in History, Memory, and Myth
edited by Joseph M. Beilein Jr. and Matthew C. Hulbert

Bluecoats and Tar Heels: Soldiers and Civilians in Reconstruction North Carolina
Mark L. Bradley

Becoming Bourgeois: Merchant Culture in the South, 1820–1865
Frank J. Byrne

Willis Duke Weatherford: Race, Religion, and Reform in the American South
Andrew McNeill Canady

Cowboy Conservatism: Texas and the Rise of the Modern Right
Sean P. Cunningham

A Tour of Reconstruction: Travel Letters of 1875
Anna Dickinson (J. Matthew Gallman, ed.)

Raising Racists: The Socialization of White Children in the Jim Crow South
Kristina DuRocher

Rethinking the Civil War Era: Directions for Research
Paul D. Escott

Lum and Abner: Rural America and the Golden Age of Radio
Randal L. Hall

Mountains on the Market: Industry, the Environment, and the South
Randal L. Hall

The New Southern University: Academic Freedom and Liberalism at UNC
Charles J. Holden

Entangled by White Supremacy: Reform in World War I–era South Carolina
Janet G. Hudson

Bloody Breathitt: Politics and Violence in the Appalachian South
T. R. C. Hutton

Cultivating Race: The Expansion of Slavery in Georgia, 1750–1860
Watson W. Jennison

De Bow's Review: *The Antebellum Vision of a New South*
John F. Kvach

Remembering The Battle of the Crater: War as Murder
Kevin M. Levin

My Brother Slaves: Friendship, Masculinity, and Resistance in the Antebellum South
Sergio A. Lussana

The Political Career of W. Kerr Scott: The Squire from Haw River
Julian Pleasants

The View from the Ground: Experiences of Civil War Soldiers
edited by Aaron Sheehan-Dean

Reconstructing Appalachia: The Civil War's Aftermath
edited by Andrew L. Slap

A Rape in the Early Republic: Gender and Legal Culture in an 1806 Virginia Trial
Alexander Smyth, edited by Randal L. Hall

Blood in the Hills: A History of Violence in Appalachia
edited by Bruce E. Stewart

Moonshiners and Prohibitionists: The Battle over Alcohol in Southern Appalachia
Bruce E. Stewart

The U.S. South and Europe: Transatlantic Relations in the Nineteenth and Twentieth Centuries
edited by Cornelis A. van Minnen and Manfred Berg

Southern Farmers and Their Stories: Memory and Meaning in Oral History
Melissa Walker

Law and Society in the South: A History of North Carolina Court Cases
John W. Wertheimer

Family or Freedom: People of Color in the Antebellum South
Emily West